THE DICTIONARY OF
LIBERAL
QUOTATIONS

Also available from Biteback Publishing
The Dictionary of Labour Quotations
The Dictionary of Conservative Quotations
The Margaret Thatcher Book of Quotations
The Biteback Dictionary of Humorous Political Quotations
The Biteback Dictionary of Humorous Sporting Quotations

Coming soon from Biteback Publishing
The Biteback Dictionary of Humorous Literary Quotations
The Biteback Dictionary of Humorous Business Quotations

THE DICTIONARY OF
LIBERAL
QUOTATIONS
— *Duncan Brack* —

Biteback Publishing

First published in Great Britain in 2013 by
Biteback Publishing Ltd
Westminster Tower
3 Albert Embankment
London SE1 7SP

ISBN 978-1-84954-538-9

10 9 8 7 6 5 4 3 2 1

A CIP catalogue record for this book is available from the British Library.

Set in Perpetua by Duncan Brack

Printed and bound in Great Britain by
CPI Group (UK) Ltd, Croydon CR0 4YY

Foreword

by Paddy Ashdown

Quotations are an essential element of political rhetoric – and of political education, and of political humour. Here in this book you will find a fine selection of Liberal quotes to inspire you, to make you think and to make you laugh.

Quotations from past leaders can raise our spirits and stir our blood. I was in the audience for David Steel's famous call to 'go back to your constituencies and prepare for government!' I wish I had been for Jo Grimond's 'marching to the sound of gunfire' speech twenty years earlier. From Gladstone defending what we would now call human rights ('remember the rights of the savage, as we call him') to Lloyd George assaulting the House of Lords ('a body of five hundred men chosen at random from amongst the unemployed') to Roy Jenkins calling for the smashing of the 'out-of-date mould which is bad for the political and economic health of Britain', the great Liberal causes of the last three centuries march through these pages.

Quotations help us learn about Liberalism. From Lord Acton's 'all power corrupts; absolute power corrupts absolutely', to John Stuart Mill's famous 'over himself, over his own body and mind, the individual is sovereign', to L.T. Hobhouse's 'liberty without equality is a name of noble sound and squalid meaning', quotations teach us the evolving history of Liberalism and Liberal thought. One quote, new to me but particularly apt for this age of extremes, is this, from the Spanish liberal Gregorio Marañón: 'It is easier to die for an idea, and I would add that it is less heroic, than to try to understand the ideas of others.'

And quotations can make us laugh. Everyone has heard Christopher Bigsby and Malcolm Bradbury's 'You know what they say: if God had been a Liberal, we wouldn't have had the ten commandments. We'd have had the ten suggestions.' But how about Cllr George Worman's explanation for his election to Orpington council: 'Faith, hope and canvassing. And the greatest of these is canvassing', or Gilbert Gray's 'I'm a Liberal – I don't just believe in miracles, I rely on them'? They not only make us smile; we recognise the truth in them.

As I wrote myself, in a quote that is – fortuitously! – included here, all political parties possess 'a heart, a history and a soul'. Here in this book you can discover much of the heart, the history and the soul of British Liberalism.

Lord Ashdown of Norton-sub-Hamdon
July 2013

Introduction

This *Dictionary of Liberal Quotations* contains almost 2,000 quotations from over 500 individuals and publications. I hope it will prove a valuable research tool for students of Liberalism and of the Liberal Democrats and its predecessor parties, a source of education and entertainment for those with a general interest in Liberal politics, and useful raw material for speeches and articles.

I and my colleagues from the Liberal Democrat History Group used two broad criteria for the inclusion of quotations: they are either by or about prominent Liberal Democrats, Liberals, Social Democrats or liberal thinkers, or they provide insights into liberal thinking and liberal concepts at different periods in history. We started, of course, from the first edition of this *Dictionary*, published in 1999 by Biteback's predecessor, Politico's. On reviewing that text, however, we decided we had included too many generic references to vaguely relevant concepts, and we have tried to focus this edition more closely on Liberalism and Liberals. And, of course, we had another fourteen years of events – including two Liberal Democrat leaders and the party's entry into government – from which to source entirely new quotes.

Individuals are listed according to the names by which they are generally known to historians and the media: thus, Paddy Ashdown, L. T. Hobhouse, Viscount Palmerston.

As with the first edition, it would not have been possible to produce this book without input from a team of dedicated quote-hunters; my thanks go to Sam Barratt, Robert Ingham, Tony Little, Michael Meadowcroft, Chris Millington, Mark Pack and Douglas Oliver, and also to all those Liberal Democrat History Group members who responded to our appeal for new quotations. Particular thanks go to Chris Millington for painstaking work on biographical details, and to Michael Meadowcroft for contributing a lifetime's worth of accumulated

Liberal quotes. Many thanks also to Iain Dale and Olivia Beattie at Biteback Publishing for their encouragement and hard work in publishing the book.

A number of sources deserve acknowledgement, including all four of the Liberal Democrat History Group's other books: the *Dictionary of Liberal Biography* (1998), *Great Liberal Speeches* (2001), the *Dictionary of Liberal Thought* (2007) and *Peace, Reform and Liberation: A History of Liberal Politics in Britain 1679–2011* (2011). Also of substantial value were Antony Jay's *Oxford Dictionary of Political Quotations*, Greg Knight's *Honourable Insults*, *Facts About British Prime Ministers*, compiled by D. Englefield, J. Seaton and I. White, Mary Tester's *Wit of The Asquiths*, Ian Bradley's *The Optimists*, Norman Gash's *Aristocracy and People 1815–65*, and Michael Foot's *Loyalists and Loners*.

No doubt some quotations will have been attributed to the wrong person, or will have been printed in slightly different forms to their original versions. And careful readers will no doubt be aware of important quotations which we have overlooked, or puzzle at the reasons why certain quotations were included. Corrections, further information, and suggestions for other quotations will be very welcome – hopefully for inclusion in the third edition!

Duncan Brack
July 2013

A

Richard Acland
1906–90; MP (Liberal, Common Wealth) Barnstaple 1935–45, (Labour) Gravesend 1947–55; founder of the Common Wealth Party 1942

I would expect no one to be more truly the ruler of the immediate post-war world than Mr J. M. Keynes.
   What It Will Be Like in the New Britain (1942)

John Emrich Edward Dalberg Acton, Lord Acton
1834–1902; historian and theologian; MP (Liberal) Carlow 1859–65, Bridgnorth 1865; created first Baron Acton 1869

Liberty, next to religion, has been the motive of good deeds and the common pretext of crime.
   Address on 'The History of Freedom in Antiquity', 26 February 1877

Liberty is not a means to a higher political end. It is itself the highest political end.
   Address on 'The History of Freedom in Antiquity', 26 February 1877

At all times sincere friends of freedom have been rare, and its triumphs have been due to minorities ... If hostile interests have wrought much injury, false ideas have wrought still more, and [true liberty's] advance is recorded in the increase of knowledge as much as in the improvement of laws.
   Address on 'The History of Freedom in Antiquity', 26 February 1877

The most certain test by which we judge whether a country is free is the amount of security enjoyed by minorities.

Address on 'The History of Freedom in Antiquity', 26 February 1877

Power tends to corrupt and absolute power corrupts absolutely. Great men are almost always bad men, even when they exercise influence and not authority.

Letter to Bishop Mandell Creighton, 3 April 1887

Liberty is not the power of doing what we like, but the right of doing what we ought.

Cited in G. E. Fasnacht, *Acton's Political Philosophy* (1952)

Liberalism is ultimately founded on the idea of conscience. A man must live by the light within and prefer God's voice to man's.

Cited in G. E. Fasnacht, *Acton's Political Philosophy* (1952)

The Whig governed by compromise; the Liberal begins the reign of ideas.

Cited in G. Watson, *The English Ideology* (1973)

To develop and perfect and arm conscience is the great achievement of history.

Attributed

The one pervading evil of democracy is the tyranny of the majority, that succeeds by force or fraud in carrying elections.

Attributed

It is easier to find people fit to govern themselves than people to govern others. Every man is the best, the most responsible, judge of his own advantage.

Attributed

John Adams
1735–1826; American President 1797–1801

There is but one element of government, and that is the people.
From this element spring all governments. For a nation to be
free, it is only necessary that she wills it. For a nation to be a
slave, it is only necessary that she wills it.
   Attributed

Paul Addison
b. 1943; historian

Sinclair had two great loyalties which account for his two main
contributions to public life. He believed in Liberalism and
revived it when it was down; and he believed in Churchill
and revived him when he was down.
   Entry on Archibald Sinclair (Liberal leader 1935–45) in *Dictionary of
   National Biography*

Aeschylus
c. 525–c. 456 BC; philosopher and playwright

Some men see things as they are and ask themselves: 'Why?' I
dream of things that never have been and ask myself: 'Why not?'
   Attributed

Aesop
c. 620–560 BC; teller of fables

Better starve free than be a fat slave.
   'The Dog and the Wolf', *Fables* (c. 6th century BC)

Prince Albert

1819–61; Prince Consort 1840–61

We are frequently inclined to plunge States into Constitutional reforms to which they have no inclination. This I hold to be *quite wrong* (*vide* Spain, Portugal, Greece), although it is Lord Palmerston's hobby.

Letter to Baron Stockmar, 2 September 1847

David Alton

b.1951; MP (Liberal, Liberal Democrat) Liverpool Edge Hill, later Liverpool Mossley Hill 1979–97; created Baron Alton of Liverpool 1997

If you are sure you want to vote Liberal, put a big 'X' next to my name; if you are not quite sure, just put a small 'x'.

Attributed

American Civil Liberties Union

Liberty is always unfinished business.

Title of 36th Report of the American Civil Liberties Union, 1955/56

Leo Amery

1873–1955; MP (Conservative) Birmingham South, later Sparkbrook 1911–45; Secretary of State for the Colonies 1924–29, for Dominion Affairs 1925–29, for India and Burma 1940–45

For twenty years, he has held a season ticket on the line of least resistance and has gone wherever the train of events has carried him, lucidly justifying his position at whatever point he has happened to find himself.

On H. H. Asquith, *Quarterly Review*, July 1914

Michael Kerr, Earl of Ancram

b. 1945; MP (Conservative) Berwickshire and East Lothian 1974,
Edinburgh South 1979–87, Devizes 1992–2010

[Paddy Ashdown] has made a lifetime career of perfecting the
arts of sanctimony and arrogance.

In the House of Commons, 13 May 1999

Anonymous

I would rather have a dangerous liberty than a placid slavery.

Attributed to a Polish nobleman by J. J. Rousseau, *Contrat Social* (1762)

He talked shop like a tenth muse.

On a Gladstone Budget speech, cited in G. W. E. Russell, *Collections
and Recollections* (1898)

'Peace, Reform and Liberation'
Be our triune aspiration,
'Til we win them for the nation.
And our land be free.

Refrain from 'The Liberal March' (sung to the tune 'Men of Harlech'),
from the 1892 election

A tick carried along on the Asquithian sheep.

Description of the Labour Party, cited in G. Knight, *Honourable Insults*
(1990)

The land, the land, 'twas God who made the land,
The land, the land, the ground on which we stand.
Why should we be beggars with the ballot in our hand?
God made the land for the people.

Chorus from 'The Land' (sung to the tune 'Marching through
Georgia'), a song originally from the followers of Henry George but
adopted by the Liberal Party in the 1910 elections and sung by Liberals
ever since

He is a man of splendid abilities, but utterly corrupt. Like a rotten mackerel, by moonlight, he shines and stinks.

On David Lloyd George, cited in G. Knight, *Honourable Insults* (1990)

Lloyd George, no doubt,
When his life ebbs out,
Will ride on a flaming chariot,
Seated in state
On a red-hot plate
'twixt Satan and Judas Iscariot;
Ananias that day
To the Devil will say,
'My claim for precedence fails,
So move me up higher,
Away from the fire,
And make way for that liar – from Wales.'

Cited in T. Wilson, *The Downfall of the Liberal Party 1914–35* (1966)

A Liberal is one who believes in social evolution but won't lift a finger to help it, whereas a Radical is one who believes in social evolution and is prepared to have a revolution to achieve it.

Cited as US definitions in T. Horabin, *Politics Made Plain* (1944)

The liberty of others extends mine to infinity.

Graffiti written during French student revolt, 1968

Liberty is necessity's conscience.

Graffiti written during French student revolt, 1968

He would be brilliant if he retained as much of what he reads as what he eats.

On Cyril Smith, cited in G. Knight, *Honourable Insults* (1990)

Joseph Arch

1826–1919; President and organiser of the National Agricultural Labourers Union; MP (Liberal), North West Norfolk 1885–86, 1892–1900

I do not believe in State Aid and land nationalisation ... Self-help and liberty, order and progress – these are what I advocate.

From Ploughtail to Parliament (reprinted 1986)

Aristotle

384–322 BC; philosopher

Tyranny seeks three things: first, to make those who are ruled consider themselves insignificant ... second, that they should utterly distrust each other ... and, third, that they should be powerless to do anything.

Politics (4th century BC)

Those who think that all virtue is to be found in their own party principles push matters to extremes; they do not consider that disproportion destroys a state.

Politics (4th century BC)

Of all the varieties of virtues, liberalism is the most beloved.

Attributed

John Arlott

1914–91; writer, broadcaster and cricket commentator; Liberal candidate

I will forgive an honest politician a very great deal but a smug hypocrite that steers my country into war, I'm agin him.

BBC Radio, *Any Questions*, November 1967

Matthew Arnold

1822–88; writer, critic and schools inspector

The Reform Bill of 1832, and local self-government, in politics;
in the social sphere, free trade, unrestricted competition,
and the making of large individual fortunes; in the religious
sphere, the Dissidence of Dissent, and the Protestantism of the
Protestant religion.

Describing the distinguishing beliefs of Liberalism, *Culture and Anarchy*
(1869)

The spurious Hellenism of our free-trading Liberal friends,
mechanically worshipping their fetish of the production of
wealth and of the increase of manufacturers and population,
and looking neither to right nor left so long as this increase
goes on … to this idea of glory and greatness the free trade
which our Liberal friends extol so solemnly and devoutly has
served … and for this it is prized. Therefore the untaxing of
the poor man's bread has, with this view of national happiness,
been used not so much to make the existing poor man's bread
cheaper, or more abundant, but rather to create more poor
men to eat it.

Culture and Anarchy (1869)

Our Liberal friends preach the right of an Englishman to be
left to do as far as possible what he likes, and the duty of his
government to indulge him and connive as much as possible and
abstain from all harness and repression.

Culture and Anarchy (1869)

And the one insuperable objection to inequality is the same
as the one insuperable objection to absolutism: namely, that
inequality, like absolutism, thwarts a vital instinct and being thus
against nature, is against our humanisation.

Preface, *Mixed Essays* (1879)

The country is profoundly Liberal; that is it is profoundly
convinced that a great course of growth and transformation lies
before it.

Cited in I. Bradley, *The Optimists* (1980)

Paddy Ashdown

b. 1941; MP (Liberal, Liberal Democrat) Yeovil 1983–2001; leader of
the Liberal Democrats 1988–99; created Baron Ashdown of Norton-sub-
Hamdon 2001; High Representative and EU Special Representative for
Bosnia & Herzegovina 2002–06

I was a soldier at the end of the golden age of imperial
soldiering; a spy at the end of the golden age of spying; a
politician while politics was still a calling…

A Fortunate Life: The Autobiography of Paddy Ashdown (2009)

Many voters want their MP to do what is right and often respect
those who do, even while disagreeing with them. The scope for
a bit of courage in politics is far greater than we think it is.

A Fortunate Life: The Autobiography of Paddy Ashdown (2009)

We have lived for far too long off … the intellectual capital of
the Jo Grimond era.

Liberal News, 19 February 1988

When I took over the leadership of the Liberal Democrats
in 1988, I said to my friends that I saw our recovery in three
distinct phases. The first was survival from a point of near
extinction; the second was to build a political force with the
strength, policy and positions to matter again in British politics;
and the third was to get on to the field and play in what I
believed would become a very fluid period of politics.

The Ashdown Diaries, Vol. 2 1997–1999, Epilogue (2001)

I am plagued by the nightmare that the party that started with Gladstone will end with Ashdown.

> After the 1989 European elections, when the Liberal Democrats were beaten into fourth place by the Greens; *The Ashdown Diaries*, Vol. 1 1988–1997, entry for 15 June 1989 (2000)

People sometimes ask me what our party stands for. The centre of our message is this: we stand for individual liberty and the international brotherhood of nations. Our fight for civil liberties in Britain – our belief in a Bill of Rights – our struggle for fair votes – our commitment to freedom of information – our demand for employee rights and shares – our determination to give people power in their own hands – all these are testimony of our faith.

> At the Liberal Democrat conference, Brighton, 15 September 1989

Let it be our party which has the courage and conviction to place the great cause of democracy at the heart of British politics once again. Let it be our party whose commitment is not to win power for itself, but to transfer power to the citizen whom we serve. Let it be our party which is determined to build a new system of politics, which responds to the divine spark in every human being.

> At the Liberal Democrat conference, Brighton, 15 September 1989

The first concern of our party must still be liberty – our challenge in the past has been how to enhance liberty whilst creating a just society – our new challenge comes from adding the words 'and a safe environment too'.

> At the Liberal Democrat conference, Brighton, 15 September 1989

I had, in my rush to create the new party, failed to understand that a political party is about more than plans and priorities and policies and a chromium-plated organisation. It also has a heart and a history and a soul – especially a very old party like the Liberals. Alan Beith and the other 'Name' rebels understood this better than me. They were right, and I had nearly wrecked the party by becoming too attached to my own vision and ignoring the fact that political parties are, at root, human organisations and not machines.

On the controversy over the short name of the merged party in 1988–89; *A Fortunate Life: The Autobiography of Paddy Ashdown* (2009)

The days of alphabet soup.

On the difficulties of establishing a name for the new party, 17 October 1989

Labour would discard any principle, abandon any conviction and adopt any policy provided it could gain votes in the process.

The Guardian, March 1990

A review of the papers. They are irretrievably awful. *The Sun*'s headline is 'Paddy Pantsdown'. Dreadful – but brilliant.

Ashdown's reaction to press coverage of his affair with his former secretary, *The Ashdown Diaries*, Vol. 1 1988–1997, entry for 6 February 1992 (2000)

[We are] the gathering point for a broader movement dedicated to winning the battle of ideas which will give Britain an electable alternative to the Conservative government. I do not believe mathematically constructed pacts and alliances are the way forward for Liberal Democrats or for others … [We should] work with others to assemble the ideas around which a non-socialist alternative to the Conservatives can be constructed.

On the future direction of the Liberal Democrats, Chard, 9 May 1992

I have been building the party to fill a certain gap in politics, which I know is there and which would give us real electoral pull. But then along comes Blair with all the power of Labour behind him, and fills exactly the space I have been aiming at for the last seven years.

On the election of Tony Blair to the Labour leadership, *The Ashdown Diaries*, Vol. 1 1988–1997, entry for 8 August 1994 (2000)

If, as it appears, I have more in common with Blair than he has with his left wing, surely the logical thing is for us to create a new, more powerful alternative force which would be unified around a broadly liberal agenda?

The Ashdown Diaries, Vol. 1 1988–1997, entry for 9 April 1996 (2000)

I was fed up at the last election with rattling around the country conferring the Westminster blessing on some unsuspecting lathe operator in the West Midlands.

The Independent, 3 April 1997

Trust is not a question of personality, it's a question of consistency. You can't … publish a manifesto one day and before the ink is dry rewrite large sections of it and then appeal to people to trust you. It would be like Moses coming down from the mountain with the ten commandments and then being told by spin doctors to ditch three of them because focus groups say they are not going down well with the Israelites.

The Independent, 8 April 1997

I am in favour of cooperating with other parties where it is in the national interest to do so but I am not talking about pacts, deals and all the rest of it – that's not on the agenda and never has been.

On *GMTV*, 28 April 1997

Some tell me this is the age of politics without ideology. They say the great 'isms' are dead. But there is one creed whose time, I am passionately convinced, has come again. This is again the liberal age.

At the Liberal Democrat conference, Southport, 15 March 1998

A taxi home, a whisky and to bed. Waiting for Blair is like waiting for Godot.

On Ashdown's attempts to persuade Tony Blair to legislate for constitutional and electoral reform; *The Ashdown Diaries*, Vol. 2 1997–1999, entry for 9 September 1998 (2001)

Surely there can be no place in a 21st-century Parliament for people with 15th-century titles and 19th-century prejudices?

On reform of the House of Lords; in the House of Commons debate on the Queen's Speech, 24 November 1998

I have one great question about you. Are you a pluralist? Or are you a control freak?

On Tony Blair, at the Liberal Democrat conference, Brighton, 24 September 1998

It is, incidentally, not necessary for parties to love their leaders – to respect them is usually enough. But it is vital for leaders to love their parties – otherwise why would we put up with it? That applies especially to our beloved Lib Dems, who are, bless them, inveterately sceptical of authority, often exasperating to the point of dementia, as difficult to lead where they don't want to go as a mule, and as curmudgeonly about success as one of those football supporters who regards his team's promotion to the premier league as insufficient because they haven't also won the FA cup! But that's what makes them liberals; and fun to be with; and inextinguishable in defeat; and bottomless in the commitment they will give you when you ask for it; and recklessly generous of your faults and quite simply the best party to lead in the world.

Open letter to leadership contenders, *The Guardian*, 11 June 1999

Eleven years ago, the first thing we did in the Liberal Democrats was to take our liberal agenda and update it. That new thinking gave us the distinctive messages, which won us the votes, that made us strong, that gave us a role to play on the field of politics as we do today. That's the order. First the ideas; then the votes; then the influence; and then the power.

Farewell speech as leader to Liberal Democrat conference, Harrogate, 21 September 1999

In Jo Grimond's time we used to have a slogan: 'We hate the Tories. But we distrust the state.' It's not a bad one for the years ahead!

Farewell speech as leader to Liberal Democrat conference, Harrogate, 21 September 1999

Through it all, you have done all I have asked of you and more. So often I left Westminster tired and dejected, to go out to meet you and campaign with you, in the knowledge that it was my job to inspire you. But ending up with you inspiring me, by your trust and your hope and your unshakeable will to win.

Farewell speech as leader to Liberal Democrat conference, Harrogate, 21 September 1999

You have given me, quite simply, the pride and the purpose of my life. To have had the privilege to lead you has been the greatest thing I have ever done – or ever will do.

Farewell speech as leader to Liberal Democrat conference, Harrogate, 21 September 1999

In September 1998, I was in the little villages of Suva Reka, near Pristina ... Every Albanian village had a graveyard – there were too many of them – with freshly dug graves, and every Albanian house, be it extremely poor, had a satellite dish. I noticed amidst the mayhem and misery that while all the graveyards pointed, according to Muslim tradition, towards Mecca, all the satellite dishes pointed towards Murdoch. I fell to wondering which of those two facts would more greatly influence the lives of the people round whom the war was raging. The answer was that Murdoch would affect their lives more than Mecca.

Final speech in the House of Commons, 25 April 2001

I am a Liberal. I am comfortable being a Liberal. It is the only answer to the conundrums of our age.

Interview, *Total Politics*, April 2009

The other two parties have conceded that it is the 'Liberal Age'. They are all Liberals now. They are all trying to be Liberals. David Cameron even proclaims himself to be a Liberal Conservative, so here's the conundrum. If this is a 'Liberal Age', why the bloody hell aren't I Prime Minister?

Interview, *Total Politics*, April 2009

George Bush may well turn out to be the last US President to have had an emotional tie to Europe. In future we are likely to be judged by Washington, not on the basis of history, but according to a rather cool, even brutal appraisal of what we can deliver when it comes to pursuing our joint interests – and here the answer is not much, if Afghanistan is anything to go by.

At the Hay Literary Festival, May 2009

An instrument of excruciating torture for the Liberal Democrats, where our hearts and emotions went one way but the mathematics the other.

On the outcome of the 2010 election, cited in R. Wilson, *Five Days to Power* (2010)

Fuck it! If this is what you're going to fight for – even with the bloody Tories – you'd better count me in.

At the meeting of the Liberal Democrat parliamentary parties and Federal Executive which approved the coalition, 11 May 2010

The thing that we have in our party title – liberal – goes back thousands of years. You should be proud of that. It should give us strength, and it should make us campaign even harder ... Henry Gibson once said, 'You do not go out to battle for freedom and truth wearing your best trousers.' Sometimes I think our party wears its best trousers too much. This is our heritage and it is also our message today – and we should be proud of it.

At the Liberal Democrat History Group meeting to launch the book *Peace, Reform and Liberation*, Birmingham, 19 September 2011

Power is not just moving laterally from nation to nation, it's also moving vertically. What's happening today is that the power that was encased, held to accountability, held to the rule of law, within the institutions of the nation state, has now migrated in very large measure on to the global stage.

TED talk, Brussels, November 2011

People say to me, 'The Chinese, of course, they'll never get themselves involved in multilateral peace-making around the world.' Oh yes? Why not? How many Chinese troops are ... serving under the UN command in the world today? 3,700. How many Americans? 11.

TED talk, Brussels, November 2011

I was not born a Liberal. I became one nearly forty years ago. When a man in a bobble hat knocked on my door and asked for my vote. To be honest I told him I wasn't interested. I was fed up with all politicians. But he was insistent. So I told him if he could persuade me Liberalism was different, he could have my vote ... So, if you ever wonder, over the next few years, as I am coaxing, cajoling, even perhaps trying to compel you; when you are dead on your feet but I need you to get out and sign up more members and deliverers, or knock on another 100 doors, or deliver another 1,000 leaflets; well, if you want to know who to blame – not me; you can blame that modest man in a bobble hat who went out one evening in the dark and the cold and knocked on somebody's door with a message of hope. A modest man who had immodest ambitions for our party and our country. Summed up in the simple, liberal demand that every citizen should be enabled to live their lives to the full.

At the Liberal Democrat conference, Brighton, March 2013

I'm sure that you, like me, have often told children and grandchildren that it's not the winning that matters, it's the taking part. Well let me let you into a little secret. That's bollocks.

At the Liberal Democrat conference, Brighton, March 2013

The Liberal Party and its members, then and now, do not pretend to be the elite. They are, for the most part, the very ordinary in the best sense of that word. And yet, somewhat to my surprise, I have felt a greater sense of privilege working with them, and been more humbled and inspired by what they were able to achieve through dedication, sacrifice and a refusal to accept the odds, than I ever felt amongst the elites of my previous careers.

A Fortunate Life: The Autobiography of Paddy Ashdown (2009)

In a life that has, I suppose, had some small excitements, nothing that I have ever experienced so terrorised me as having to stand up as a young, inexperienced, wet-behind-the-ears leader of my party to question her [Margaret Thatcher] in the House of Commons when she was at the full plenitude of her powers, with the inevitable result that I would be ritually handbagged twice a week in front of the microphones of the nation. Thank God there was no television in the Chamber then.

Tribute to Mrs Thatcher in the House of Lords, 10 April 2013

We believe that government's first role is not to help people but to help people help themselves. We prefer the hand-up to the hand-out.

Attributed

The most frightening period of my life.

Attributed; on the first two years of the Liberal Democrats

H. H. Asquith

1852–1928; MP (Liberal) East Fife 1886–1918, Paisley 1920–24; Home Secretary 1892–95, Chancellor of the Exchequer 1905–08, Prime Minister 1908–16; leader of the Liberal Party 1908–26; created Earl of Oxford and Asquith 1925

A mischievous and injurious scheme.

On the proposal for votes for women, in the House of Commons, 27 April 1892

In politics I think he may fairly be described as an idealist in aim and optimist by temperament. Great causes appealed to him. He was not ashamed, even in old age, to see visions and to dream dreams.

Tribute in the House of Commons to Henry Campbell-Bannerman following his death in April 1908

Too many pubs.

When asked to summarise his arguments for the Licensing Bill, 1908, cited in M. Tester, *Wit of The Asquiths* (1974)

We must wait and see.

Used repeatedly during a debate on the Parliament Act Procedure Bill, in the House of Commons, 4 April 1910. Later used to characterise Asquith's attitude to the First World War and other issues

The Army will hear nothing of politics from me – and in return I expect to hear nothing of politics from the Army.

Following the Curragh Mutiny, Ladybank, 4 April 1914

We shall never sheathe the sword which we have not lightly drawn until Belgium receives in full measure all and more than all that she has sacrificed, until France is adequately secured against the menace of aggression, until the rights of the smaller nationalities of Europe are placed upon an unassailable foundation, and until the military domination of Prussia is wholly and finally destroyed.

At the Guildhall, London, 9 November 1914

There is nothing to be got by being a Liberal today. It is not a profitable or remunerative career.

To the National Liberal Federation, 26 November 1920

Youth would be an ideal state if it came a little later in life.

The Observer, 15 April 1923

It is fitting that we should have buried the Unknown Prime Minister by the side of the Unknown Soldier.

> On the interment of Andrew Bonar Law's ashes at Westminster Abbey, November 1923, cited in R. Blake, *The Unknown Prime Minister* (1955)

We are a dying party, set between the upper and the nether millstones.

> After defeat in the 1924 election, cited in C. Cook, *The Age of Alignment: Electoral Politics in Britain 1922–29* (1975)

We have now for nearly three years been trying the experiment of 'Liberal Reunion'. There is not one of us that does not know that in practice it has turned out to be a fiction, if not a farce.

> Memorandum, 6 October 1926, cited in T. Wilson, *The Downfall of the Liberal Party 1914–35* (1966)

There is only one way in which liberalism can ever be killed, and that is by suicide.

> At Greenock, 15 October 1926

A great political party which is not for the time being in a majority should never allow itself to succumb to the temptation to degenerate into a bargaining counter.

> At Greenock, 15 October 1926

The Liberal Party … can point to the richest record of actual achievement in the removal of abuses and the extension of freedom, in securing, step by step, that predominance of the general over the particular interest, which I have described as one of the greatest principles.

> At Greenock, 15 October 1926

Look neither to the right nor to the left, but keep straight on.

> At Greenock, 15 October 1926

There is no more striking illustration of the immobility of British institutions than the House of Commons.

Fifty Years of Parliament, Vol. 2 (1926)

The War Office kept three sets of figures – one to mislead the public, another to mislead the Cabinet, and the third to mislead itself.

Cited in A. Horne, *The Price of Glory* (1962)

A Chimborazo or Everest among the foothills of the Baldwin Cabinet.

On Winston Churchill, cited in R. Jenkins, *Asquith* (1964)

He is a wonderful creature, with a curious dash of schoolboy simplicity, and having what someone said of genius – a zig-zag streak of lightning in the brain.

On Winston Churchill, cited in M. Tester, *Wit of The Asquiths* (1974)

A chip off the old Blockhead.

Description of the son of a Tory peer, cited in M. Tester, *Wit of The Asquiths* (1974)

They had hardly even a prejudice in common.

On an alliance between Morley and Harcourt, cited in M. Tester, *Wit of The Asquiths* (1974)

Rather a dusty lot.

On the Gladstonian Cabinet, cited in M. Tester, *Wit of The Asquiths* (1974)

It is an impossible audience … It is like speaking by torchlight to corpses in a charnel-house.

On addressing the House of Lords, cited in M. Tester, *Wit of The Asquiths* (1974)

In public politics as in private life, character is better than brains, and loyalty more valuable than either; but I shall have to work with the material that has been given to me.

Attributed, in conversation to Margot Asquith

It may seem a truism to say that the Liberal Party inscribes among its permanent watchwords the name of liberty ... but liberty itself, like so many of the rallying cries in the secular struggle of parties, is a term which grows by what it feeds on, and acquires in each generation a new and larger content.

Attributed

Mr Asquith says in a manner sweet and calm,
Another little drink won't do us any harm.

Music-hall song

Margot Asquith

1864–1945; political hostess and author; wife of H. H. Asquith

I was reminded of George Eliot's remark, 'When a man wants a peach, it is no good offering him the largest vegetable marrow.'

On hearing that Campbell-Bannerman, in planning the Liberal administration of 1905, intended to make R. B. Haldane Home Secretary instead of Lord Chancellor, cited in R. Jenkins, *Asquith* (1964)

I was tired of cleverness – the clever among Henry's colleagues were not always loyal, and the loyal, with notable exceptions, were not too clever.

Autobiography (1920)

If not a great soldier, he is at least a great poster.

On Lord Kitchener, *More Memories* (1933)

No amount of education will make women first-rate politicians. Can you see a woman becoming a Prime Minister? I cannot imagine a greater calamity for these islands than to be put under the guidance of a woman in 10 Downing Street.

Off The Record (1943)

Lord Birkenhead is very clever but sometimes his brains go to his head.

On F. E. Smith, *The Listener*, 11 July 1953

He never saw a belt without hitting below it.

On David Lloyd George, *The Listener*, 11 July 1953

The t is silent, as in Harlow.

To Jean Harlow, who had been mispronouncing her name, cited in T. S. Matthews, *Great Tom* (1973)

What a pity when Christopher Columbus discovered America that he ever mentioned it.

Cited in M. Tester, *Wit of The Asquiths* (1974)

That clash of flint with steel.

On a dispute between Lord Rosebery and Sir William Harcourt, cited in M. Tester, *Wit of The Asquiths* (1974)

It caught on like wildfire with the semi-clever and moderately educated – the Imperialists, Dukes, Journalists and Fighting Forces.

On Joseph Chamberlain's proposal for tariff reform, cited in M. Tester, *Wit of The Asquiths* (1974)

I think there is something horribly vulgar in trying to get too familiar with men's souls.

To General Booth, founder of the Salvation Army, cited in M. Tester, *Wit of The Asquiths* (1974)

He has not a ray of humour, and hardly any sensibility. If he were a horse I certainly would not back him.

On Sir Charles Dilke, cited in M. Tester, *Wit of The Asquiths* (1974)

Henry is as indifferent to the press as St Paul's Cathedral is to midges.

> On her husband, cited in M. Tester, *Wit of The Asquiths* (1974)

I always knew Lloyd George had won the war, but until I read his memoirs, I did not know he had won it single-handed.

> Letter to T. Jones, cited in M. Tester, *Wit of The Asquiths* (1974)

The amount of silly things that I have heard clever people say makes me wonder what is left for the stupid.

> Cited in M. Tester, *Wit of The Asquiths* (1974)

His modesty amounts to a deformity.

> On H. H. Asquith, cited in G. Knight, *Honourable Insults* (1990)

The most sophisticated untrue unsound gerry-built quick clever affectionate vulgarian I've ever seen.

> On Andrew Bonar Law, cited in the *Independent on Sunday*, 18 April 1999

Clement Attlee

1883–1967; MP (Labour) Limehouse 1922–50, Walthamstow West 1950–55; leader of the Labour Party 1935–55; deputy Prime Minister 1942–45, Prime Minister 1945–51; created Earl Attlee and Viscount Prestwood 1955

He [Churchill] has been a very ardent lover of this elderly spinster, the Liberal Party. The elder sister – the National Liberals – was married long ago; she is now deceased. This now is the younger sister, but she is getting on. I can never make out whether the Rt Hon. Member for Woodford is going to play Petruchio or Romeo. He has given her a slap in the face, then offers her a bunch of flowers.

> In the House of Commons, 1950, cited in D. Dutton, *A History of the Liberal Party* (2004)

All of the things that the Liberals have worked for we have
carried out.

Used in Labour election literature, 1951

A dead fly.

Describing Violet Bonham Carter, 1951, cited in M. Tester, *Wit of The
Asquiths* (1974)

Aung San Suu Kyi

b. 1945; Burmese politician, held under house arrest for much of 1989–
2010

It's very different from living in academia in Oxford. We called
someone vicious in the *Times Literary Supplement*. We didn't know
what vicious was.

Cited in *The Observer* on her return to Myanmar (Burma) in 1988

It is not power that corrupts but fear. Fear of losing power
corrupts those who wield it and fear of the scourge of
power corrupts those who are subject to it.

Freedom from Fear (1991)

The quest for democracy in Burma is the struggle of a people to
live whole, meaningful lives as free and equal members of the
world community. It is part of the unceasing human endeavour
to prove that the spirit of man can transcend the flaws of his
own nature.

Freedom from Fear (1991)

The people of Burma view democracy not merely as a form of
government but as an integrated social and ideological system
based on respect for the individual. When asked why they feel so
strong a need for democracy, the least political will answer: 'We
just want to be able to go about our own business freely and
peacefully, not doing anybody any harm, just earning a decent
living without anxiety and fear.' In other words they want the

basic human rights which would guarantee a tranquil, dignified existence free from want and fear.

Freedom from Fear (1991)

It was predictable that as soon as the issue of human rights became an integral part of the movement for democracy the official media should start ridiculing and condemning the whole concept of human rights, dubbing it a western artefact alien to traditional values.

Freedom from Fear (1991)

It is a puzzlement to the Burmese how concepts which recognise the inherent dignity and the equal and inalienable rights of human beings, which accept that all men are endowed with reason and conscience and which recommend a universal spirit of brotherhood, can be inimical to indigenous values.

Freedom from Fear (1991)

The proposition that the Burmese are not fit to enjoy as many rights and privileges as the citizens of democratic countries is insulting. It also makes questionable the logic of a Burmese government considering itself fit to enjoy more rights and privileges than the governments of those same countries.

Freedom from Fear (1991)

In societies where men are truly confident of their own worth, women are not merely tolerated but valued.

At the Forum on Women, China, 1995

B

Francis Bacon

1561–1626; writer and philosopher; MP for various constituencies 1584–1617; created Baron Verulam 1618, Viscount St. Albans 1621; Lord Chancellor 1618–21

He that will not apply new remedies must expect new evils; for time is the greatest innovator.

Essays, third edition (1625)

Walter Bagehot

1826–77; Liberal economist and constitutional writer; editor of *The Economist* 1860–77

The path of great principles is marked through history by trouble, anxiety, and conflict.

Saturday Review, 16 February 1856

It has been the bane of many countries which have tried to obtain freedom, but failed in the attempt, that they have regarded popular government rather as a means of intellectual excitement than as an implement of political work.

Saturday Review, 16 February 1856

No real English gentleman, in his secret soul, was ever sorry for the death of a political economist.

Estimates of some Englishmen and Scotchmen (1858)

He believes, with all his heart and soul and strength that there is such a thing as truth; he has the soul of a martyr with the intellect of an advocate.

On W. E. Gladstone, *National Review*, July 1860

There is no method by which men can be both free and equal.

The Economist, 5 September 1863

In such constitutions [e.g. England's] there are two
parts ... first, those which excite and preserve the reverence of
the population – the dignified parts ... and next, the efficient
parts – those by which it, in fact, works and rules.

The English Constitution (1867)

A cabinet is a combining committee – a hyphen which joins,
a buckle which fastens, the legislative part of the state to the
executive part of the state.

The English Constitution (1867)

It has been said that England invented the phrase, 'Her Majesty's
Opposition'; that it was the first government which made a
criticism of the administration as much a part of the polity as
administration itself. This critical opposition is the consequence
of cabinet government.

The English Constitution (1867)

It is often said that men are ruled by their imaginations; but it
would be truer to say that they are governed by the weakness of
their imaginations.

The English Constitution (1867)

The Queen ... must sign her own death-warrant if the two
Houses unanimously send it up to her.

The English Constitution (1867)

Above all things our royalty is to be reverenced, and if you begin
to poke about it you cannot reverence it ... Its mystery is its
life. We must not let in daylight upon magic.

The English Constitution (1867)

The Sovereign has, under a constitutional monarchy such as
ours, three rights – the right to be consulted, the right to

encourage, the right to warn. A king of great sense and sagacity would want no others.

The English Constitution (1867)

A severe though not unfriendly critic of our institutions said that 'the cure for admiring the House of Lords was to go and look at it'.

The English Constitution (1867)

The House of Commons lives in a state of perpetual potential choice: at any moment it can chose a ruler and dismiss a ruler. And therefore party is inherent in it, is bone of its bone, and breath of its breath.

The English Constitution (1867)

An Opposition, on coming into power, is often like a speculative merchant whose bills become due. Ministers have to make good their promises, and they find difficulty in doing so.

The English Constitution (1867)

It is an inevitable defect, that bureaucrats will care more for routine than for results.

The English Constitution (1867)

The natural impulse of the English people is to resist authority.

The English Constitution (1867)

In plain English, what I fear is that both our political parties will bid for the support of the working man; that both of them will promise to do as he likes, if he will only tell them what it is; that, as he now holds the casting vote in our affairs, both parties will beg and pray him to give that vote to them. I can conceive of nothing more corrupting or worse for a set of poor Ignorant people than that two combinations of well-taught and rich men should constantly offer to defer to their decision, and compete for the office of executing it.

The English Constitution, second edition (1872)

We have in England an elective first magistrate as truly as the Americans have an elective first magistrate. The Queen is only at the head of the dignified part of the constitution. The prime minister is at the head of the efficient part.

The English Constitution, second edition (1872)

If we know that a nation is capable of enduring continuous discussion, we know that it is capable of practising with equanimity continuous tolerance.

Physics and Politics (1872)

In happy states, the Conservative party must rule upon the whole a much longer time than their adversaries. In well-framed politics, innovation – great innovation that is – can only be occasional. If you are always altering your house, it is a sign either that you have a bad house, or that you have an excessively restless disposition – there is something wrong somewhere.

The Chances for a Long Conservative Regime in England (1874)

The being without an opinion is so painful to human nature that most people will leap to a hasty opinion rather than undergo it.

The Economist, 4 December 1875

Good government depends at least as much on an impartial respect for the rights of all as it does on energy in enforcing respect for the authority which protects those rights.

The Economist, 27 May 1876

The characteristic danger of great nations, like the Romans or the English, which have a long history of continuous creation, is that they may at last fail from not comprehending the great institutions which they have created.

Fortnightly Review, 1 November 1876

Capital must be propelled by self-interest; it cannot be enticed by benevolence.

Economic Studies (1880)

If he were a horse, nobody would buy him; with that eye, no one could answer for his temper.

'Lord Brougham' in *Biographical Studies* (1881)

Mikhail Bakunin

1814–76; Russian anarchist

The liberty of man consists solely in this, that he obeys the laws of nature, because he has himself recognised them as such, and not because they have been imposed upon him externally by any foreign will whatsoever, human or divine, collective or individual.

Dieu et l'État (1882)

Freedom is the absolute right of all adult men and women to seek permission for their action only from their own conscience and reason, and to be determined in their actions only by their own will, and consequently to be responsible only to themselves, and then to the society to which they belong, but only insofar as they have a made a free decision to belong to it.

Dieu et l'État (1882)

James Baldwin

1924–87; American writer

Freedom is not something that anybody can be given; freedom is something people take and people are as free as they want to be.

'Notes for a Hypothetical Novel', *Nobody Knows My Name* (1961)

Stanley Baldwin

1867–1947; MP (Conservative) Bewdley 1908–37; Chancellor of the Exchequer 1922–23, Prime Minister 1923–24, 1924–29, 1935–37, Lord

President of the Council 1931–35; created Earl Baldwin of Bewdley and
Viscount Coverdale of Coverdale 1937

A Rolls-Royce mind, without a driver.
> On Sir John Simon, cited in R. Douglas, *History of the Liberal Party
> 1895–1970* (1971)

He spent his whole life in plastering together the true and the
false, and therefrom manufacturing the plausible.
> On David Lloyd George, cited in G. Knight, *Honourable Insults* (1990)

A. J. Balfour

1848–1930; MP (Conservative) Hertford 1874–85, Manchester East
1885–1906, City of London 1906–22; First Lord of the Treasury 1891–
92, 1895–1905, Prime Minister 1902–05, Foreign Secretary 1916–19;
created Earl of Balfour, Viscount Traprain of Whittingehame 1922

A mere cork, dancing on a current which he cannot control.
> On Henry Campbell-Bannerman, letter to Lady Salisbury, 1906, cited
> in B. Dugdale, *Arthur James Balfour* (1939)

Asquith's lucidity of style is a positive disadvantage when one
has nothing to say.
> Cited in G. Knight, *Honourable Insults* (1990)

He is, and always was, in everything except essentials, a
tremendous Tory.
> On Gladstone, cited in P. Clarke, *A Question of Leadership* (1991)

Conservative prejudices are rooted in a great past and Liberal
ones in an imaginary future.
> Cited in D. Englefield, J. Seaton & I. White, *Facts About the British Prime
> Ministers* (1996)

Honor Balfour

1912–2001; journalist; Liberal candidate

Not only am I fighting the press boycott but the boy Prescott.

> On her experience as an Independent Liberal candidate in the Darwen
> by-election, 1943 – the local paper refused to report her campaign
> because she was defying the wartime electoral truce, whereas Stanley
> Prescott was her Conservative opponent; attributed

Jackie Ballard

b. 1953; MP (Liberal Democrat) Taunton 1997–2001

Male politicians get away with being far more scruffy, ugly and
overweight than female politicians, which annoys me.

> *Independent on Sunday*, 28 March 1999

Desmond Banks

1918–97; President, Liberal Party 1968–69; created Baron Banks of
Kenton 1975

Just as there are one or two Liberals on the Right who believe in
nothing but free trade and laissez-faire so there are Liberals on the
Left like Lady Megan [Lloyd George] who view the Labour Party
through rose-tinted spectacles. If once she learns to appreciate
the point of view of those Liberals with [her views], who firmly
believe in modern Liberalism as it has evolved from Asquith and
Lloyd George through the Yellow Book to *Full Employment in a
Free Society*, ownership for all and co-ownership in industry, yet
who detest Labour Party theory and much of its practice, then
the hopes of Party unity will be high. Modern Liberals, though
they reject laissez-faire which Asquith described as administrative
nihilism, have not rejected the principle of the freedom of world
trade which Asquith did so much to uphold. Nor are they any
less conscious of the need to defend the liberty of the subject
against all assaults. Liberals are prepared with Lady Megan to

use the weapon of state intervention but as [we were] reminded in our last issue 'they must use it cautiously and never with gay abandon'.

Editorial, *The Middle Road*, February 1951

The conception of the free movement of men, goods, capital and ideas over the frontiers of the nations is a great one, and the Liberal Party must support every movement in that direction. The taxation of land values has, perhaps, been to some extent neglected by the Party in recent years. Adam Smith and Henry George are certainly prophets to be honoured among Liberals. But they are prophets, not gods – and not the only ones at that.

Editorial, *The Middle Road*, April 1951

But it takes so long to write 'disenfranchised Liberal' on the ballot paper.

Response to the suggestion that Liberals should spoil their ballot papers where there was no Liberal candidate, general election, 1964

John Bannerman

1901–69; chairman, Scottish Liberal Party 1954–64; created Lord Bannerman of Kildonan 1967

It's boy David.

Describing David Steel on his by-election victory, 1965; subsequently used by the *Scottish Daily Express* in its report of the by-election

Anthony Barber

1920–2005; MP (Conservative) Doncaster 1951–64, Altrincham & Sale 1965–74; Chancellor of the Exchequer 1970–74; created Baron Barber of Wentbridge 1975

The Liberals have no chance of forming a government and cut no ice in Parliament. The hard fact is that the Liberal Party is

as irrelevant to the reality of present-day politics as a pair of
Victorian opera glasses to a moon probe.

Orpington and Kentish Times, 7 February 1964

Francis Thornhill Baring

1796–1866; MP (Whig/Liberal) Portsmouth 1826–65; Chancellor of the
Exchequer 1839–41; created Baron Northbrook 1866

A body of men connected with high rank and property, bound
together by hereditary feeling and party ties, as well as higher
motives, who in bad times keep alive the sacred name of
freedom.

Describing Whigs, 1830, cited in B. Mallet, *Thomas George, Earl of
Northbrook: A Memoir* (1908)

Frédéric Bastiat

1801–50; French economist

If goods do not cross frontiers, armies will.

Attributed

Tim Beaumont

1928–2008; President, Liberal Party 1969–70; created Baron Beaumont
of Whitley 1968

I am a Liberal because, as John Pardoe crystallised it, the hatred
of Tories is the beginning of wisdom and to be Old Labour was
to be centralist and undemocratic and to be New Labour is
not to be on the side of the poor and afflicted.

Cited in D. Brack (ed.), *Why I am a Liberal Democrat* (1996)

Max Aitken, Lord Beaverbrook

1879–1964; press baron; MP (Conservative) Ashton-under-Lyme 1910–16; created Baron Beaverbrook 1917; Lord Privy Seal 1943–45

Don't thank God. Thank Clem Davies.

> Response to his employee Alan Wood's comment, 'Thank God!', on hearing that Neville Chamberlain had resigned and been replaced by Winston Churchill, 10 May 1940 – Davies had played a key role in Chamberlain's downfall, cited in A. Wyburn-Powell, *Clement Davies: Liberal Leader* (2003)

Churchill was perhaps the greater man but George was more fun.

> On David Lloyd George, cited in K. O. Morgan, *David Lloyd George: Welsh Radical as World Statesman* (1963)

He does not care in which direction the car is travelling, so long as he remains in the driving seat.

> On David Lloyd George, *The Decline and Fall of Lloyd George* (1963)

Henry Ward Beecher

1813–87; American preacher and reformer

Liberty is the soul's right to breathe, and, when it cannot take a long breath, laws are girdled too tight.

> *Proverbs from Plymouth Pulpit* (1887)

Alan Beith

b. 1943; MP (Liberal, Liberal Democrat) Berwick-upon-Tweed 1973–; Liberal Chief Whip 1976–85, deputy leader of the Liberal Party 1985–88, deputy leader of the Liberal Democrats 1992–2003

If it means an intolerance to people who are simply different in their outlook and style to the rest of us, then I think it is rather a dangerous concept and there is no way you can enforce every law, every minute of every day.

> On the concept of zero tolerance in law enforcement, *The Independent*, 11 April 1997

Fundamental to Liberalism is the belief in the freedom of the individual. That freedom is threatened from many directions: by over-mighty states, by private concentrations of power, by the actions of other individuals, or by circumstances which leave the individual without access to power or opportunity. A preoccupation of Liberalism has therefore been the creation of a democratic system of government which can protect individual liberty and whose institutions are themselves restrained from usurping the freedom of the individual.

> Foreword to the Liberal Democrat policy paper *It's About Freedom* (2002)

The instinct of a Liberal is to distribute power as widely as possible, and to hold to account all those who exercise it.

> Attributed

Hilaire Belloc
1870–1953; historian, poet and novelist; MP (Liberal) Salford South 1906–10

Gentlemen, I am a Catholic ... if you reject me on account of my religion, I shall thank God that He has spared me the indignity of being your representative.

> To the voters of South Salford, 1906, cited in R. Speaight, *The Life of Hilaire Belloc* (1957)

A man can no more make a good speech in such a place than sing a song in it.

> On the House of Commons, 29 July 1930, cited in *The Political Diary of Hugh Dalton* (1986)

The choice lies between property on the one hand and slavery, public or private, on the other. There is no third issue.

An Essay on the Restoration of Property (1936)

Arnold Bennett

1867–1931; writer

Seventy minutes had passed before Mr Lloyd George arrived at his proper theme. He spoke for a hundred and seventeen minutes, in which period he was detected only once in the use of an argument.

Things That Have Interested Me (1921)

Every Briton is at heart a Tory – especially every British Liberal.

Commenting on the contemporary political scene, in *Journal*, December 1929

Nicholas Bennett

b. 1949; MP (Conservative) Pembroke 1987–92

Liberal Democrat support would be impressive only if it was measured on the Richter scale.

Cited in G. Knight, *Honourable Insults* (1990)

Jeremy Bentham

1748–1832; philosopher

The greatest happiness of the greatest number is the foundation of morals and legislation.

The Commonplace Book (1843)

Every law is an infraction of liberty.

Principles of the Civil Code in *Collected Works*, Vol. 1 (1843)

The only object of government ought to be the greatest possible happiness of the community ... It fulfils this object by creating rights, which it confers upon individuals: rights of personal security, rights of protection for honour, rights of property, rights of receiving aid in case of need.

Principles of the Civil Code in *Collected Works*, Vol. 1 (1843)

Right ... is the child of law: from real laws come real rights; but from imaginary laws, from laws of nature, fancied and invented by poets, rhetoricians, and dealers in moral and intellectual poisons, come imaginary rights, a bastard brood of monsters.

Anarchical Fallacies in *Collected Works*, Vol. 3 (1843)

Natural rights is simple nonsense: natural and imprescriptible rights, rhetorical nonsense – nonsense upon stilts.

Anarchical Fallacies in *Collected Works*, Vol. 3 (1843)

He rather hated the ruling few than loved the suffering many.

On James Mill, cited in H. N. Pym, *Memories of Old Friends, being Extracts from the Journals and Letters of Caroline Fox* (1882)

Isaiah Berlin

1909–97; philosopher

Liberty is liberty, not equality or fairness or justice or human happiness or a quiet conscience.

Two Concepts of Liberty (1958)

It is this – the 'positive' conception of liberty: not freedom from, but freedom to – which the adherents of the 'negative' notion represent as being, at times, no better than a specious disguise for brutal tyranny.

Two Concepts of Liberty (1958)

The fundamental sense of freedom is freedom from chains, from imprisonment, from enslavement by others. The rest is extension of this sense, or else metaphor.

Four Essays on Liberty (1969)

Injustice, poverty, slavery, ignorance – these may be cured by reform or revolution. But men do not live only by fighting evils. They live by positive goals, individual and collective, a vast variety of them, seldom predictable, at times incompatible.

Four Essays on Liberty (1969)

Those who have ever valued liberty for its own sake believed that to be free to choose, and not to be chosen for, is an inalienable ingredient in what makes human beings human.

Four Essays on Liberty (1969)

Few new truths have ever won their way against the resistance of established ideas save by being overstated.

Vico and Herder (1976)

No society is free unless it is governed by two interrelated principles: first, that no power but only rights can be regarded as absolute; second, that there are frontiers within which men should be inviolable.

Attributed

Leonard Bernstein

1918–90; American conductor, pianist and composer

A liberal is a man or a woman or a child who looks forward to a better day, a more tranquil night, and a bright, infinite future.

New York Times, 30 October 1988

Aneurin Bevan

1897–1960; MP (Labour) Ebbw Vale 1929–60; Minister for Health
1945–51

We know what happens to people who stay in the middle of the
road. They get run down.

The Observer, 6 December 1953

Lloyd George was a bigger man than Churchill, and one of the
biggest things about Churchill was that he knew it.

Cited in M. Foot, *Loyalists and Loners* (1986)

William Beveridge

1879–1963; academic; MP (Liberal) Berwick-upon-Tweed 1944–45;
created Baron Beveridge of Tuggal 1946

The object of government in peace and in war is not the glory of
rulers or of races, but the happiness of the common man.

Social Insurance and Allied Services (the Beveridge Report) (1942)

Want is one only of five giants on the road of reconstruction …
the others are Disease, Ignorance, Squalor and Idleness.

Social Insurance and Allied Services (the Beveridge Report) (1942)

This is the greatest advance in our history. There can be no
turning back. From now on Beveridge is not the name of a man;
it is the name of a way of life, and not only for Britain, but for
the whole of the civilised world.

To Harold Wilson on the publication of the Beveridge Report, cited in
H. Wilson, *Memoirs: Making of a Prime Minister 1916–64* (1986)

Ignorance is an evil weed which dictators may cultivate among
their dupes, but which no democracy can afford among its
dictators.

Full Employment in a Full Society (1944)

If full employment is not won and kept, no liberties are secure, for to many they will not seem worthwhile.

Full Employment in a Full Society (1944)

The ultimate aims of Liberalism are unchanged – equal enjoyment of all essential liberties secured by the rule of law, material progress for the sake of increasing spiritual life, toleration for variety of opinion, the common interest of all citizens over-riding every sectional privilege at home, peace and goodwill and international trade abroad. These aims endure. Today they must be pursued by new methods, by positive radical methods based on experience, suited to changed conditions. Liberalism is a faith, not a formula.

Why I am a Liberal (1945)

In many practical measures for improving the material conditions and the security of the masses of the people, Liberal and Labour will go together, as with them will go many Tory reformers. But as distinct from Labour, Liberals will always have more consciously in mind as their aim, not material progress but spiritual liberty; they will emphasise the importance of the individual and the need to let each man develop on his own line, so long as he does not harm others.

Why I am a Liberal (1945)

The outstanding merit of Liberalism as a political creed – that it stands for the general interest – means that the Liberal Party, unlike both its rivals, cannot count on automatic support from any sectional interest. It must build its own organisation for itself and its ideals.

Why I am a Liberal (1945)

Liberties are not all equally important. The error of the individualists is to treat them as if they were. The essence of Liberalism is to distinguish between essential liberties to be preserved at all costs, and lesser liberties which should be preserved only so far as they are consistent with social justice and social progress.

Why I am a Liberal (1945)

Bible

The vile person shall be no more called liberal, nor the churl said to be bountiful.

Isaiah 32, 6

But the liberal deviseth liberal things; and by liberal things shall he stand.

Isaiah 32, 8

Ambrose Bierce

1842–1914; American writer

Conservative, n. A statesman who is enamoured of existing evils, as distinguished from the Liberal, who wishes to replace them with others.

The Cynic's Word Book (1906)

Liberty, n. One of Imagination's most precious possessions.

The Devil's Dictionary (1911)

Christopher Bigsby and Malcolm Bradbury

Writers; Bigsby: b. 1941; Bradbury: 1932–2000

Liberals think that goats are just sheep from broken homes.

From BBC TV, *The After Dinner Game*, 1975

You know what they say: if God had been a liberal, we wouldn't have had the ten commandments. We'd have had the ten suggestions.

From BBC TV, *The After Dinner Game*, 1975

Bill of Rights
1689

[The] Lords Spiritual and Temporal and Commons ... being now assembled in a full and free representative of this nation ... do in the first place (as their ancestors in like case have usually done) for the vindicating and asserting their ancient rights and liberties declare

That the pretended power of suspending of laws or the execution of laws by regal authority without consent of Parliament is illegal.

That the pretended power of suspending of laws or the execution of laws by regal authority as it hath been assumed and exercised of late, is illegal.

That the commission for erecting the late court of commissioners for ecclesiastical causes and all other commissions and courts of like nature are illegal and pernicious.

That Levying money for or to the use of the crown by pretence of prerogative without grant of Parliament for longer time or in other manner that the same is or shall be granted is illegal.

That it is the right of the subjects to petition the king, and all commitments and prosecutions for such petitioning are illegal.

That the raising or keeping a standing army within the kingdom in time of peace unless it be with the consent of Parliament is against law.

That subjects which are Protestants may have arms for their defence suitable to their conditions and as allowed by law.

That election of members of Parliament ought to be free.

That the freedom of speech and debates or proceedings in Parliament ought not to be impeached or questioned in any court or place out of Parliament.

That excessive bail ought not to be required, nor excessive fines imposed, nor cruel and unusual punishments inflicted.

That jurors ought to be duly impaneled and returned and jurors which pass upon men in trials for high treason ought to be freeholders.

That all grants and promises of fines and forfeitures of particular persons before conviction are illegal and void.

And that for redress of all grievances and for the amending, strengthening, and reserving of the laws, Parliament ought to be held frequently.

And they do claim, demand and insist upon, all and singular, the premises as their undoubted rights and liberties...

The Bill of Rights, 1689, from *The Statutes of the Realm* (1819); the spelling has been modernised

Nigel Birch

1906–81; MP (Conservative) Flintshire, later Flintshire West 1945–70; Economic Secretary, HM Treasury 1957–58; created Baron Rhyl of Holywell 1970

An extremely respectable elderly spinster soliciting outside a pub on a wet Monday evening.

On Jo Grimond's attitude to the Labour Party, *The Times*, 27 September 1965

Birmingham Liberal Association

A body of well-intentioned elderly people, who have been unable to make any impression on local opinion ... [with] no coherent or continuing policy. The offices are uninviting; the staff are inadequate; and the atmosphere indicative of a decaying cause.

Report of the Enquiry Committee into the state of Birmingham Liberal Association, February 1946

Augustine Birrell

1850–1933; MP (Liberal) Fife West 1889–1900, Bristol North 1906–18;
President, Board of Education 1905–07, Chief Secretary for Ireland 1907–16

The Master should have added that he can go further, for
it is obvious that the affairs of the world are built upon the
momentous fact that God also is a Trinity man.

> 1902, at a dinner at Trinity College, Cambridge, at which the Master
> proposed a toast to the King and Prime Minister, both Trinity men,
> cited in a letter from Harold Laski to Oliver Wendell Holmes,
> 4 December 1926

Wordsworth has been called the High Priest of Nature. Burke
may be called the High Priest of Order – a lover of settled ways,
of justice, peace and security. His writings are a storehouse of
wisdom, not the cheap shrewdness of the mere man of the world,
but the noble, animating wisdom of one who has the poet's heart
as well as the statesman's brain. Nobody is fit to govern this
country who has not drunk deep at the springs of Burke.

> *Obiter Dicta* (1910)

Liberalism is not a creed but a frame of mind.

> Attributed to Birrell in J. Morley, *Recollections* (1917)

What a grateful thought that there is not an acre in this vast and
varied landscape that is not represented at Westminster by a
London barrister.

> On the view from a Fife hilltop, including Asquith's, Haldane's and his
> own constituencies, cited in H. H. Asquith, *Memories and Reflections*, Vol.
> 2 (1928)

William Blackstone

1723–80; jurist and judge; MP Hindon 1761–68, Westbury 1768–70

The absolute rights of man, considered as a free agent, endowed
with discernment to know good from evil, and with power

of choosing those measures which appear to him to be most desirable, are usually summed up on one general appellation, and denominated the natural liberty of mankind. This natural liberty consists properly in a power of acting as one thinks fit, without any restraint or control, unless by the law of nature: being a right inherent in us by birth, and one of the gifts of God to man at his creation, when he endued him with the faculty of freewill.

Commentaries on the Laws of England (1765–69)

It is better that ten guilty persons escape than one innocent suffer.

Commentaries on the Laws of England (1765–69)

Andrew Bonar Law

1858–1923; MP (Conservative) Glasgow Blackfriars & Hutchesontown 1900–06, Camberwell, Dulwich 1906–10, Bootle 1911–18, Glasgow Central 1918–23; Chancellor of the Exchequer 1916–19, Prime Minister 1922–23

An example of destructive violence to which there is no parallel since the Long Parliament.

On the record of the Asquith government, at the Royal Albert Hall, 26 January 1912

I am afraid I shall have to show myself as very vicious, Mr Asquith, this session. I hope you will understand.

Letter to H. H. Asquith, 9 April 1912

George will always be his own party.

On David Lloyd George, 1922, cited in D. Englefield, J. Seaton & I. White, *Facts About the British Prime Ministers* (1996)

Mark Bonham Carter

1922–94; MP (Liberal) Torrington 1958–59; created Baron Bonham
Carter of Yarnbury 1986

It is the task of a radical party to make a re-appraisal of the
British position and having made it to lead the country in new
directions. There is nothing shameful in not being a great power,
nor is it necessarily boring. For the bulk of our history we
have had to make terms with our more powerful neighbours
and develop a way of life in conformity with our means. Since
the great powers of the twentieth century have little room to
manoeuvre, and since their posture is of necessity pretty rigid,
an escape from the world's predicament may well be found
by those who, having experienced greatness, have recently
descended into the middle ranks. They can afford to experiment
with new types of political association; indeed they must. It is
for them to develop forms of international cooperation, perhaps
a pattern of international democracy, which may allow the tiny
world we share with so many other societies at such contrasting
levels of development to develop without the total destruction
of us all, but which, at the same time, will have to take into
account the enduring fact that, although some societies will
always regard others as bad, to treat them as intolerable is today
to jeopardise the survival of mankind.

   'Liberals and the Political Future', *Radical Alternative*, 1962

Violet Bonham Carter

1887–1969; President, Women's Liberal Federation 1923–25, 1939–45;
President, Liberal Party 1945–47; created Baroness Asquith of Yarnbury
1964

We are asked to choose between one man suffering from
sleeping sickness, and another from St Vitus's Dance.

   On the collapse of the coalition government into factions led by Bonar
   Law and Lloyd George, 1922, cited in M. Tester, *Wit of The Asquiths*
   (1974)

Mr Lloyd George has split one party, and there is evidently some chance of his wrecking another. Perhaps, before many months have passed, he will be trying to build a raft – out of the splinters of both.

1922, cited in M. Tester, *Wit of The Asquiths* (1974)

We hear much talk about the Lion lying down with the Lamb. I can only say for myself that I have never seen Mr Lloyd George look less voracious – or my father more uneatable.

On Liberal reunification for the 1923 election, cited in M. Tester, *Wit of The Asquiths* (1974)

We Liberals have nothing so gaudy to show as their red flags and blue blood.

On the Labour Party following the defections from the Liberal Party of Lord Haldane and Lady Warwick, 1924, cited in M. Tester, *Wit of The Asquiths* (1974)

[The Conservatives have] settled down quite comfortably with Mr Churchill now, and he is very useful to them; but it's taken a world war to make them touch him with a bargepole. Let us be fair to them – they are not always wrong – but they are always wrong at the right moment and right twenty years too late. The task of statesmanship is to forestall events, not to be dragged helpless at their flying heels.

On the Conservative Party, election broadcast, 23 June 1945

A Britain without Liberalism would be a Britain that had lost its soul.

June 1945, cited in J. McCallum & A. V. Readman, *The British General Election of 1945* (1947)

We are not satisfied with this milk-and-water Beveridge they call National Insurance – we like our beverage neat.

1945, cited in M. Tester, *Wit of The Asquiths* (1974)

The Conservative Party have all suddenly become Liberal, under another name of course. Once again they have caught the Liberals bathing, and stolen their clothes – or so we read in the press. We do not begrudge them our Liberal clothes, if only they would wear them!

> On the Tories' Industrial Charter, cited in M. Tester, *Wit of The Asquiths* (1974)

Even the election didn't really dishearten me – I still believed we could stage a come-back – a great revival. Well, now quite frankly I do not believe that can happen (certainly not by 1950) … One must face the *possibility* of Parliamentary extinction.

> Letter to Megan Lloyd George, 17 November 1947

It is an action so subtle and intricate, and beyond me, that I think it would be understood only by Freud.

> Referring to Megan Lloyd George's decision to vote against a motion criticising the Labour government on the rising cost of living which she herself had tabled, 1950, cited in M. Tester, *Wit of The Asquiths* (1974)

Sir Stafford Cripps has a brilliant mind – until he makes it up.

> 1951, cited in M. Tester, *Wit of The Asquiths* (1974)

Mr Bevan is such a gift horse to his opponents that it would be ungrateful of us to look him in the mouth.

> On Aneurin Bevan at Holyport, 1951, cited in M. Tester, *Wit of The Asquiths* (1974)

A political refrigerator.

> Describing Clement Attlee, Colne Valley 1951, cited in M. Tester, *Wit of The Asquiths* (1974)

If Mr Attlee believes me to be a Conservative, he must believe me to be a liar – and a lunatic as well … Who but a stark mad

Conservative would spend, as I have done, some twenty years in the wilderness pretending to be a Liberal.

At Colne Valley, 1951, cited in M. Tester, *Wit of The Asquiths* (1974)

I don't feel like a dead fly – I mean to do some flying, and some buzzing, and even possibly some stinging in the next few weeks!

After Clement Attlee described her as 'a dead fly', 1951, cited in
M. Tester, *Wit of The Asquiths* (1974)

[I] almost persuaded myself during the '51–56 Government [that] Toryism was shading into Liberalism ... Now I feel there is a reversion to type.

After the Suez crisis, letter to W. Monckton, cited in K. Morgan, *The People's Peace* (1990)

When I went to Torrington, I had a strange feeling that I was a member of an army of liberation, setting out to free territory which had been held by Quislings and collaborators, whose day was at an end. There are still thousands of Liberals living in occupied territory, whom we have yet to liberate. The message which goes out to them today is 'Hold on, hold out, we are coming', and we are!

At the National Liberal Club, March 1958, following her son's victory in the Torrington by-election, cited in J. Thorpe, *In My Own Time* (1999); the 'Quislings and collaborators' were National Liberals

Wade is ill, Jeremy is ill, Clem [Davies] is a chronic absentee and useless when present. [Grimond] wrote imploringly to Bowen to be with him for the Berlin debate on Monday and to speak – and Bowen replied that he had 'a function'. He does damn all in the House. As Jo says – why go into it?

On the state of the Liberal Party in the House of Commons, July 1961, cited in D. Dutton, *A History of the Liberal Party* (2004)

Lloyd George needed, in order to deploy his great gifts, a great stage, footlights, and, above all, an audience. But he was not an actor – he was a medium. He lived and fed on his immediate surroundings – in fact he seemed almost to be created by them, sometimes to his advantage, and sometimes to his detriment.

Romanes Lecture, 1963, cited in M. Tester, *Wit of The Asquiths* (1974)

If goods do not cross frontiers, armies will.

On free trade, *Winston Churchill as I Knew Him* (1965); more commonly attributed to Bastiat

Government decisions should be reached behind closed doors. Watching the Government planners trying to make up their minds in public is not only demoralising but amounts to indecent exposure.

On the much-trailed decision to cancel orders for the TSR2 and other advanced UK military aircraft, 1967, cited in M. Tester, *Wit of The Asquiths* (1974)

She ... flashed into our lives like some dazzling bird of paradise, filling us with amazement, amusement, excitement: sometimes with a vague uneasiness as to what she might do next ... She was a law unto herself.

On her stepmother, Margot Asquith, cited in M. Tester, *Wit of The Asquiths* (1974)

My father liked thinking alone – Winston Churchill liked thinking aloud.

Cited in M. Tester, *Wit of The Asquiths* (1974)

We have held the Liberal faith. We are not as some of the ex-Liberal families are – scattered among the various parties like confetti.

A reference to the Lloyd George family, cited in M. Tester, *Wit of The Asquiths* (1974)

On my first day, [the Lords] spent a whole afternoon discussing the Dogs' Bill ... It was a Bill to prevent dogs misbehaving on the pavements. I haven't an idea of what the official Liberal line was on the Dogs' Bill. My Liberal instincts were to favour freedom of choice for the dogs. Why shouldn't dogs be free to choose between the gutter and the pavement – just as Lord Snow is free to choose between Eton and a comprehensive school?

Cited in M. Tester, *Wit of The Asquiths* (1974)

Their policies are often determined by habit, heredity, custom, colours. They like at meetings – as we all do in Church – to sing the hymns they know. New tunes disturb them. Like old soldiers, they feel most at home when fighting the election battle before the last.

On political activists, cited in M. Tester, *Wit of The Asquiths* (1974)

Neutrality is not in my makeup. I have never sat on the fence since I was born. I don't feel comfortable on a fence, besides – there are no fences to sit on in the world today.

Cited in M. Tester, *Wit of The Asquiths* (1974)

Horatio Bottomley

1860–1933; MP (Liberal) Hackney South 1906–12, (Independent) 1918–22; fraudster and propagandist

No, reaping.

Reply to a prison visitor, who saw him sewing mail bags and asked, 'Ah, Bottomley, sewing?', 1922, cited in J. Lewis, *Horatio Bottomley* (1953)

Duncan Brack, Richard S. Grayson and David Howarth

Liberal Democrat activists, academics and policy-makers; Brack, b. 1960; Grayson b. 1969; Howarth b. 1958; MP (Liberal Democrat) Cambridge 2005–10

It is about reinventing the British state so that it delivers social justice and environmental sustainability through a decentralised and participatory democracy.

On social liberalism; Introduction, *Reinventing the State: Social Liberalism for the 21ˢᵗ Century* (2007)

Ian Bradley

b. 1950; Liberal candidate, writer and theologian

[T]he greatest obstacles of all to the creation of a truly liberal society are the forces of cynicism, fatalism and despair. We need to meet those forces head on in a crusading spirit and with a conviction of the utter worth of human life and endeavour.

The Strange Rebirth of Liberal England (1985)

Louis Dembitz Brandeis

1856–1941; American Supreme Court judge 1916–39

Experience teaches us to be most on our guard to protect liberty when the government's purpose is beneficent. Men born to freedom are naturally alert to repel invasion of their liberty by evil-minded rulers. The greatest dangers to liberty lurk in insidious encroachment by men of zeal, well-meaning but without understanding.

Attributed

John Bright

1811–89; MP (Liberal) Durham 1843–47, Manchester 1847–57, Birmingham 1857–85, (Liberal Unionist) Birmingham Central 1885–89; President of the Board of Trade 1868–70, Chancellor of the Duchy of Lancaster 1873–74, 1880–82; radical orator

I have no interest in the extravagance of Government; I have no interest in receiving appointments under any Government; I have no interest in pandering to the views of any Government; I have nothing to gain by being the tool of any party. I come here before you as the friend of my own class and order, as one of the people; as one who would on all occasions, be the firm defender of all your rights and asserter of all those privileges to which you are justly entitled.

> At Durham, 17 July 1843, cited in B. Cash, *John Bright: Statesman, Orator, Agitator* (2012)

The principles of free trade are so simple that the mind of no unbiased man who hears them will have any hesitation in receiving them as true ... We ask that the world should be our workshop, and the wide world our market.

> At the Covent Garden Theatre, 27 March 1844, cited in B. Cash, *John Bright: Statesman, Orator, Agitator* (2012)

The angel of death has been abroad throughout the land; you may almost hear the beating of its wings.

> On the effects of the Crimean War, in the House of Commons, 23 February 1855

Palaces, baronial castles, great halls, stately mansions, do not make a nation. The nation in every country dwells in the cottage; and unless the light of your Constitution can shine there, unless the beauty of your legislation and the excellence of your statesmanship are impressed there on the feelings and condition of the people, rely on it you have yet to learn the duties of government.

> At Birmingham, 29 October 1858

A gigantic system of outdoor relief for the aristocracy of Great Britain.

> Describing British foreign policy, at Birmingham, 29 October 1858, cited in J. E. T. Rogers (ed.), *The Speeches of John Bright* (1883)

I am for peace, retrenchment and reform, the watchword of the great Liberal Party thirty years ago.

> At Birmingham, 28 April 1859; the phrase has been traced to Washington Irving, *The Sketchbook: John Bull* (1820)

England is the mother of all Parliaments.

> At Birmingham, 18 January 1865

[He] has retired into what may be called his political Cave of Adullam – and he has called about him everyone that was in distress and everyone that was discontented.

Attacking Robert Lowe and fellow Whig opponents of parliamentary reform, referring to 1 Samuel 22, in the House of Commons, 13 March 1866

You may have an historical monarchy decked out in the dazzling splendour of royalty; you may have an ancient nobility settled in grand mansions and on great estates; you may have an ecclesiastical hierarchy, hiding with its worldly pomp that religion whose first virtue is humility; but notwithstanding all of this, the whole fabric may be rotten and doomed ultimately to fall, if the great mass of the people on whom it is supported is poor, and suffering, and degraded.

At Edinburgh, 5 November 1868

If government were just, if taxes were moderate and equitably imposed, if land were free, if schools were as prominent institutions in our landscapes and in our great towns as prisons and workhouses are, I suspect we should find the people gradually gaining more self-respect.

At Edinburgh, 5 November 1868

The workman of England is no longer a human machine. He is a man into whom has been infused a new life, and to whom is given a new and wholesome responsibility. Every voting working man in England is now a ruler of men, and a joint ruler of many nations.

On the extension of the franchise, at Rochdale Working Men's Club, 1877

This policy [imperialism] may lead to a seeming glory to the Crown, and may give scope for patronage and promotion and pay and pensions to a limited and favoured class, but to you, the people, it brings expenditure of blood and treasure, increased debt and taxes, and the added risks of war in every quarter of the globe.

At Manchester, October 1879

The Government from that time [the Great Reform Act of 1832] has been, with the exception of about twelve years, Liberal in name, and has steadily become more and more Liberal to the great advantage of the nation.

Diary entry in 1880, cited in R. A. J. Walling (ed.), *The Diaries of John Bright* (1930)

From her [Rome's] history, and indeed from all history, I learn that loud boasting, great wealth, great power, extended dominion, successive conquests, mighty fleets and armies, are not immovable foundations of national greatness. I would rely rather on an educated and moral people, and on a system of government free at home, and scrupulously moral and just in its dealings with every other government and people.

Cited in G. M. Trevelyan, *The Life of John Bright* (1925)

I could not be otherwise than a Liberal. I knew that I came from the stock of martyrs, that one of my ancestors had been in prison for several years because he preferred to worship in the humble meeting house of his own favoured sect rather than in the church of the law-favoured sect.

Cited in G. M. Trevelyan, *The Life of John Bright* (1925)

For the disbanding of great armies and the promotion of peace, I rely on the abolition of tariffs, on the brotherhood of the nations resulting from free trade in the products of industry.

Cited in J. L. Sturgis, *John Bright and the Empire* (1969)

You find it in Holy Writ that the Earth is the Lord's, and the fullness thereof. We have put Holy Writ into an Act of Parliament.

After the repeal of the Corn Laws in 1846, cited in A. Briggs, *Victorian People* (1971)

It was not a good Bill but it was a great Bill when it passed.

> On the Great Reform Bill, 1831, cited in N. Gash, *Aristocracy and People 1815–65* (1979)

And he adores his maker.

> On being told that Disraeli should be admired for being a self-made man, attributed; also attributed to Henry Clapp (1814–75), with his target being journalist Horace Greeley

Leon Brittan

b. 1939; MP (Conservative) Cleveland & Whitby 1974–83, Richmond 1983–88; Home Secretary 1983–85; European Commissioner 1989–99; created Baron Brittan of Spennithorne 2000

I said that if he [Nick Clegg] wasn't happy with the Conservatives and wasn't happy with Labour, all that left was the Liberal Democrats, 'so you've really got to make up your mind: do you want to join a party of power or a party of influence? There's nothing wrong with influence, it's very important, and you can direct policies in useful directions, but it's very different from being in power. And if you join the Liberal Democrats, you'll only have influence, whereas if you join the Conservatives or Labour, you'll at some stage be in power.'

> Brittan was Clegg's boss at the European Commission 1996–99, cited in C. Bowers, *Nick Clegg: The Biography* (2011)

Christopher Brocklebank-Fowler

b. 1934; MP (Conservative, SDP) King's Lynn, later Norfolk North West 1970–83

It is very unlikely that the majority of our membership would accept merger with the Liberals when it is clear, both from Roy Jenkins's Dimbleby Lecture and from the Limehouse Declaration, that the SDP was founded in response to a discernible need for a radical new political party which has drawn its membership from the Labour Party, the Conservative Party, some disenchanted Liberals, and a majority who previously were not members of any political party.

On a merger proposal put to the 1983 SDP conference, *The Social Democrat*, 19 August 1983

Claire Brooks

1931–2008; Liberal councillor and activist

I do not want to wake up one morning to find I am a member of a party of disgruntled, conscience-stricken Tories and half-baked Socialists.

At the 1958 Liberal Assembly, Torquay, cited in A. Watkins, *The Liberal Dilemma* (1966)

Henry Brougham

1778–1868; MP (Whig) Camelford 1810–12, Winchelsea 1815–30, Yorkshire 1830; created Baron Brougham and Vaux 1830; Lord Chancellor 1830–34

Education makes a people easy to lead, but difficult to drive; easy to govern but impossible to enslave.

Observations on the Education of the People (1825)

The great unwashed.

Attributed

William Browne

1692–1774; physician and writer

The King to Oxford sent a troop of horse,
For Tories own no argument but force:

With equal skill to Cambridge books he sent,
For Whigs admit no force but argument.

    Cited in J. Nichols, *Literary Anecdotes*, Vol. 3 (1812–16)

Malcolm Bruce

b. 1944; MP (Liberal, Liberal Democrat) Gordon 1983–

The concept of supremacy of Parliament is an outdated
obscenity. It has been used by corrupt politicians to suppress
and deny rights and opinions that do not conform to the ruling
establishment.

    At the Liberal Democrat conference, Blackpool, 17 September 1990

Arthur Bryant

1899–1985; historian

Liberty does not consist merely of denouncing Tyranny, any
more than horticulture does of deploring and abusing weeds, or
even pulling them out.

    Illustrated London News, 24 June 1939

L. Bulley

Women's Liberal Federation member

Every bright and clever woman in my Liberal society has left
us. Can you wonder at our intense gratitude to men like Philip
Snowden and Ramsay MacDonald and Labour associations who
value their women?

    Letter to Margaret Lloyd George, c. 1914, cited in M. Pugh, *The
Making of Modern British Politics 1867–1939* (1982)

Edmund Burke

1729–97; statesman and writer; MP (Whig) Wendover 1765–74, Bristol
1774–80, Malton 1780–94

In all forms of Government the people is the true legislator.

A Tract on the Popery Laws (c. 1765)

People must be governed in a manner agreeable to their temper
and disposition; and men of free character and spirit must be
ruled with, at least, some condescension to this spirit and this
character.

Observations on a Late Publication entitled 'The Present State of the Nation'
(1769)

It is a general popular error to imagine the loudest complainers
for the public to be the most anxious for its welfare.

Observations on a Late Publication entitled 'The Present State of the Nation'
(1769)

I am not one of those who think that the people are never
wrong. They have been so, frequently and outrageously, both
in other countries and in this. But I do say, that in all disputes
between them and their rulers, the presumption is at least upon
a par in favour of the people.

Thoughts on the Cause of the Present Discontents (1770)

When bad men combine, the good must associate; else they will
fall, one by one, an unpitied sacrifice in a contemptible struggle.

Thoughts on the Cause of the Present Discontents (1770)

To complain of the age we live in, to murmur at the present
possessor of power, to lament the past, to conceive extravagant
hopes of the future, are the common dispositions of the greatest
part of mankind.

Thoughts on the Cause of the Present Discontents (1770)

We must soften into a credulity below the milkiness of infancy to think all men virtuous. We must be tainted with a malignity truly diabolical, to believe all the world to be equally wicked and corrupt.

Thoughts on the Cause of the Present Discontents (1770)

The greater the power, the more dangerous the abuse.

Comment on the Middlesex election, 7 February 1771

Your representative owes you, not his industry only, but his judgement; and he betrays, instead of serving you, if he sacrifices it to your opinion.

At Bristol, 3 November 1774

Abstract liberty, like other mere abstractions, is not to be found.

On Conciliation with America (1775)

Freedom and not servitude is the cure of anarchy; as religion, and not atheism, is the true remedy of superstition.

On Conciliation with America (1775)

It is the love of the people; it is their attachment to their government, from the sense of the deep stake they have in such a glorious institution, which gives you your army and your navy, and infuses into both liberal obedience, without which your army would be a base rabble, and your navy nothing but rotten timber.

On Conciliation with America (1775)

Parties must ever exist in a free country.

On Conciliation with America (1775)

The use of force alone is but temporary. It may subdue for a moment; but it does not remove the necessity of subduing again; and a nation is not governed, which is perpetually to be conquered.

On Conciliation with America (1775)

I was persuaded that government was a practical thing made for the happiness of mankind, and not to furnish out a spectacle of uniformity to gratify the schemes of visionary politicians.

Letter to the Sheriffs of Bristol (1777)

Among a people generally corrupt, liberty cannot long exist.

Letter to the Sheriffs of Bristol (1777)

Liberty too must be limited in order to be possessed.

Letter to the Sheriffs of Bristol (1777)

People crushed by law have no hopes but from power. If laws are their enemies, they will be enemies to laws; and those, who have much to hope and nothing to lose, will always be dangerous, more or less.

Letter to Charles James Fox, 8 October 1777

Bad laws are the worst sort of tyranny.

At Bristol, Previous to the Late Election (1780)

I feel an inseparable reluctance in giving my hand to destroy any established institution of government, upon a theory, however plausible it may be.

On Fox's East India Bill, in the House of Commons, 1 December 1783

The people never give up their liberties but under some delusion.

At Buckinghamshire, 1784

A state without the means of some change is without the means of its conservation.

Reflections on the Revolution in France (1790)

This sort of people are so taken up with their theories about the rights of man, that they have totally forgotten his nature.

Reflections on the Revolution in France (1790)

The age of chivalry has gone. That of sophisters, economists, and calculators, has succeeded; and the glory of Europe is extinguished forever.

Reflections on the Revolution in France (1790)

Kings will be tyrants from policy when subjects are rebels from principle.

Reflections on the Revolution in France (1790)

Society is indeed a contract ... it becomes a partnership not only between those who are living, but between those who are living, those who are dead, and those who are to be born.

Reflections on the Revolution in France (1790)

Good order is the foundation of all good things.

Reflections on the Revolution in France (1790)

Nothing turns out to be so oppressive and unjust as a feeble government.

Reflections on the Revolution in France (1790)

Those who have been once intoxicated with power, and have derived any kind of emolument from it, even though for but one year, can never willingly abandon it.

Letter to a Member of the National Assembly (1791)

Tyrants seldom want pretexts.

Letter to a Member of the National Assembly (1791)

You can never plan the future by the past.

Letter to a Member of the National Assembly (1791)

And having looked to government for bread, on the very first scarcity they will turn and bite the hand that fed them.

Thoughts and Details on Scarcity (1800)

It is necessary only for the good man to do nothing for evil to triumph.

Attributed

John Burns

1858–1943; MP (Labour/Liberal) Battersea 1892–1918; President of the Local Government Board 1906–14, President of the Board of Trade 1914

I have seen the Mississippi. That is muddy water. I have seen the St Lawrence. That is crystal water. But the Thames is liquid history.

Daily Mail, 25 January 1943

Josephine Butler

1828–1906; campaigner for women's education, the vote and the repeal of the Contagious Diseases Acts

Uniformity is not a beautiful thing. There is no uniformity in God's creation, either in the natural or the spiritual world. The insistence on uniformity crushes out individuality and hinders initiative. It clips the wings of the best human gifts and capacities.

The Storm-Bell, 1899, cited in *An Autobiographical Memoir* (1909)

Race prejudice is a poison which will have to be cast out if the world is ever to be Christianised, and if Great Britain is to maintain the high and responsible place among the nations which has been given to her.

Native Races and the War (1900) (on the Boer War), cited in *An Autobiographical Memoir* (1909)

Samuel Butler

1835–1902; author, painter and musician

The simple-minded and child-like earnestness of his character, an earnestness which might be perceived by the solemnity with

which he spoke even about trifles. It is hardly necessary to say
he was on the Liberal side in politics.

On the learned public schoolmaster, Dr Skinner, *The Way of All Flesh*
(1903)

Frank Byers

1915–84; MP (Liberal) North Dorset 1945–50; Liberal Chief Whip
1946–50; created Baron Byers of Lingfield 1964; leader of the Liberal
peers 1967–84

The man with the deep-frozen smile.

On Edward Heath, *Guardian Report of the Liberal Assembly 1965*

George Byron

1788–1824; Romantic poet; became 6th Baron Byron 1798

Hereditary Bondsmen! know ye not
Who would be free themselves must strike the blow?

Childe Harold's Pilgrimage (1812)

Talk not of seventy years of age. In seven
I have seen more changes, down from monarchs to
The humblest individual under heaven,
Than might suffice a moderate century through.
I knew that nought was lasting, but now even
Change grows too changeable without being new.
Nought's permanent among the human race,
Except the Whigs not getting into place.

A reference to successive Whig election defeats; *Don Juan*, Canto XI
(1819–24)

C

Vince Cable

b. 1943; MP (Liberal Democrat) Twickenham 1997–; deputy leader of the Liberal Democrats 2006–10, Secretary of State for Business, Innovation & Skills 2010–

The House has noticed the Prime Minister's remarkable transformation in the past few weeks from Stalin to Mr Bean: creating chaos out of order, rather than order out of chaos.

On Gordon Brown, in the House of Commons, 28 November 2007

Economic storms ... test out the underlying seaworthiness of the vessels of state. The fleet has been plying a gentle swell for some years and making impressive progress. But big waves are already exposing some weaknesses. SS *Britannia*, said to be unsinkable, has sprung a leak ... Passengers and crews are starting to panic and have noticed that most of the life rafts are reserved for those in First Class.

The Storm (2009)

Nineteenth-century history, taught in the O level curriculum, also led to the conclusion that Liberals were progressive and a Good Thing, while Conservatives – Disraeli excepted – were reactionary and a Bad Thing.

Free Radical (2009)

The lesson of Charles Kennedy's political success on the Iraq War was the need to muscle in on the story; to take risks; to challenge; to avoid being sucked into any cosy establishment consensus; and to tap into popular idealism, anger and frustration – the politics of protest.

Free Radical (2009)

I draw encouragement from the fact that some of our greatest leaders came into their political prime in their sixties or seventies. And I cannot be the only pensioner in the country to have discovered deep reserves of energy, curiosity and ambition when convention suggests that we are 'too old'.

Free Radical (2009)

According to the papers, I'm miserable, alienated, and on the brink of resignation. But that's simply not where I am.

Interview, *The Guardian*, 9 August 2010

Banks operate like a man who either wears his trousers round his chest, stifling breathing, as now, or round his ankles, exposing his assets. We want their trousers tied round their middle: steady lending growth; particularly to productive British business, especially small-scale enterprise.

At the Liberal Democrat conference, Birmingham, 19 September 2011

The European project was constructed to rescue Europe from extreme nationalism and conflict. There is no guarantee that won't return.

New Statesman, 15 October 2012

Charles Pratt, Lord Camden

1714–94; MP (Whig) Downton 1757–61; created Baron Camden of Camden Place 1765; Lord Chancellor 1766–70; created Earl of Camden and Viscount Bayham of Bayham Abbey 1786 .

Taxation and representation are inseparable … whatever is a man's own is absolutely his own; no man hath a right to take it from him without his consent either expressed by himself or representative; whoever attempts to do it, attempts an injury; whoever does it, commits a robbery; he throws down and destroys the distinction between liberty and slavery.

In the House of Lords, 10 February 1766

Menzies Campbell

b. 1941; MP (Liberal, Liberal Democrat) Fife North East 1987–, leader of the Liberal Democrats 2006–07

I should have liked to be leader of the Liberal Democrats, but the party wants rather more emollient qualities in its leader than I possess.

Financial Times, 3 June 1999

Too many of our most worthy and well-meaning activists are Roundheads, while Liberal Democrats should be the Cavaliers of British politics.

Financial Times, 3 June 1999

The threat was manufactured not in the sands of Iraq, but in the corridors of Whitehall. The tyranny of oppression has been replaced by the tyranny of terrorism. The misjudgement of war, matched only by the mishandling of occupation.

At the Liberal Democrat conference, Blackpool, 19 September 2005

I am going to lead the party to crusade against poverty – the poverty of income and the poverty of aspiration. Fairness and freedom are the inalienable right of every citizen.

Following victory in the 2006 leadership election, 2 March 2006

Radical action doesn't feature on Labour's agenda. Gordon Brown spent the last decade wanting to move into No. 10. But the most extraordinary thing he has done since he finally got the job is to praise Margaret Thatcher. It's like a soap opera. It's certainly an identity crisis. Gordon wants to be like Maggie. But he doesn't want to be like Tony. Tony also wanted to be like Maggie. But Maggie only wanted to be like Ronnie. Now Dave, he wants to be like Tony. But he doesn't want to be like William, or Iain, or Michael. And certainly not like Maggie either. Confused? You must be. But you can be clear on this: I don't want to be like any of them.

At the Liberal Democrat conference, Brighton, 20 September 2007

A truly liberal society guarantees the freedom of all religions, but it accepts the tyranny of none. People must be free to live without threat or fear. To say the things, write the words and live the lives they choose. Does that offend some people? Yes, of course. But the price of freedom is the risk of offence, and, for me, that price is always worth paying ... the Liberal Democrats must be the voice of those who are not heard – of those who are marginalised, and of those who are rejected.

At the Liberal Democrat conference, Brighton, 20 September 2007

What frustrated me most was how the media's obsession with my age obscured the party's radical policy agenda and the progress it had made under my leadership.

Menzies Campbell: My Autobiography (2008)

The public got it right. It is a great pity the politicians got it wrong.

On the Iraq war, *The Independent*, 25 July 2010

Henry Campbell-Bannerman

1836–1908; MP (Liberal) Stirling Burghs 1868–1908, Secretary of State for War 1886, 1892–95, leader of the Liberal Party 1899–1908, Prime Minister 1905–08

What is Liberalism? I should say it means the acknowledgement in practical life of the truth that men are best governed who govern themselves; that the general sense of mankind, if left alone, will make for righteousness; that artificial privileges and restraints upon freedom, so far as they are not required in the interest of the community, are hurtful; and that the laws, while, of course, they cannot equalise conditions, can at least avoid aggravating inequalities, and ought to have for their object the securing to every man the best chance he can have of a good and useful life.

Speech, 1898

When is a war not a war? When it is carried on by methods of barbarism in South Africa.

At the National Reform Union dinner, 14 June 1901

I am no believer in the doctrine of the clean slate.

Replying to Lord Rosebery's speech of 16 December 1901, at Leicester, 19 February 1902

We are Liberals. We believe in free trade because we believe in the capacity of our countrymen.

At Bolton 1903, cited in I. Bradley, *The Optimists* (1980)

Good government could never be a substitute for government by the people themselves.

At Stirling, 23 November 1905

Enough of this tomfoolery. It might have answered very well in the last Parliament, but it is altogether out of place in this.

To the Unionist leader A. J. Balfour, in the House of Commons, 1906, cited in R. Hattersley, *The Edwardians* (2004)

There's the last kick. My dear fellow, I don't mind. I've been Prime Minister for longer than I deserve.

On signing his letter of resignation, 3 April 1908

The Sledgehammer.

Nickname for H. H. Asquith, cited in D. Englefield, J. Seaton & I. White, *Facts About the British Prime Ministers* (1996)

He showed how little political and parliamentary education he had because he thought it was sufficient defence of any public utterance to say that it was true.

On Lord Rosebery, cited in G. Knight, *Honourable Insults* (1990)

No more tact than a hippopotamus … Haldane always prefers the backstairs. But it does not matter. The clatter can be heard all over the house.

> On R. B. Haldane, cited in A. Jay, *Oxford Dictionary of Political Quotations* (1996)

Thomas Carlyle

1795–1881; writer, historian and philosopher

I note the English Whig has, in the second generation, become an English Radical; who, in the third again, it is to be hoped, will become an English Rebuilder.

> *Sartor Resartus* (1858)

Gladstone appears to be one of the contemptiblest men I ever looked on. A poor Ritualist; an almost spectral kind of phantasm of man, nothing in him but forms and ceremonies and kinds of wrappings.

> 1873, cited in J. Green, *Dictionary of Insulting Quotations* (1996)

Cobden is an inspired bagman, who believes in a calico millennium.

> Cited in T. W. Reid, *Life, Letters and Friendships of Richard Monckton*, Vol. 1 (1890)

Vote by ballot is the dyspepsia of society.

> Cited in S. Heffer, *Moral Desperado* (1995)

Alistair Carmichael

b. 1965; MP (Liberal Democrat) Orkney & Shetland 2001–; Liberal Democrat Chief Whip 2010–

I fought the Lords and the Lords won.

> On the failure of legislation for an elected House of Lords, Liberal Democrat conference, Brighton, 21 September 2012

His favourite song is Supertramp's 'The Logical Song' because of the line, 'Watch what you say / now they'll be calling you a radical, a liberal – fanatical, criminal'. 'I think,' he grins, 'that's the company that liberals should be in, the radicals, the fanaticals – maybe not the criminals. But liberalism shouldn't be about the safe option, it should always be a risky thing to take on.'

Interview, *Total Politics*, November 2012

Mike Carr

b. 1946; teacher; MP (Liberal Democrat) Ribble Valley 1991–92

Here lies the poll tax, killed in Ribble Valley.

Victory speech at the Ribble Valley by-election, March 1991; two weeks later the government announced the scrapping of Council Tax; cited in R. Ingham & D. Brack (eds), *Peace, Reform and Liberation* (2011)

John Cartwright

1740–1824; naval officer and campaigner for parliamentary reform (often called 'the father of Reform')

One man shall have one vote.

People's Barrier Against Undue Influence (1780)

How is despotism to be reformed? This is the point we have to consider. We are to remember that the despotism being legislative, it must be the very agent of its own reformation.

Letter to Christopher Wyvill, 1811

Thomas Nixon Carver

1865–1961; American economist

The trouble with radicals is that they only read radical literature, and the trouble with conservatives is that they don't read anything.

Described as Carver's Law by J. K. Galbraith, *A Life in Our Times* (1981)

Barbara Castle

1910–2002; MP (Labour) Blackburn 1945–79; Minister for Transport
1965–68, Secretary of State for Employment and Productivity 1968–70,
Social Services 1974–76; created Baroness Castle of Blackburn 1990

These Foot brothers all merge into one collective Foot type:
rational, radical and eminently reasonable. They even speak in
the same voice and the same tones; they are natural Liberals.

Diary, 20 March 1975

Lord Hugh Cecil

1869–1956; MP (Conservative) Greenwich 1895–1906, Oxford
University 1910–37; created Baron Quickswood 1941

There is no more ungraceful figure than that of a humanitarian
with an eye to the main chance.

On Henry Campbell-Bannerman, *The Times*, 24 June 1901

Joseph Chamberlain

1836–1914; MP (Liberal, Liberal Unionist) Birmingham 1876–85,
Birmingham West 1885–1914; President of the Board of Trade 1882–85,
Secretary of State for the Colonies 1895–1903; founder of the Liberal
Unionist Party, 1886

If I were to write the heading of the next chapter of the Liberal
programme I would write 'Free Schools', 'Free Land' and 'Free
Church'.

At the Temperance Hall, Birmingham, 19 February 1872

All monopolies, which are sustained in any way by the state,
ought to be in the hands of the representatives of the people, by
whom they should be administered and to whom their profits
should go.

Speech to Birmingham Town Council, 13 January 1874

I am inclined to increase the duties and responsibilities of the local authority, and will do everything in my power to constitute these local authorities, real local parliaments supreme in their special jurisdiction.

Speech to Birmingham Town Council, 13 January 1874

The advanced Liberals ... form an important element in the Liberal Party ... Without them it would be difficult to distinguish the party of the moderate Tories who do not practise their principles from the party of the moderate Liberals who have no principles to practise ... If it is really the desire of the country that nothing should be done, the Conservatives are the proper persons to carry out its wishes.

Gladstone's first government had been defeated in the general election earlier in the year, *Fortnightly Review*, October 1874

England is said to be the paradise of the rich; we have to take care that it is not suffered to become the purgatory of the poor.

At Bingley Hall, 28 June 1876

The essential feature of the proposed Federation is the principle which must henceforth govern the actions of the Liberals as a political party, namely, the direct participation of all members of the party in the formation and direction of policy.

At the inaugural meeting of the National Liberal Federation, 1877

The opponents of the Caucus are not to be convinced – they hate it for its virtues – because it puts aside and utterly confounds all that club management and Pall Mall selection which has been going on for so long and which has made the Liberal Party the molluscous, boneless, nerveless thing it is. The caucus is force, enthusiasm, zeal, activity, movement, popular will and the rule of the majority – the Seven Deadly Sins in fact.

Letter to John Morley, 29 September 1878

It may be the work of Tories to crush out disaffection; it is the better and higher work of Liberals to find out the cause of disaffection and to remove it.

At Birmingham Town Hall, referring to terrorist outrages in Ireland, November 1880

Lord Salisbury constitutes himself the spokesman of a class – of the class to which he himself belongs, who toil not neither do they spin, whose fortunes, as in his case, have originated by grants made in times gone by for the services which courtiers rendered kings, and have since grown and increased while they have slept by levying an increased share on all that other men have done by toil and labour to add to the general wealth and prosperity of the country.

At Birmingham, 30 March 1883; the biblical reference is to 6 Matthew 28

The politics of the future are social politics, and the problem is still how to secure the greatest happiness of the greatest number and especially of those whom all previous legislation and reform seem to have left very much where they were before.

Letter to a friend in 1883, cited in J. L. Garvin, *The Life of Joseph Chamberlain* (1932)

But then I ask what ransom will property pay for the security which it enjoys? ... There is a doctrine in many men's mouths and in a few men's practice that property has obligations as well as rights. I think in the future we shall hear a great deal more about the obligations of property, and we shall not hear quite so much about its rights.

At Birmingham Town Hall, 5 January 1885

The great problem of our civilisation is still unsolved. We have to account for and to grapple with the mass of misery and destitution in our midst, co-existent as it is with the evidence of abundant wealth and teeming prosperity. It is a problem which some men would put aside by references to the eternal laws of supply and demand, to the necessity of freedom of contract, and to the sanctity of every private right of property. But, gentlemen, these phrases are the convenient cant of selfish wealth.

At Warrington, 8 September 1885

The Liberal Party of the past has been the popular party. It has been reinforced from time to time by successive Reform Bills, and now after the greatest of them all, it would be false to its trust and unworthy of its high mission if it did not strive to bring the institutions of the country into harmony with the wants and aspirations of the people; if it did not seek continuously the greatest happiness of the greatest number; if it did not serve the poor with at least as much zeal as it brings to the protection of the rich; and if it did not enforce the obligations of property as strenuously as it defends its rights.

At Warrington, 8 September 1885

While I am myself afraid of anything in the nature of centralisation or state interference, I have no jealousy at all of the growth and spread of these municipal institutions, which are the great honour and glory of this country.

On the growth in the powers and responsibilities of local government, *The Times*, 21 September 1885

Progress is the law of the world; and Liberalism is the expression of this law in politics.

Cited in A. Reid (ed.), *Why I am a Liberal* (1885)

The goal to which the advance will probably be made at an accelerated pace is that in the direction of which the legislation of the last quarter of a century has been tending – the intervention in other words, of the State on behalf of the weak against the strong, in the interests of labour against capital, of want and suffering against luxury and ease.

Preface to *The Radical Programme*, generally known as the 'Unauthorised Programme' (1885)

Of course it is Socialism. The Poor Law is Socialism; the Education Act is Socialism; the greater part of municipal work is Socialism; and every kindly act of legislation by which the community has sought to discharge its responsibilities and obligations to the poor is Socialism, but it is none the worse for that.

> At Warrington on his Radical Programme, 1885, cited in J. L. Garvin, *The Life of Joseph Chamberlain* (1932)

The experience of the great towns is encouraging. By their wise and liberal use of the powers entrusted to them, they have, in the majority of cases, protected the health of the community; they have provided means of recreation and enjoyment and instruction, and they have done a great deal to equalise social advantages.

> Drawing on his experiences as mayor of Birmingham, at Hull, 1885; cited in H. J. Schulz, *English Liberalism and the State: Individualism or Collectivism* (1972)

I am told if I pursue this course that I shall break up the party ... but I care little for the party ... except to promote the objects which I publicly avowed when I first entered Parliament.

> On his programme for social reform – the radical wing's 1885 'Unauthorised Programme', unpopular with Gladstone, cited in D. Brack et al. (eds), *Dictionary of Liberal Biography* (1998)

What is that the working classes of the country want? What is it that they have the right to demand? I will see if I can put your aspirations, your expectations, into short clear and succinct language. You shall tell me if I fail. I say, in the first place, you want good wages and constant employment. I say, in the second place, you want more leisure and better means of enjoying it. And I say, in the third place, I think you want some provision for your old age, so that when declining years come you may not be forced to look forward to the cold charities of the poorhouse as the end and reward of a long life of toil. That is my labour programme. Is it reasonable? Can the government do anything to assist? I say that there is no doubt as to the answer.

The first time a major British politician advocated old-age pensions, at Ashton Manor, 17 March 1891

What is the use of supporting your own government only when it is right?

Cited in W. S. Churchill, *My Early Life* (1930)

What folly it is to talk about the moral and intellectual elevation of the masses when the conditions of life are such as to render elevation impossible! What can the schoolmaster or the minister of religion do, when the influences of home undo all he does? We find bad air, polluted water, crowded or filthy homes, and ill-ventilated courts everywhere prevailing in the midst of our boasted wealth, luxury and civilisation.

Cited in E. P. Hennock, *Fit and Proper Persons* (1973)

All private effort, all individual philanthropy sinks into insignificance compared with the organised power of a great representative assembly like this.

Speech to Birmingham Town Council, on his third election as mayor, cited in E. P. Hennock, *Fit and Proper Persons* (1973)

Henry 'Chips' Channon

1897–1958; MP (Conservative) Southend, later Southend West 1935–58

[A speech in the House of Commons by] Sir Archie Sinclair always provides a pleasant interval during which one can go out for a drink or a cup of tea.

On the Liberal leader Sir Archibald Sinclair, *Diary*, 19 December 1938

Crinks Johnstone died suddenly last night from a stroke. He was only forty-nine, and can really be described as having dug his grave with his teeth, for all his life he over-ate and drank … rather liked him, though I long ago recognised that he was a Liberal hypocrite.

On the Liberal MP Harcourt Johnstone, *Diary*, 2 March 1945

Noam Chomsky
b. 1928; American linguistics academic and philosopher

If we don't believe in freedom of expression for people we despise, we don't believe in it at all.

Interview, BBC 2, 25 November 1992

Randolph Churchill
1849–95; MP (Conservative) Woodstock 1874–85, Paddington South 1885–95; Chancellor of the Exchequer 1886

His amusements, like his politics, are essentially destructive.

On W. E. Gladstone, referring to his hobby of tree felling, at Blackpool, 24 January 1884, cited in R. Blake, *The Conservative Party from Peel to Churchill* (1970)

I decided some time ago that if the G. O. M. went for Home Rule, the Orange card would be the one to play. Please God it may turn out the ace of trumps and not the two.

The G. O. M. was W. E. Gladstone, the Grand Old Man; letter to Lord Justice FitzGibbon, 16 February 1886

An old man in a hurry.

On W. E. Gladstone, address to the electors of South Paddington, 19 June 1886

Slaves were free, Conscience was free, Trade was free. But hunger and squalor and cold were also free and the people demanded something more than liberty ... How to fill the void was the riddle that split the Liberal Party.

On the end of Gladstonian Liberalism, cited in W. S. Churchill, *Lord Randolph Churchill*, Vol. 1 (1906)

Winston Churchill

1874–1965; MP (Conservative) Oldham 1900–06, (Liberal) 1904–05, Manchester North West 1905–08, Dundee 1908–22, (Constitutionalist, Conservative) Epping 1924–45, (Conservative) Woodford 1945–64; Home Secretary 1910–11, Chancellor of the Exchequer 1924–29, Prime Minister 1940–45, 1951–55

I am an English Liberal. I hate the Tory Party, their men, their words and their methods.

1903, cited in R. Churchill, *Winston S. Churchill*, Vol. 2 (1967)

A party of great vested interests banded together in a formidable federation; corruption at home, aggression to cover it up abroad; sentiment by the bucketful, patriotism by the imperial pint; the open hand at the public exchequer, the open door at the public house; dear food for the millions, cheap food for the millionaire.

On the Conservative Party, 13 May 1904, cited in A. Roberts, *Eminent Churchillians* (1994)

It is not possible to draw a hard-and-fast line between individualism and collectivism. You cannot draw it either in theory or in practice. That is where the Socialist makes a mistake. Let us not imitate that mistake. No man can be a collectivist alone or an individualist alone. He must be both an individualist and a collectivist. The nature of man is a dual nature. The character of the organisation of human society is dual. Man is at once a unique being and a gregarious animal. For some purposes he must be collectivist, for others he is, and he will for all time remain, an individualist ... No view of society can possibly be complete which does not comprise within its scope both collective organisation and individual incentive ... I look forward to the universal establishment of minimum standards of life and labour, and their progressive elevation as the increasing energies of production may permit.

At St Andrew's Hall, Glasgow, 11 October 1906, reprinted as *Liberalism and the Social Problem* (1909)

I do not want to see impaired the vigour of competition, but we can do much to mitigate the consequences of failure. We want to draw a line below which we will not allow persons to live and labour yet above which they may compete with all the strength of their manhood. We want to have free competition upwards; we decline to allow free competition to run downwards.

At St Andrew's Hall, Glasgow, 11 October 1906, reprinted as *Liberalism and the Social Problem* (1909)

Socialism seeks to pull down wealth; Liberalism seeks to raise up poverty. Socialism would destroy private interests; Liberalism would preserve private interests ... by reconciling them with public right. Socialism would kill enterprise; Liberalism would rescue enterprise from the trammels of privilege and preference. Socialism assails the pre-eminence of the individual; Liberalism seeks ... to build up a minimum standard for the mass. Socialism exalts the rule; Liberalism exalts the man. Socialism attacks capitalism; Liberalism attacks monopoly.

At Dundee, 14 May 1908, reprinted as 'The Social Policy of Liberalism', 27 November 1909

The moving equilibrium of the forces of collectivism and individualism, not a contradiction or a compromise, but a harmony, is the very essence of that social progress to which Liberalism commits itself with fresh faith and with growing courage, as the nature of her task becomes clearer to consciousness, and draws its inspiration from a firmer grasp upon the principles of social justice.

At Dundee, 14 May 1908, reprinted as 'The Social Policy of Liberalism', 27 November 1909

The cool-blooded class hatred shown for some years in the corporate counsels of the House of Lords.

> During the Budget crisis – Churchill warned the Lords that, having started the class war, 'they'd better be careful', 1909, cited in M. Foot, *Loyalists and Loners* (1986)

Like a powerful graceful cat walking delicately and unsoiled across a rather muddy street.

> On A. J. Balfour moving from Asquith's to Lloyd George's Cabinet, 1916, *Great Contemporaries* (1937)

The difference between him and Arthur is that Arthur is wicked and moral, Asquith is good and immoral.

> Comparing A. J. Balfour and H. H. Asquith, cited in E. T. Raymond, *Mr Balfour* (1920)

Anyone can rat, but it takes a certain amount of ingenuity to re-rat.

> On moving back to the Conservative Party, from the Liberal Party, during the 1920s, cited in K. Halle, *Irrepressible Churchill* (1966)

It is a remarkable thing that within a few minutes the old relationship was completely re-established ... The relationship of master and servant – and I was the servant.

> Recounting a meeting with David Lloyd George, 1926, cited in R. Boothby, *Recollections of a Rebel* (1978)

Gladstone read Homer for fun, which I thought served him right.

> *My Early Life* (1930)

He would not stoop; he did not conquer.

> Assessment of Rosebery, *Great Contemporaries* (1937)

I must say I think this is a fine hour in the life of the Liberal Party, because, from the moment when they realised that rearmament was necessary, they have seemed to bring together both the material and moral strength of the country, and I believe that at the moment they represent what is the heart and soul of the British nation.

In the House of Commons, 3 April 1939

When the English history of the first quarter of the twentieth century is written, it will be seen that the greater part of our fortunes in peace and in war were shaped by this one man.

On David Lloyd George, *Evening Standard*, 4 October 1951

They are so few and so futile.

On the Liberal Party in later years, cited in G. Knight, *Honourable Insults* (1990)

He could cast a chill over all and did not hesitate to freeze and snub.

On the Earl of Rosebery, cited in D. Englefield, J. Seaton & I. White, *Facts About the British Prime Ministers* (1996)

Marcus Tullius Cicero

106–43 BC; Roman orator, statesman and writer

Freedom suppressed and again regained bites with keener fangs than freedom never endangered.

De Officiis (44 BC)

Liberty consists in the power of doing that which is permitted by law.

Attributed

Extreme patriotism in the defence of liberty is no vice, and moderation in the pursuit of justice is no virtue.

Attributed; later used by Barry Goldwater

Alan Clark

1928–99; MP (Conservative) Plymouth Sutton 1974–92, Kensington
and Chelsea 1997–99; Minister for Trade 1986–89, Minister of State,
Ministry of Defence 1989–92

He's so engaging, such good company. Like me, he despises the
Liberals. Like me, he admires the Lady. What is to become of
him? I said, 'You must be Prime Minister' and later, 'You *will*
be Prime Minister'. It's extraordinary how this extravagant
compliment invariably gives pleasure, however ludicrously
improbable, to whomsoever it is addressed. But in David's case
it could happen. And we could do a lot worse.

On supper with David Owen, *Diary*, 15 July 1983

I don't see what all the fuss was about. P. was an unmemorable
figure really, with his (demi-bogus) West-Country vowels and
homespun philosophy. But he personified, I suppose, a kind of
soft-centred Cornish provincialism.

Reflecting on the memorial service for David Penhaligon, *Diary*, 10
January 1987

The trouble is, once the Libs get stuck in, really stuck in, they
are devilish hard to dislodge. Their trick is to *degrade* the whole
standard of political debate. The nation, wide policy issues,
the sweep of history – forget it. They can't even manage to
discuss broad economic questions, as they don't understand
the problems – never mind the answers. The Liberal technique
is to force people to lower their sights, teeny little provincial
problems about bus timetables, and street lighting and the
grant for a new community hall. They compensate by giving
the electorate uplift with constant plugging of an identity
concept – no matter how miniscule – to which they try to
attach a confrontational flavour: 'Newton Ferrers Mums outface
Whitehall' and a really bouncy commonplace little turd (or big
turd in the case of Penhaligon) as candidate, and they're in.

On a visit to Truro, *Diary*, 3 March 1990

You are the only one with balls.

> Comparing Jackie Ballard MP to other contenders for the Liberal
> Democrat leadership, cited in *The Independent*, 29 May 1999

Kenneth Clarke

b. 1940; MP (Conservative) Rushcliffe 1970–; Home Secretary 1992–93,
Chancellor of the Exchequer 1993–97, Secretary of State for Justice 2010–12

I saw David Owen on television the other day. He was heckling a
small number of bystanders in Torquay. And then I realised they
weren't bystanders – they were his party.

> Cited in G. Knight, *Honourable Insults* (1990)

John Cleese

b. 1939; actor, comedian and writer

Look, this isn't the first of the Python repeats. It's a party
political, so I'll give you five seconds to switch over.

> Opening line of Alliance party political broadcast, April 1987

If you think PR's boring, you're a very silly person.

> Liberal Democrat party political broadcast, September 1998

Nick Clegg

b. 1967; MEP (Liberal Democrat) East Midlands 1999–2004, MP (Liberal
Democrat) Sheffield Hallam 2005–; leader of the Liberal Democrats
2007–, Lord President of the Council and deputy Prime Minister 2010–

If the legislation is passed I will lead a grassroots campaign of
civil disobedience to thwart the identity cards programme ...
I, and I expect thousands of people like me, will simply refuse
ever to register.

> On ID cards, 30 October 2007

I became a liberal not in a library, but over the dinner table, in the car, in the park – in conversation with my mum.

Liberal Democrat Voice, 16 November 2007

No.

When asked if he believed in God, BBC Radio 5 Live rapid-fire interview, 19 December 2007

I am a Liberal by temperament, by instinct and by upbringing.

Yorkshire Post, 22 December 2007

Marrying our proud traditions of economic and social liberalism, refusing to accept that one comes at the cost of the other. On that point, if not all others, the controversial *Orange Book* in 2004 was surely right.

Speech, 12 January 2008

No more than thirty. It's a lot less than that.

On being asked how many women he had slept with ('How many are we talking: ten, twenty, thirty?'), interview, *GQ*, 31 March 2008

Only liberalism possesses a clear understanding of the way in which power has flowed upwards and downwards from the central state. Only liberalism marries a passion for devolution within Britain with a commitment to international institutions and the international rule of law.

The Liberal Moment (2009)

[L]iberalism does not shun collective action where it is necessary. But it is much more alert to the dangers of heavy-handed collective action: authoritarianism, secrecy, a lack of transparency and accountability. Once a collective good has been identified as important, there is always the danger that the means, even if they are illiberal, will be justified in pursuit of those collective ends. That is why, for instance, Labour has been so untroubled by the infringement of civil liberties, arguing instead that the supposed end of collective security justifies the illiberal means. A liberal would never make such an argument.

The Liberal Moment (2009)

The progressive forces in Britain must regroup under a new banner. I believe that liberalism offers the rallying point for a resurgent progressive movement in Britain.

The Liberal Moment (2009)

Nation states need to pool decision-making with others if they want to extend real sovereignty over the world around them. Terrorism, climate change, immigration, commerce, crime – all operate at a level beyond the clutches of the nineteenth century nation state. This insight has always escaped the Conservatives.

The Liberal Moment (2009)

In some cases we will be quite bold, or even savage, on current spending, precisely to be able to retain spending where you need it in areas where the economy is weak in infrastructure.

Interview, *The Observer*, 19 September 2009; often quoted as calling for 'savage cuts' in spending

AV is a baby step in the right direction – only because nothing can be worse than the status quo. If we want to change British politics once and for all, we have got to have a quite simple system in which everyone's votes count. We think AV-plus is a feasible way to proceed. At least it is proportional – and it retains a constituency link. The Labour Party assumes that changes to the electoral system are like crumbs for the Liberal Democrats from the Labour table. I am not going to settle for a miserable little compromise thrashed out by the Labour Party.

Interview, *The Independent*, 22 April 2010; often (mis)quoted as describing AV itself as 'a miserable little compromise'

David Cameron has joined a bunch of nutters, anti-Semites, people who deny climate change exists, homophobes.

On Tory allies in the European Parliament, TV election debate, 22 April 2010

I think, if Labour do come third in terms of number of votes cast, then people would find it inexplicable that Gordon Brown himself would carry on as Prime Minister. As for who I'd work with I've been very clear – more clear than David Cameron or Gordon Brown – I will work with the man from the moon, I don't care; with anyone who can deliver the greater fairness that I think people want.

27 April 2010, cited in *The Guardian*, 4 May 2010

There is a gulf in values between myself and David Cameron. They have no progressive reform agenda at all – only an unbearable sense of entitlement that it's just their time to govern.

Interview, *The Guardian*, 1 May 2010

I have always accepted the first part of Roy Jenkins's analysis, which says that, historically, Labour and Liberal Democrats are two wings of a progressive tradition in British politics.

Interview, *The Guardian*, 1 May 2010

Maybe he one day – perhaps we will have to wait for his memoirs – could account for his role in the most disastrous decision of all, which is the illegal invasion of Iraq.

To Jack Straw in the House of Commons, 21 July 2010

You shouldn't trust any government, actually including this one. You should not trust government – full stop. The natural inclination of government is to hoard power and information; to accrue power to itself in the name of the public good.

Interview, *The Observer*, 13 February 2011

Our opponents try to divide us with their outdated labels of left and right. But we are not on the left and we are not on the right.

We have our own label: Liberal. We are liberals and we own the freehold to the centre ground of British politics. Our politics is the politics of the radical centre.

At the Liberal Democrat conference, Sheffield, March 2011

If we keep doing this we won't find anything to bloody disagree on in the bloody TV debates!

To David Cameron, overheard comment, 25 March 2011

The current government is a coalition of necessity … It is not a 'national' government, but it is a government formed in the national interest … In the next phase of the coalition, both partners will be able to be clearer in their identities … You will see a strong liberal identity in a strong coalition government. You might even call it muscular liberalism.

Speech, 11 May 2011

States, markets and communities can give people power. But they can also hoard power – in state bureaucracies, market monopolies and social norms. Labour is a party of state power. Conservatives believe in the power of the free market. These are honourable political traditions. But they are not ours. For us the litmus test of any institution, law or reform is whether it gives more power to people to lead their own version of a good life. The exercising of power by people – individually and together – is the basis of social progress.

Foreword to *Facing the Future*, Liberal Democrat policy document, August 2011

We made a promise before the election that we would vote against any rise in fees under any circumstances. But that was a mistake. It was a pledge made with the best of intentions – but we shouldn't have made a promise we weren't absolutely sure we could deliver … There's no easy way to say this: we made a pledge … we didn't stick to it – and for that I am sorry.

On tuition fees, 20 September 2012

The freedom to be who you are. The opportunity to be who you could be. That, in essence, is the Liberal promise.

At the Liberal Democrat conference, Brighton, September 2012

I'm a liberal interventionist. It goes back to Gladstone – you can't be indifferent to people suffering, even if they may be in countries which seem a long way from us ... I think we should never turn out back on the idea that we have duties to other people, and that where we can, we should help ... where you can, where there are good humanitarian reasons, as a liberal you should intervene muscularly to promote good liberal values.

Cited in C. Bowers, *Nick Clegg: The Biography* (2011)

I really just believe in the basic tenets of liberalism ... which starts from the premise that there's something wonderful about every person, there's something marvellous about their potential and talents, and you've got to do everything you possibly can in politics to emancipate individuals, to give them privacy, give them freedom, give them the ability to get ahead.

Cited in C. Bowers, *Nick Clegg: The Biography* (2011)

Libertarianism is a one-eyed approach to liberalism.

29 November 2012

Georges Clemenceau

1841–1929; Prime Minister of France 1906–09, 1917–20

What do you expect when I'm between two men of whom one thinks he is Napoleon and the other thinks he is Jesus Christ?

On being asked why he always gave in to Lloyd George (the first mentioned), at the Paris Peace Conference, 1918; the second was Woodrow Wilson; cited in a letter from H. Nicolson to his wife, 20 May 1919

Voltairine de Cleyre

1866–1912; American feminist and anarchist

So long as the people do not care to exercise their freedom,
those who wish to tyrannise will do so; for tyrants are active and
ardent, and will devote themselves in the name of any number
of gods, religious and otherwise, to put shackles upon sleeping
men.

Attributed

Richard Cobden

1804–65; MP (Liberal) Stockport 1841–47, West Riding of Yorkshire
1847–57, Rochdale 1859–65; founder of the Anti-Corn Law League 1839

Free trade, by perfecting the intercourse and securing the
dependence of countries one upon another, must inevitably
snatch the power from the governments to plunge their people
into wars.

Letter to Mr Ashworth, 1842

We advocate the abolition of the Corn Law, because we believe
that to be the foster-parent of all other monopolies; and if we
destroy that – the parent, the monster monopoly – it will save
us the trouble of devouring all the rest.

On the repeal of the Corn Laws, 8 February 1844

Be diligent therefore in disseminating knowledge on the
question. The repeal of the Corn Laws will be carried when men
understand it. And when you understand it, if you are an honest
man, you will feel it; if you feel it, at least as I have, you will not be
able to be quiet without doing something to put down this great
injustice. I exhort you in each of your several circles to spread
abroad light on the subject. Knowledge is the power – knowledge
alone – by which we shall bring this foul system to the dust.

On the repeal of the Corn Laws, 8 February 1844

I have always had an instinctive monomania against this system
of foreign interference, protocolling, diplomatising, etc., and I
shall be glad if you and your other Free Trade friends ... would
try to prevent the Foreign Office from undoing the good
which the Board of Trade has done to the people. But you
must not disguise from yourself that the evil has its roots in the
pugnacious, energetic, self-sufficient, foreigner-despising and
pitying character of that noble insular creature, John Bull.

> Letter to John Bright in 1847, over Palmerstonian intervention in
> Spain, cited in J. Morley, *The Life of Richard Cobden*, Vol. 2 (1881)

Our cry should be neutrality and isolation unless attacked, this
cry must be put forth ... by the manufacturers and merchants
of the country upon whom the efforts of war would fall with
serious force.

> Letter to Edward Baines, 1 March 1848

We are a servile, aristocracy-loving, lord-ridden people, who
regard the land with as much reverence as we still do the
peerage and the baronetage.

> 1849, cited in N. Gash, *Aristocracy and People 1815–65* (1979)

One copy of *The Times* contains more useful information than
the whole of the historical books of Thucydides.

> At the Manchester Athenaeum, 27 December 1850

I rather think there is quite as much agitation about
parliamentary reform in the House of Commons as in the
country. It has got into the House of Commons, and they don't
know what to do with it. It is bandied from side to side, and all
parties are professing to be reformers; everybody is in favour of
an extension of the suffrage; and, upon my honour, I think in my
heart no one likes it much, and they don't care much about it.

> At Rochdale, 18 August 1859

The great rule of conduct for us in regard to foreign nations is, in extending our commercial relations, to have with them as little political connection as possible.

The Political Writings of Richard Cobden (1867)

It is certain that in this world the virtues and the forces go together, and the vices and the weaknesses are inseparable.

Cited in C. Brinton, *English Political Thought in the Nineteenth Century* (1933)

The world never yet beheld such a compound of jobbing, swindling, hypocrisy, and slaughter, as goes to make up the gigantic scheme of villainy called the 'British rule in India' ... I have no faith in such an undertaking being anything but a calamity and curse to the people of England.

Cited in I. Bradley, *The Optimists* (1980)

As little intercourse as possible betwixt *Governments*, as much connection as possible between the *Nations* of the world.

Cited in I. Bradley, *The Optimists* (1980)

Jesse Collings

1831–1920; MP (Liberal) Ipswich 1880–86, (Unionist) Birmingham Bordesley 1886–1918

Three acres and a cow.

A phrase used to describe the amendment on land reform which brought down the Salisbury government in January 1886; its origins lie in J. S. Mill's *Principles of Political Economy* (1848) and date back to Daniel Defoe's *A Tour through the Whole Island of Great Britain* (1724–27)

Michael Collins

1890–1922; Irish republican leader

He would ... sell his nearest and dearest for political prestige.

On David Lloyd George, cited in G. Knight, *Honourable Insults* (1990)

John Colville
1915–87; diplomat and civil servant

[Sir John Simon's] idea of making himself socially agreeable was
to quote Homer at length and follow it up with an exposition of
Binomial Theorem.

Man of Valour (1972)

Benjamin Constant
1767–1830; French philosopher and novelist

The option to do anything which does not hurt others, or in
freedom of action, in the right not to be obliged to profess
any belief of which one is not convinced, even though it be the
majority view, or in religious freedom, in the right to make
public one's thought, using all the means of publicity, provided
that that publicity does not harm any individual or provoke
any wrong act, finally in the certainty of not being arbitrarily
treated, as if one had exceeded the limits of individual rights,
that is to say, in being guaranteed not to be arrested, detained,
or judged other than according to law and with all due process.

On the rights of the individual, *Principles of Politics Applicable to All
Representative Governments* (1815)

Patrick Cormack
b. 1939; MP (Conservative) Cannock, later Staffordshire South West then
Staffordshire South 1970–2010; elevated to the peerage in 2010

The Liberal Democrats are the vegans of British politics ... they
are not fit to eat the red meat of British politics.

In the House of Commons, 13 May 1999

Harry Cowie
b. 1930; director of research, Liberal Party 1959–64

Planned intervention by the State is acceptable to Liberals so long as it is open to democratic control and so long as it is concerned with creating conditions in which the individual can develop his personality to the full.

Why Liberal? (1964)

William Cowper
1731–1800; poet

Freedom has a thousand charms to show,
That slaves, howe'er contented, never know.

Table Talk (1782)

Ivor Crewe and Anthony King
Academics; Crewe b. 1945; Vice Chancellor, University of Essex 1995–2007; King b. 1934; Professor of Government, University of Essex 1969–

Many of those closest to Owen attributed to him almost God-like qualities of farsightedness, vision and strategic grasp. They saw him as, in effect, a supremely gifted military commander. In fact, he was nothing of the sort. He was an incompetent. If there was a shell-crater full of water anywhere on the battlefield, Owen unerringly led his dwindling band of troops directly into it. No wonder that in the end they all drowned.

On David Owen's behaviour over merger, cited in *SDP* (1995)

It was perhaps appropriate that what one journalist had dubbed 'the Monster Raving Ego Party' should in the end have been destroyed by the Monster Raving Loony Party.

On the decision to wind up the Owenite 'continuing SDP', after its candidate had been beaten into seventh place in the Bootle by-election, May 1990, cited in *SDP* (1995)

Benedetto Croce

1866–1952; philosopher, historian, critic and President, Italian Liberal
Party 1947

It is necessary to preach the benefits of authority to the people
and those of liberty to the princes.

Politics and Morals (1945)

Richmal Crompton

1890–1969; writer

I'm tryin' to tell you 'bout this gen'ral election. There's four
sorts of people tryin' to get to be rulers. They all want to make
things better, but they want to make 'em better in different
ways. There's Conservatives an' they want to make things better
by keepin' 'em just like what they are now. An' there's Lib'rals
and they want to make things better by alterin' them jus' a bit,
but not so's anyon'd notice, an' there's Socialists, an' they want
to make things better by takin' everyone's money off 'em an'
there's Communists an' they want to make things better by
killin' everyone but themselves.

Henry to William in 'William the Prime Minister' from *William the Bad*
(1930)

Oliver Cromwell

1599–1658; parliamentary military and political leader; Lord Protector
1653–58

I had rather have a plain russet-coated captain that knows what
he fights for, and loves what he knows, than that which you call
a gentleman and is nothing else.

Letter to Sir William Spring, September 1643

Sir, the State, in choosing men to serve it, takes no notice of
their opinions; if they be willing faithfully to serve it, – that

satisfies. I advised you formerly to bear with men of different minds from yourself: if you had done it when I advised you to it, I think you would not have had so many stumbling blocks in your way.

Letter to the Reverend Mr Hitch, at Ely, and to Major-General Crawford, 10 March 1643

Therefore the considering of what is fit for the kingdom does belong to the Parliament, provided they be well composed in their creation and election.

At the Putney debates, 1 November 1647

For that which you mention concerning liberty of conscience, I meddle not with any man's conscience.

To the Governor of Ross, 19 October 1649

It will be found an unjust and unwise jealousy, to deprive a man of his natural liberty upon a supposition he may abuse it. When he doth abuse it, judge.

To the Governor of Edinburgh Castle, 12 September 1650

Liberty of Conscience, and Liberty of the Subject, – two as glorious things to be contended for, as any that God hath given us...

Speech to the First Protectorate Parliament, 4 September 1654

That Parliaments should not make themselves perpetual is a Fundamental.

Speech to the First Protectorate Parliament, 12 September 1654

Liberty of Conscience is a natural right; and he that would have it, ought to give it.

Speech to the First Protectorate Parliament, 12 September 1654

Anthony Crosland
1918–77; MP (Labour) Gloucestershire South 1950–55, Grimsby 1959–
77; Foreign Secretary 1976–77

On most issues of policy we have long been incredibly
conservative, e.g. on Europe and (until last spring) on defence
we have been far more conservative than the Liberals ... It is
Grimond, and not any of our own leaders, who makes speeches
about the public schools, the House of Lords and social privilege
generally.

Letter to H. Gaitskell, November 1960

These delicate souls who flee for the Liberals at the first sound
of Tory and Fleet Street grapeshot.

On Lord Chalfont and other defectors to the Liberal Party, 1974, cited
in S. Crosland, *Tony Crosland* (1982)

A social democrat is someone who is about to join the Tory
Party.

Cited in M. Foot, *Loyalists and Loners* (1986)

Richard Crossman
1907–74; MP (Labour) Coventry East 1945–74; leader of the House of
Commons 1966–68, Secretary of State for Social Services and Minister
for Health 1968–70

This afternoon in the House was really exciting since Jo
Grimond's resignation as Liberal leader had been announced
and Jeremy Thorpe was to make his first appearance. The
Liberal Party had virtually degenerated into a personality cult
of Grimond. Jeremy is charming and young but I doubt if he'll
carry the weight to unite the Liberals.

Diary, 19 January 1967

Maud Cunard
1872–1948; society hostess

Herbert Asquith is black and wicked and has only a nodding
acquaintance with the truth.
Cited in *Chips: The Diaries of Henry Channon*, 7 January 1944 (1996)

John Philpot Curran
1750–1817; Irish judge

Eternal vigilance is the price of liberty.
Speech on the Right of the Election of the Lord Mayor of Dublin, 10
July 1790

George Nathaniel Curzon, Lord Curzon
1859–1925; MP (Conservative) Southport 1886–98; Viceroy of India
1899–1905; Foreign Secretary 1919–24; created Baron Curzon 1898,
Earl Curzon 1911, Marquis Curzon of Kedleston 1921

When a group of Cabinet Ministers begins to meet separately
and to discuss independent action, the death-tick is audible in
the rafters.
November 1922, shortly before the fall of Lloyd George's coalition
government, cited in D. Gilmour, *Curzon* (1994)

D

Ralf Dahrendorf

1929–2009; philosopher and sociologist; created Baron Dahrendorf of
Clare Market 1993

Democracy ... is not about the emergence of some unified view
from 'the people', but is about organising conflict and living
with conflict.

Class and Class Conflict in Industrial Society (1959)

The elementary desire to be free is the force behind all liberties.

The New Liberty (1975)

Mature citizens demand direct participation in their
affairs ... we will not have the new liberty unless we create a
new kind of effective general public.

The New Liberty (1975)

Liberty remains a response to the fact that we live in a world of
uncertainty.

The New Liberty (1975)

Is it not conceivable that values borrowed largely from
economic development miss some important points? Could
it not be that tomorrow's 'rationality' and 'reasonableness' are
not about work and production, but about a different shape
for human lives? The derision with which social democrats like
to greet such suggestions is hardly enough: before long it may
sweep them away.

After Social Democracy (1980)

The issue today is not to be social democratic, must as this may
agitate the victims of adversary politics. The issue is what comes

after social democracy. If this is not to be a Blue, Red or Green aberration, it will have to be an imaginative, unorthodox and distinctive liberalism which combines the common ground of social-democratic achievements with the new horizons of the future of liberty.

After Social Democracy (1980)

Britain's Social Democratic Party offers the country a better yesterday.

On the launch of the SDP, March 1981

Between the new socialists and the new conservatives there are the social democrats who believe that by tinkering with the system we can make it work for some time to come. In an immediate and fairly short-term sense they may well be right, but they have no answer to the underlying issues mentioned here. The new pragmatists are merely survival politicians, essentially about the past rather than about the future.

'The New Social State: a Liberal Perspective', cited in D. Steel (ed.), *Partners in One Nation* (1985)

In most cases the Greens are merely the translation of a social movement into a political organisation. The social movement responds to one of the disparities in people's social position, the threats to the environment of life. Since these threats affect everybody, a 'party' to represent them is an obvious contradiction in terms ... There remains what the Greens themselves call the 'fundamentalist' wing which can be described almost as a party to end all parties.

The Modern Social Conflict (1988)

There is no state of affairs in which Liberalism has been completely realised. Liberalism is forever process, the process by which human beings explore new opportunities for more people.

'The Future Tasks of Liberalism: a Political Agenda', paper at Liberal International Congress, Pisa, September 1988

101

Poverty is described as a violation of human rights which is no less abhorrent than arbitrary arrest. Liberals must beware of such confusion of language. Perhaps extreme poverty is as abhorrent as arbitrary arrest. It will be argued that poverty and unemployment are an unacceptable denial of citizenship for some. But human rights are human rights and economic and social position is economic or social position. It is misleading to confuse the two or to attempt to balance one by the other. There is no excuse for violations of civil rights, neither in the apparent full employment of Communist countries nor the widespread destitution of developing countries. The Liberal demand for elementary human rights is unconditional and non-negotiable.

'The Future Tasks of Liberalism: a Political Agenda', paper at Liberal International Congress, Pisa, September 1988

The so-called right to self-determination is often an invitation to usurpers to give their abuses of power the semblance of legitimacy. For the liberal, there are no collective rights, because all collectivities need representation, and all representatives are temptable by the arrogance of power, and thus liable to take away rights rather than give them protection. Rights are entitlements of individuals, and more often than not they serve to protect persons against self-appointed or self-anointed 'representatives' including those who claim to speak on behalf of whole peoples.

'The Future Tasks of Liberalism: a Political Agenda', paper at Liberal International Congress, Pisa, September 1988

I prefer to think of myself as a radical liberal for whom the social entitlements of citizenship are as important a condition of progress as the opportunities for choice which require entrepreneurial initiative and an innovative spirit.

Reflections on the Revolution in Europe (1990)

Participation is clearly central to the idea of citizenship, but it is participation with purpose, and the purpose is change.

Attributed

Utopia is always illiberal, because it leaves no room for error or correction.

Attributed

Daily Chronicle

There must be at bottom some kind of definite and coherent body of doctrine, from which the various reforms urged are necessary and logical inferences. We know, of course, that it will be said the English people are not logical but practical, and that the party of progress must therefore be practical too, and scout the mere theorist, with his systems and formulas. But ... the older type of Liberalism was strong just because it was based on definite ideas – because its advocates (to use Mr Morley's words) 'could explain in the large dialect of a definite scheme what were their aims and whither they were going'.

On the New Liberalism, 29 July 1892

Daily Mail

Hardly a beard or a fisherman's sweater, let alone the skin-tight black pants of the hip Left-Wing ... [Instead] a practical working conference of normal balanced young people from all walks of life who were making a serious attempt to grapple with the problems of our day but who, in doing so, did not take themselves too seriously.

Charles Greville, on the 1962 Young Liberal conference, cited in
C. Lakin, *New Outlook*, No. 11, August 1962

Daily Mirror

The dead duck of modern politics.

On the Liberal Party, 1951

Daily Telegraph

The most English minister that ever governed England.
> Obituary of Viscount Palmerston, October 1865

The final and total eclipse of the Liberal Party.
> Comment on the result of the 1950 general election, cited in
> H. G. Nicholas, *The British General Election of 1950* (1951)

The sage of the credit crunch.
> Description of Vince Cable, 11 October 2008

If the Lib Dems had men in grey suits, they would be led by Jim Wallace.
> On the top 50 most influential Liberal Democrats, 18 September 2011

R. W. Dale

1829–95; Birmingham Congregationalist minister

The split of the Liberal Party has made an immense difference to my private life. There are two clubs, and I belong to neither.
> On the split over Irish Home Rule in 1886, cited in A. W. W. Dale, *The Life of R. W. Dale* (1898)

Hugh Dalton

1887–1962; MP (Labour) Peckham 1924–29, Bishop Auckland 1929–31, 1935–59; Chancellor of the Exchequer 1945–47; created Baron Dalton of Forest and Frith 1960

The Liberal Party is a living corpse.
> *Oxford Guardian*, 21 February 1939

George Dangerfield

1904–86; journalist and writer

England has scarcely known a greater demagogue than this pre-war Lloyd George. His face, in its rare moments of repose, was elfin and commonplace, like a Barrie play: animated, it was something between an incomparable drama and a high-class vaudeville act. It was tragic and sorrowful and charming and comic by turns; it was lofty and it was low: emotions chased themselves across it like wind across a rain puddle, breaking it up into a hundred images.

The Strange Death of Liberal England (1935)

To reduce the Liberal Party to a definition would be like attempting to reduce the glandular contours of a circus Fat Lady by simply talking her thin. It was an irrational mixture of Whig aristocrats, industrialists, dissenters, reformers, trade unionists, quacks and Mr Lloyd George: it preserved itself from the destructive contradictions of daily reality by an almost mystical communion with the doctrine of laissez-faire and a profound belief in the English virtue of compromise.

The Strange Death of Liberal England (1935)

Dante Alighieri

1265–1321; Italian poet

For what is liberty but the unhampered translation of will into act?
Attributed

Clarence Darrow

1857–1938; American civil rights lawyer

Freedom comes from human beings, rather than from laws and institutions.
Attributed

Clement Davies

1884–1962; MP (Liberal, National Liberal, Independent, Liberal)
Montgomeryshire 1929–62; leader of the Liberal Party 1945–56

I want something said so distinctly that any ordinary man can then understand and be able to say that that is our distinguishing mark.

1950, cited in M. Baines, 'Survival of the British Liberal Party 1932–59', D.Phil, Oxford University, 1989

An intense passion of duty unites us in this fateful hour in an honourable freedom in which the undying flame of Liberalism burns.

During the 1950 general election campaign, cited in H. G. Nicholas, *The British General Election Campaign of 1950* (1951)

The greatest step towards peace which has ever been taken.

On the Schuman Plan for a European Coal and Steel Community, as the first step towards a federal Europe, 1950, cited in H. Cowie, *Why Liberal?* (1964)

There is no party but a number of individuals who, because of their adherence to the Party, come together only to express completely divergent views.

On the Liberal Party, 1950, cited in J. Stevenson, *Third Party Politics* (1993)

My own position is one of supine weakness for if I give full expression to a definite course of action that at once leads to trouble and a definite split.

Letter to Gilbert Murray, 1950, cited in J. G. Jones, *National Library of Wales Journal*, 23, No. 4

Somehow, the two progressive parties *must* get together to save the world.

Said to Philip Noel-Baker, 10 March 1951, and relayed in a letter to Megan Lloyd George, 20 March 1951

However small are our numbers we have a task to perform, and that cannot be performed if we sink our independence and see the party gradually welded into the structure of another party.

On his refusal to join the Churchill government in 1951

I have nothing to offer materially, no position, no career, and certainly not safety. I can only offer faith, and with that faith I demand a sacrifice.

On the attractions of the Liberal Party, at the National Liberal Club, 21 November 1951

Ivor Davies

1915–86; publisher and perennial Liberal candidate

Some of our friends have lulled themselves into the belief that there is going to be a great landslide towards us in the post-war peace. They are about as foolish as they possibly could be. The public will forget our warnings and our wisdom in the flush of victory.

Reflecting Davies' criticisms of the Liberal Party leadership during the Second World War, cited in G. de Groot, *Liberal Crusader: The Life of Sir Archibald Sinclair* (1993)

Robin Day

1923–2000; broadcaster; Liberal candidate for Hereford 1959

I rapidly changed gear. I dropped Liberal philosophy and picked up local non-party issues. (Many years later this was called community politics.)

Grand Inquisitor: Memoirs (1989)

Edward Stanley, 14th Earl of Derby

1799–1869; MP (Whig) Stockbridge 1822–26, Preston 1826–30, Windsor 1831–32, (Whig, Tory) Lancashire North 1832–44; became

Lord Stanley of Bickerstaffe 1844, 14th Earl of Derby 1851; Prime
Minister 1852, 1858–59, 1866–68

When I came into Parliament, Mr Tierney, a great Whig
authority, used always to say that the duty of an opposition was
very simple – it was to oppose everything and propose nothing.
    In the House of Commons, 4 June 1841

A political chameleon which offers a different hue and colour
to the spectator according to the side from which he gazes. I
defy any man, even the most ardent of his supporters, to say,
when he professes confidence in the noble Viscount, what upon
any great domestic question of the day is the policy to which he
pledges himself.
    On Viscount Palmerston, in the House of Lords, 16 March 1857

Meddle and muddle.
    On Lord John Russell's Poland policy, 1863, in the House of Lords, 4
    February 1864

Don't you see that we have dished the Whigs?
    Referring to the 1867 Reform Bill, cited in W. F. Moneypenny & G. E.
    Buckle, *Life of Disraeli*, Vol. 2 (1920)

Navnit Dholakia

b. 1937; created Baron Dholakia of Waltham Brooks 1997; President,
Liberal Democrats 2000–04

At some stage I was invited by a friend to meet him in a pub on
the seafront for a drink. I went there. There was a small group
huddled in a corner. My friend was nowhere to be seen. Then
a young man came to me. He explained that this was a meeting
of the Young Liberals but they could not proceed because they
were short of one person to form a quorum. I paid my half a
crown and even now call myself a quorum Liberal.
    Cited in D. Brack (ed.), *Why I am a Liberal Democrat* (1996)

The progress we have made in achieving some sort of
multiculturalism is too valuable to be gambled in a cynical
manner by politicians, in an attempt to play to their perception
that the majority of the public believe that we cannot live as
a community of communities, despite all our history and our
pride in tolerance.

'Towards Cultural Pluralism', cited in J. Margo (ed.), *Beyond Liberty*
(2007)

It is right that we should celebrate British citizenship, and
the rights and responsibilities that come with it. If we built
active community participation in our democratic process,
supplemented with a sense of a united community, then
ethnicity and multiculturalism would be less contentious.

'Towards Cultural Pluralism', cited in J. Margo (ed.), *Beyond Liberty*
(2007)

A. V. Dicey

1835–1922; constitutional writer

We olden-time English Liberals did not rest our case on any
abstract theory, such as Rousseau's *Contrat Social*, nor did
we attach much value to written expositions of theoretical
principles, such as the American Declaration of Independence.
We based our plea on the broad ground that in the long run
the world fared better if people were left to manage their own
affairs, to do the best they could for themselves, and to fight
their own way without legal or social interference ... The
whole theory of modern Liberals is that the State is to take
in hand the control of the masses, and override the rights of
individuals ... Common sense tells me that there is less practical
risk of individual liberty being seriously endangered under a
Conservative than under a Liberal administration ... Once you
desert the solid ground of individual freedom, you can find no
resting place till you reach the abyss of Socialism.

Fortnightly Review, new series, XXXVIII (October 1885)

Charles Dickens

1812–1870; author

My faith in the people governing is, on the whole, infinitesimal;
my faith in the people governed is, on the whole, illimitable.

At the Birmingham and Midland Institute, 27 September 1869

Charles Dilke

1843–1911; MP (Liberal) Wallingford (1865–88), Chelsea 1868–86, Forest
of Dean 1892–1911; President of the Local Government Board 1882–85

In many matters municipalities may be expected to go right
even where States go wrong, because in the smaller area there is
direct and immediate responsibility to a ratepaying electorate.

'A Radical Programme', *New Review*, Vol. 3, part II (1890)

Madelon Dimont

Assistant SDP Press Officer at the Crosby by-election

But perhaps the spirit of the campaign was best summed up by
Bill Rodgers, striding in from the rain with a bottle of plonk and
a paper bag. 'Claret and chips for lunch,' he announced.

On the Crosby by-election, November 1981, *SDP Newsletter*, No. 4,
February 1982

Benjamin Disraeli

1804–81; MP (Conservative) Maidstone 1837–41, Shrewsbury 1841–47,
Buckinghamshire 1847–76; Chancellor of the Exchequer 1852, 1858–59,
1866–68, Prime Minister 1868, 1874–80; created Earl of Beaconsfield
1876

'A sound Conservative government,' said Taper, musingly. 'I
understand: Tory men and Whig measures.'

Coningsby (1844)

The Rt Hon. Gentleman caught the Whigs bathing, and walked away with their clothes.

On Peel's conversion to free trade, in the House of Commons, 28 February 1845

Lady St Julians: 'Men who breakfast out are generally Liberals. Have you not observed that? I wonder why?'
Lady Firebrace: 'It shows a restless, revolutionary mind that can settle to nothing, but must be running after gossip the moment they are awake.'

Sybil (1845)

No Reform! New Taxes! Canton blazing! Persia invaded!

Satirising the Liberal government's call for 'peace, retrenchment and reform', 1857, cited in A. Hawkins, *British Party Politics, 1852–1886* (1998)

We have legalised confiscation, consecrated sacrilege, and condoned high treason.

On Gladstone's Irish policy, in the House of Commons, 27 February 1871

As I sat opposite the Treasury Bench the ministers reminded me of one of those marine landscapes not very unusual on the coasts of South America. You behold a range of exhausted volcanoes.

Describing Gladstone's cabinet, at Manchester, 3 April 1872

If you look at the history of this country since the advent of Liberalism forty years ago, you will find that there has been no effort so continuous, so subtle, supported by so much energy, and carried on with so much ability and acumen, as the attempts of Liberalism to effect the disintegration of the Empire of England.

At Crystal Palace, 1872, cited in R. Blake, *The Conservative Party from Peel to Churchill* (1972)

A sophisticated rhetorician inebriated with the exuberance of his own verbosity, and gifted with an egotistical imagination that can at all times command an interminable and inconsistent series of arguments to malign an opponent and to glorify himself.

On W. E. Gladstone, at Knightsbridge, reported in *The Times*, 29 July 1878

Posterity will do justice to that unprincipled maniac Gladstone – an extraordinary mixture of envy, vindictiveness, hypocrisy and superstition; and with one commanding characteristic – whether Prime Minister or Leader of the Opposition, whether preaching, praying, speechifying or scribbling – never a gentleman.

Letter to Lord Derby, 1878, cited in W. F. Moneypenny & G. E. Buckle, *Life of Benjamin Disraeli*, Vol. 6 (1920)

If Gladstone fell into the Thames that would be a misfortune. If anybody pulled him out, that would be a calamity.

On the difference between a misfortune and a calamity; attributed, cited in H. Pearson, *Lives of the Wits* (1962)

The school of Manchester.

On the free trade politics of Cobden and Bright, cited in R. Blake, *Disraeli* (1966)

If a traveller were informed that such a man was Leader of the House of Commons, he might begin to comprehend how the Egyptians worshipped an insect.

On Lord John Russell, cited in G. Knight, *Honourable Insults* (1990)

He has not a single redeeming defect.

On W. E. Gladstone, cited in D. Englefield, J. Seaton & I. White, *Facts About the British Prime Ministers* (1996)

You owe the Whigs a great gratitude, my Lord, and therefore I think you will betray them. For your lordship is like a favourite footman on easy terms with his mistress. Your dexterity seems a happy compound of the smartness of an attorney's clerk and the intrigue of a Greek of the lower empire.

On Lord Palmerston, cited in J. Green, *Dictionary of Insulting Quotations* (1996)

A man who is not a Liberal at sixteen has no heart; a man who is not a Conservative at sixty has no head.

Attributed

Elliott Dodds

1889–1977; journalist, writer; President, Liberal Party 1948–49

Liberalism is a progressive force, and as it advances it learns, finding at every turn of the road new vistas of challenge and opportunity. We may leave to our Socialist friends the claim to possess a perfect plan of the ideal society. Liberals make no such boast. They believe in the free play of individuality, and they have a shrewd idea as to what will happen to these pretty bubbles when human nature (ignored by our Socialist Utopians) applies the pin.

Foreword to *The Social Gospel of Liberalism* (1925)

Cooperation ... to be real must be spontaneous. The spirit of fellowship cannot be enforced. Inter-dependence must be based in independence. Neither the ant-heap nor the bee-hive is a model for man, who was made in the image of God. Only as a 'free man,' enjoying full opportunity to employ the gifts with which his Creator has endowed him and the power to make his own choices, can he work with his fellows in building up the Good Society where self-development and service go hand in hand. To be such a 'free man' he must enjoy Liberty, Property and Security. These are his human title-deed. And it because Liberalism insists on all three of them that it is unique in its appeal.

Let's Try Liberalism (1944)

More and more, in our own country, power is being drained away
from the independent centres of initiative and enterprise, and
sucked into the centre. More and more we are succumbing to the
tyranny of bigness and tending to despair of checking the growth
of monopoly. More and more, our people, herded together in
great urban agglomerations, are losing their roots. More and
more power is passing from our local authorities to Whitehall.
More and more, though wages and social conditions have
materially improved, the workers, from being machine tenders,
are coming to be regarded as machines. More and more, men
are becoming dependent on the State and losing their appetite
for independence. There is one way of escape – and one alone
– the Third Way, the way of deconcentration and giving men roots,
the spreading of property, power, responsibility and control.

The Third Way (1951)

The Liberal purpose – let it be said again – is the creation of
opportunity for men and women to become self-directing,
responsible persons.

Liberty and Welfare (1957)

Liberals value the 'small man' not mainly because he represents
something indispensable in our national life. He is a person;
he renders personal service; he manages his own business;
he knows and is known by his customers; he lives where he
makes his livelihood; he belongs to the local community and
contributes to its life.

On decentralisation; cited in D. Brack & E. Randall (eds), *Dictionary of
Liberal Thought* (2007)

We are advocating State action of the most drastic and radical
character to disestablish privilege and abolish the barriers
which prevent the gains due to industrial progress from being
shared by the whole people. We seek to plan – yes, to plan – a
framework in which freedom may flourish.

On his alternative to centralised state planning; cited in D. Brack & E.
Randall (eds), *Dictionary of Liberal Thought* (2007)

Fyodor Dostoevsky
1821–81; Russian writer

'The higher Liberalism' and the 'higher liberal', that is, a liberal without any definite aim, is only possible in Russia.

The Possessed (1873)

Elizabeth Douglas-Home
1909–90; wife of Sir Alec Douglas-Home

Honestly, Jo, if you can't run your personal life, how do you run the Liberal Party?

After Jo Grimond and the Douglas-Homes had attended the funeral of John F. Kennedy together, 1963, cited in D. R. Thorpe, *Alec Douglas-Home* (1996)

William Durant
1885–1981; philosopher

When liberty destroys order, the hunger for order will destroy liberty.

Attributed

As soon as liberty is complete, it dies in anarchy.

Attributed

Maurice Duverger
b. 1917; French political scientist

The fate of the Centre is to be torn asunder, buffeted and annihilated.

Political Parties (1954)

E

Robert Eccleshall
Academic and writer

If Liberalism is now partly invisible, this is because so many of
its assumptions and ideals have infiltrated political practice and
public awareness ... There is one area, however, in which people
are motivated by recognisably Liberal principles to urge further
political reforms. In contemporary Britain there is an energetic
campaign to give substance to the claim – initially formulated
and persistently sustained by Liberals – that citizens have an
equal right to liberty.

British Liberalism (1986)

Historically ... Liberalism displays hostility to the undeserved
benefits of aristocratic privilege and also wishes to promote the
moral elevation of the labouring classes.

British Liberalism (1986)

Umberto Eco
b. 1932; Italian philosopher and novelist

When it comes to the debt crisis, and I'm speaking as someone
who doesn't understand anything about the economy, we
must remember that it is culture, not war, that cements our
[European] identity. The French, the Italians, the Germans,
the Spanish and the English have spent centuries killing each
other. Today we have been at peace for seventy years and no one
realises how amazing that is any more. Indeed the very idea of a
war between Spain and France, or Italy and Germany, provokes
hilarity. The United States needed a civil war to unite properly.

I hope that culture and the [European] market will do the same for us.

The Guardian, 27 January 2012

The Economist

Her Majesty's New Opposition
The caption of a photograph of the SDP's Gang of Four, December 1981

Douglas Eden

SDP activist and academic

The principal task of the SDP is therefore utterly to replace the Labour Party. The SDP has a mission to fill the yawning gap in our political system and, together with our Liberal allies, make certain the Conservatives are faced with a democratic alternative attuned to modern times and the real world.

The Future of Social Democracy (1983)

Emily Eden

1797–1869; novelist and traveller

If he were soaked in boiling water and rinsed until he were twisted into a rope, I do not suppose a drop of fun would ooze out.

Referring to W. E. Gladstone in a letter to Lord Clarendon, 1860

Edward VII
1841–1910; King 1901–10

Calculated to set class against class and to inflame the passions of the working and lower orders against people who happened to be owners of property.

On Lloyd George's 1909 Budget, cited in M. Foot, *Loyalists and Loners* (1986)

Peggy Edwards
b. 1917; Liberal activist and Matlock councillor

I am sick and tired of the bloke Greaves banging on about the dangers of the Alliance and the virginal purity of the Liberals. Can't anyone tell him to get lost?

Referring to Tony Greaves, then Organising Secretary of the Association of Liberal Councillors, in a letter to a Liberal MP, January 1982

George Eliot
1819–80; writer

'You did not answer me when I wrote to you to London about your standing. There is no other Tory candidate spoken of …'
'But I shall not be a Tory candidate.'
Mrs Transome felt something like an electric shock. 'What then?' she said almost sharply. 'You will not call yourself a Whig?'
'God forbid! I'm a Radical.'
Mrs Transome's limbs tottered; she sank into a chair. Here was a distinct confirmation of the vague but strong feeling that her son was a stranger to her.

Felix Holt the Radical (1866)

Ralph Waldo Emerson
1803–82; American essayist and poet

If you cannot be free, be as free as you can.
Journals (1836)

Conservatism goes for comfort, reform for truth.
Lecture at Boston, 1841

Wild liberty breeds iron conscience; natures with great
impulses have great resources, and return from afar.
'Power', *The Conduct of Life* (1860)

Epictetus
c. 55–c. 135; philosopher

What is it that every man seeks? To be secure, to be happy, to do
what he pleases without restraint and without compulsion.
Discourses

Only the educated are free.
Discourses

T. J. Evans
Biographer of Liberal MP Rhys Hopkin Morris

He stood for a cause [Liberty and Freedom] that may now
have been largely won, but being won, still needs the eternal
vigilance which is the price of liberty.
Rhys Hopkin Morris: The Man and his Character (1956)

In both religion and judgement he was an Independent, and
could be relied upon to cling, regardless of the consequences, to
that which he considered to be right.
Rhys Hopkin Morris: The Man and his Character (1956)

F

Tim Farron
b. 1970; MP (Liberal Democrat) Westmorland & Lonsdale 2005–;
President, Liberal Democrats 2011–

If you listen to some, then apparently because I am in coalition
with the Conservatives, or 'in bed with the Tories', then I must
be a Tory. Are they mad? Look, for flip's sake, I share a bed with
my wife, it doesn't make me a woman.
> At the Liberal Democrat conference, Sheffield, 11 March 2011

Anyone with a memory better than a goldfish will remember
they spent thirteen years behaving like Tories. That shouldn't
be forgotten simply because they've spent the last eight months
behaving like bloomin' Trots.
> On the Labour Party, interview, *The Cambridge Student*, 29 March 2011

The Labour Party, to me, is a conservative party. Was then and
is now.
> Interview, *The Guardian*, 18 November 2011

Freedom is not something that happens by accident. It happens
by intervention, or by refereeing the situation. And of course
the greatest block to anyone's freedom, normally, is poverty and
a lack of resources.
> Interview, *The Guardian*, 18 November 2011

How do you get to be a Liberal Democrat MP? It's not as if
you can be flown into a safe seat – because there aren't any. So
how do you become one? By being a nutter and working your
socks off and doing the traditional Liberal Democrat grassroots-
building-up-a-seat-from-nothing process.
> Interview, *The House*, March 2013

A bit like cockroaches after a nuclear war, just a bit less smelly, we are made of sterner stuff.

> On the Liberal Democrats' ability to survive, interview, *The House*, March 2013

Millicent Garrett Fawcett

1847–1929; suffragette and educational reformer

I am a Liberal, because Liberalism seems to me to mean faith in the people, and confidence that they will manage their own affairs far better than those affairs are likely to be managed for them by others.

> Cited in A. Reid (ed.), *Why I am a Liberal* (1885)

Lynne Featherstone

b. 1951; businesswoman; MP (Liberal Democrat) Hornsey & Wood Green 2005–; Parliamentary Under-Secretary of State, Home Office 2010–12, Department for International Development 2012–

Of course you can disagree with equal marriage. You can believe that it can only be between a man and a woman. You can ultimately resist getting married to someone of the same sex if you don't want to when this becomes law. What you surely cannot do is simply rail against the fact that not everyone subscribes to your point of view and then try to stop others living life in a different way than your religion dictates.

> Supporting the coalition government's proposals for same-sex marriage, 26 December 2012

Financial Times

A Tigger leading a crowd of wols and rabbits.

> On Paddy Ashdown, 1990

A fruitful source of ideas, some of which are bright and some of which are incomprehensible.

On the Liberal Democrats' manifesto, 1992

H. A. L. Fisher

1865–1940; academic; MP (Liberal) Sheffield Hallam 1916–18, Combined English Universities 1918–26; President of the Board of Education 1916–22

Is it not notorious … how great a part is played by catch-phrases and relatively unimportant local issues in our local elections?

The Common Weal (1924)

[Patriotism] is, indeed, of all the great qualities of mankind that which has been most vulgarised by abuse.

The Common Weal (1924)

Purity of race does not exist. Europe is a continent of energetic mongrels.

A History of Europe (1935)

Nothing commends a radical change to an Englishman more than the belief that it is really conservative.

A History of Europe (1935)

Eva Mackintosh Foot

1878–1946; Foot family matriarch

Come along now, the world is waiting to be saved.

To her husband Isaac, when he was neglecting the Liberal Party for books, cited in S. Hoggart & D. Leigh, *Michael Foot: A Portrait* (1981)

Isaac Foot

1880–1960; MP (Liberal) Bodmin 1922–24, 1929–35; President, Liberal Party 1947–48

Free Trade did not fall in open battle. This Caesar fell by the stroke of the dagger of Casca Chamberlain and the sword-thrust of Brutus Runciman.

> At London, 1932, cited in S. Hoggart & D. Leigh, *Michael Foot: A Portrait* (1981)

Great as freedom may be, it has to rest upon a basis of government.

> In the House of Commons, 5 June 1935

I can answer your question, but I can't give you the brains to understand it.

> In answer to hecklers, cited in S. Hoggart & D. Leigh, *Michael Foot: A Portrait* (1981)

Tell them it is a lie. Tell them it is a damned lie. Tell them it is no less of a damned lie because it is uttered by a Tory gentleman of title.

> On how to handle a Conservative election ploy, cited in S. Hoggart & D. Leigh, *Michael Foot: A Portrait* (1981)

Who's that knocking at the door?
Who's that knocking at the door?
If it's Astor and his wife
We'll stab 'em with a knife
And they won't be Tories any more.

> Foot family song, aimed at Lady Astor, in 1920s and 1930s, cited in S. Hoggart & D. Leigh, *Michael Foot: A Portrait* (1981)

Michael Foot

1913–2010; MP (Labour) Plymouth Devonport 1945–55, Ebbw Vale,
later Blaenau Gwent 1960–92; Secretary of State for Employment 1974–
76, leader of the House of Commons 1976–79; leader of the Labour
Party 1980–83

Books were weapons, the most beloved and sharpest. And
there, spread before us, were enemies enough for a lifetime:
historical figures and their modern counterparts melted into
one; protectionists, papists, apologists for Lord North and the
Chamberlain family; Spanish tyrants and Stuart kings; Simonites
and appeasers; men of Munich and Suez; sons of Belial or
Beelzebub, normally disguised as West Country Tories, an
exceptionally reprehensible bunch.

On his childhood, cited in S. Hoggart & D. Leigh, *Michael Foot: A
Portrait* (1981)

I am a Liberal because I believe it is Liberalism in its more
radical moods which established the social and democratic
institutions which this country already enjoys.

'Why I am a Liberal', *New Statesman*, 4 April 1936

He's passed from rising hope to elder statesman without any
intervening period whatsoever.

On David Steel, in the House of Commons, 28 March 1979

Their party starts with an act of dishonour.

On the SDP, cited in M. Jones, *Michael Foot* (1994)

If a party selling soap or soft drinks asked people to send cash on
the kind of pretences adopted by the SDP, they'd be had up for
fraud … It reminds me of the famous or infamous prospectus of
the South Sea Bubble.

At Ebbw Vale, 11 April 1981

Philip Fothergill

1906–59; President, Liberal Party 1950–52

There is arising a new Liberal Party, formally rooted in the splendid traditions of the past, but with a sense of unity and self-confidence attracting a flood of new recruits and using novel methods of raising money and organising opinion.

At the Liberal Assembly, Bournemouth, 1947, cited in J. Rasmussen, *The Liberal Party: A Study of Retrenchment and Revival* (1965)

Liberals remain steadfast … because they know in their very bones that the institutions of freedom would suffer untold damage if their organisations were allowed to collapse.

Political Quarterly, Vol. 24, No. 3

George Foulkes

b. 1942; MP (Labour) Ayrshire South, later Carrick, Cumnock & Doon Valley 1979–2005; MSP Lothians 2007–11; created Baron Foulkes of Cumnock 2005

The heterosexual wing of the Liberal Party.

On the SDP, cited in G. Knight, *Honourable Insults* (1990)

Charles James Fox

1749–1806; MP (Whig) Midhurst 1768–74, Westminster 1780–1806; Foreign Secretary 1782, 1783, 1806

He was uniformly of an opinion which, though not a popular one, he was ready to aver, that the right of governing was not property but a trust.

On Pitt the Younger's scheme for parliamentary reform, 1785, cited in J. L. Hammond, *Charles James Fox* (1903)

How much the greatest event it is that ever happened in the world! And how much the best!

Letter to Mr Fitzpatrick on the fall of the Bastille, 30 July 1789

What have you done? Taken upon you by your own authority to suppress them – to erect every man, not merely into an inquisitor, but into a judge, a spy, an informer – to set father against father, brother against brother, and neighbour against neighbour, and in this way you expect to maintain the peace and tranquillity of the country! You have gone upon the principles of slavery in all your proceedings: you neglect in your conduct the foundation of all legitimate government, the rights of the people: and, setting up this bugbear, you spread a panic for the very purpose of sanctifying this infringement while, again, the very infringement engenders the evil which you dread. One extreme naturally leads to another.

On the authoritarian backlash in England provoked by the French Revolution, 1792, cited in J. M. Dent, *The Speeches of Charles James Fox: French Revolutionary War Period*

If the love of liberty was not to be maintained in England; if the warm admiration of it was not to be cherished in the hearts of the people; if the maintenance of liberty was not to be inculcated as a duty; if it was not to be reverenced as our chief good, as our boast and pride and richest inheritance;– what else had we worthy of our care? Liberty was the essence of the British constitution.

On the suspension of the Habeas Corpus Act, in the House of Commons, 17 May 1794

And now to Politics, a good amusement, though a bad employment.

Letter from Naples, 1797

I die happy.

Last words, cited in Lord John Russell, *Life and Times of C. J. Fox*, Vol. 3 (1860)

I will not close my politics in that foolish way.

On the suggestion of a peerage, cited in Fox's entry in the *Dictionary of National Biography*

The people of this country have a better ground of loyalty to the House of Brunswick than that of Divine Right, namely, that they are sovereigns of their own election; that their right is not derived from superstition, but from the choice of the people themselves; that it originated in the only genuine fountain of all power, the will of the many.

Attributed

Henry Fox, Lord Holland

1705–74; MP (Whig) Hindon 1735–41, Windsor 1741–61, Dunwich 1761–63; leader of the House of Commons 1755–56, 1762–63; created Baron Holland of Foxley 1763; father of Charles James Fox

Let nothing be done to break his spirit. The world will do that business fast enough.

On C. J. Fox, attributed

Felix Frankfurter

1882–1965; American Supreme Court judge 1939–62

The history of liberty has largely been the history of the observance of procedural standards.

McNabb *v.* United States, 1943

It is a fair summary of history to say that the safeguards of liberty have been forged in controversies involving not very nice people.

Dissenting opinion in United States *v.* Rabinowitz, 1950

Benjamin Franklin

1706–90; American statesman, writer, scientist etc.

They that can give up essential liberty to obtain a little
temporary safety deserve neither liberty nor safety.

Historical Review of Pennsylvania (1759)

Michael Frayn

b. 1933; dramatist and humorist

To be absolutely honest, what I really feel bad about is that I
don't feel worse. There's the ineffectual liberal's problem in a
nutshell.

The Observer, 8 August 1965

Michael Freeden

b. 1944; academic and writer on political ideology

Now liberals face a dilemma concerning what is non-negotiable
in their own doctrines: is it the equal respect for human rights
as liberals had formulated them, or is it the equal respect for
the liberty of both individuals and groups to engage in practices
they regard as wholesome and desirable? Multiculturalism
has set the universal and the particular at loggerheads within
liberal ideology. That debate is still alive within liberalism,
though all too frequently sotto voce in embarrassed half-tones;
that it is also unresolved attests to the inescapable internal
incompatibility of some liberal beliefs, notwithstanding the
characteristic liberal trust in rational harmony.

'More than freedom', cited in J. Margo (ed.), *Beyond Liberty* (2007)

Clement Freud

1924–2009; MP (Liberal) Isle of Ely, later Cambridgeshire North East
1973–87; writer and chef

Attila the Hen.

Describing Margaret Thatcher, on BBC Radio 4, 1979

Long live the amateur politician – amateur as in loving the work
one does – who does what he thinks is right, what makes sense,
and what will be to the general good of his constituents.

The Independent, 14 April 1997

Robert Frost

1874–1963; poet

I'm liberal. You, you aristocrat
Won't know exactly what I mean by that.
I mean so altruistically moral
I never take my own side in a quarrel.

Often quoted as 'a Liberal is someone too broad-minded to take his
own side in a quarrel', *A Witness Tree* (1942)

I never dared to be a radical when young
For fear it would make me a conservative when old.

'Ten Mills', *A Further Range* (1936)

Roger Fulford

1902–83; historian

In the politics of recent times there has been only one miracle,
that is the survival of the Liberal Party.

The Liberal Case (1959)

Thomas Fuller
1654–1734; physicist

Lean liberty is better than fat slavery.
Gnomologia (1732)

G

J. K. Galbraith
1908–2006; American economist

Liberalism is, I think, resurgent. One reason is that more and more people are so painfully aware of the alternative.
New York Times, 8 October 1989

The modern conservative is engaged in one of man's oldest exercises in moral philosophy; that is, the search for a superior moral justification for selfishness.
Attributed

Mahatma Gandhi
1869–1948; Indian leader

The moment the slave resolves that he will no longer be a slave, his fetters fall. He frees himself and shows the way to others. Freedom and slavery are mental states.
Non-Violence in Peace and War (1948)

The cause of liberty becomes a mockery if the price to be paid is the wholesale destruction of those who are to enjoy liberty.
Non-Violence in Peace and War (1948)

Freedom is not worth having if it does not include the freedom to make mistakes.
Attributed

A. G. Gardiner

1865–1946; writer; editor of the *Daily News* 1902–19

The Churchill audacity – that union of recklessness and calculation that snatches victory out of the jaws of danger.

An essay on Winston Churchill c. 1914, cited in M. Foot, *Loyalists and Loners* (1986)

He is always unconsciously playing a part – an heroic part. And he is himself an astonished spectator. He sees himself moving through the smoke of battle – triumphant, terrible, his brow clothed with thunder, his legions looking to him for victory, and not looking in vain. He thinks of Napoleon; he thinks of his great ancestor.

An essay on Winston Churchill c. 1914, cited in M. Foot, *Loyalists and Loners* (1986)

Hans-Dietrich Genscher

b. 1927; German Free Democratic Party politician; Foreign Minister and Vice Chancellor of Germany 1974–82 and 1982–92

I recently had to speak before a committee of inquiry. I was asked: 'Name, date of birth, profession?' I answered: 'Greatest foreign minister of all time.' It was embarrassing for me, but I was under oath.

The Guardian, 31 December 1992

George III

1738–1820; King 1760–1820

When he has wearied me for two hours he looks at his watch, to see if he may not tire me for an hour more.

On Whig Prime Minister George Grenville, 1765, cited in H. Walpole, *The Reign of George III* (1845)

I would sooner meet Grenville at the point of the sword than let
him into my closet.

Letter to Lord Hardwicke, 10 July 1767

Henry George

1839–97; American economist and social reformer

So long as all the increased wealth which modern progress
brings goes to build up great fortunes, to increase luxury and
make sharper the contrast between the House of Have and the
House of Want, progress is not real and cannot be permanent.

Progress and Poverty (1879)

I have never advocated or asked for special rights or special
sympathy for working men. What I stand for is equal rights for
all men.

1897

In all kinds of forms of government, the ultimate political power
is always found in the hands of the masses. And in reality, it is
certainly not the kings or aristocrats, and certainly not the
landowners or capitalists, who enslave the people everywhere.
The people are enslaved by their ignorance.

Attributed

Edward Gibbon

1737–94; historian

In the end more than they wanted freedom, they wanted
security. When the Athenians finally wanted not to give to
society but for society to give to them, when the freedom they
wished for was freedom from responsibility, then Athens ceased
to be free.

Decline and Fall of the Roman Empire (1776–88)

The principles of a free constitution are irrevocably lost when the legislature is nominated by the executive.

Decline and Fall of the Roman Empire (1776–88)

W. S. Gilbert

1836–1911; parodist and librettist

I often think it's comical,
How Nature always does contrive,
That every boy and every girl,
That's born into the world alive,
Is either a little Liberal,
Or else a little Conservative!

Iolanthe (1882)

Catherine Gladstone

1812–1900; wife of William Gladstone

Oh William dear, if you were not such a great man you would be a terrible bore.

Cited in D. Bebbington, *William Ewart Gladstone: Faith and Politics in Victorian Britain* (1993)

Herbert Gladstone

1854–1930; MP (Liberal) Leeds 1880–85, Leeds West 1885–1910;
Liberal Chief Whip 1899–1905, Home Secretary 1905–10, Governor
General and High Commissioner, South Africa, 1910–14; created
Viscount Gladstone 1910

In strict confidence our stroke oar neither sets the time nor rows his weight. And the worst of it is he does not know it.

Referring to H. H. Asquith, draft letter to Lord Robert Cecil, 22 April 1922

William Ewart Gladstone

1809–98; MP (Tory) Newark 1832–46, (Peelite) Oxford University
1847–65, (Liberal) South Lancashire 1865–68, Greenwich 1868–80,
Midlothian 1880–95; Chancellor of the Exchequer 1852–55, 1859–66,
1873–74, 1880–82; Prime Minister 1868–74, 1880–85, 1886, 1892–94

Ireland, Ireland! That cloud in the west, that coming storm.
Letter to his wife, 12 October 1845

The negation of God erected into a system of Government.
Letter to the Earl of Aberdeen, referring to the state prosecutions of
the Neapolitan government, 1851

It is, when strictly judged, an act of public immorality to form
and lead an opposition on a certain plea, to succeed and then in
office to abandon it.
On the abandonment of protectionism by Derby's 1852 government,
letter to Lord Aberdeen, 1852

I venture to say that every man who is not presumably
incapacitated by some consideration of personal unfitness or of
political danger, is morally entitled to come within the pale of
the constitution.
Arguing in favour of the extension of the franchise, in the House of
Commons, 11 May 1864

I am come among you 'unmuzzled'.
In Manchester, after his defeat for the parliamentary seat of Oxford
University, 18 July 1865

What do I understand by the Liberal principle? I understand,
in the main, it is a principle of trust in the people only
qualified by prudence. By the principle which is opposed to
the Liberal principle, I understand mistrust of the people, only
qualified by fear.
Speeches and Addresses Delivered at the Election of 1865 (1865)

You cannot fight against the future. Time is on our side. The great social forces which move onward in their might and majesty ... are against you. They are marshalled on our side.

> In the debate on the Russell government's Reform Bill, which was not enacted, House of Commons, 27 April 1866

My mission is to pacify Ireland.

> On receiving the news that he was to form his first cabinet, 1 December 1868, cited in H. C. G. Matthew, *Gladstone 1809–1874* (1986)

Swimming for his life, a man does not see much of the country through which the river winds.

> *Diary*, 31 December 1868

Your business is not to govern the country but it is, if you think fit, to call to account those who do govern it.

> On the role of the House of Commons, in the House of Commons, 29 January 1869

For myself, not in education only, but in all things, I prefer voluntary to legal machinery, where the thing can be well done either way.

> On a proposal to introduce Board Schools into Hawarden in 1873, cited in J. Morley, *The Life of William Ewart Gladstone* (1903)

We have been borne down in a torrent of gin and beer.

> Letter to his brother, explaining the Liberals' election defeat, 6 February 1874

Good ends can rarely be attained in politics without passion: and there is now, the first time for a good many years, a virtuous passion.

> Letter to Lord Granville on the Bulgarian atrocities, August 1876, cited in A. Ramm (ed.), *The Political Correspondence of Mr Gladstone and Lord Granville 1868–86* (1962)

Human justice is ever lagging after wrong, as the prayers in Homer came limping after sin.

Contemporary Review, December 1876

Let the Turks now carry away their abuses in the only possible manner, namely by carrying off themselves ... one and all, bag and baggage, shall I hope clear out from the province they have desolated and profaned.

Bulgarian Horrors and the Question of the East (1876)

The love of freedom itself is hardly stronger in England than the love of aristocracy.

Nineteenth Century (1877)

The best thing that government can do for the people is to help them to help themselves.

The Times, 5 February 1877

National injustice is the surest road to national downfall.

At Plumstead, 30 November 1878

I am a firm believer in the aristocratic principle – the rule of the best. I am an out-and-out inegalitarian.

Letter to John Ruskin, December 1878

Remember the rights of the savage, as we call him. Remember that the happiness of his humble home, remember that the sanctity of life in the hill villages of Afghanistan among the winter snows, is as inviolable in the eye of Almighty God as can be your own. Remember that He who has united you together as human beings in the same flesh and blood, has bound you by the law of mutual love; that that mutual love is not limited by the shores of this island, is not limited by the boundaries of Christian civilisation; that it passes over the whole surface of the earth, and embraces the meanest along with the greatest in its unmeasured scope.

At Dalkeith, 26 November 1879

I hope it may perhaps possibly be my privilege and honour to assist in procuring for you some of those provisions of necessary liberation from restraint; but beyond that, it is your own energies, of thought, and action, to which you will have to trust.

Third Midlothian speech at West Calder, 27 November 1879

No Chancellor of the Exchequer is worth his salt who is not ready to save what are meant by the candle-ends and cheese-parings in the cause of his country.

At Edinburgh, 29 November 1879

Just legislation and economy at home, to preserve to the nations of the world the blessings of peace, to strive to cultivate and maintain the Concert of Europe, avoid needless and entangling engagements, acknowledge the equal rights of all nations, and the foreign policy of England should always be inspired by the love of freedom.

Gladstone's principles of foreign policy, *Midlothian Speeches 1879*

Nonconformity supplies the backbone of English Liberalism.

Gleanings of Past Years (1879)

[The British Constitution] presumes more boldly than any other the good sense and the good faith of those who work it.

Gleanings of Past Years (1879)

[An] Established Clergy will always be a Tory Corps d'Armée.

Letter to Bishop Goodwin, September 1881

The resources of civilisation against its enemies are not yet exhausted.

At Leeds, referring to the Irish Land League, 7 October 1881

There never was a Churchill from John of Marlborough down that had either morals or principles.

On Randolph Churchill, 1882, cited in R. F. Foster, *Lord Randolph Churchill* (1981)

Ideal perfection is not the true basis of English legislation. We look at the attainable; we look at the practical, and we have too much English sense to be drawn away by those sanguine delineations of what might possibly be attained in Utopia, from a path which promises to enable us to effect great good for the people of England.

On the Reform Bill, in the House of Commons, 28 February 1884

Yes; these people are struggling to be free; and they are struggling rightly to be free.

On the Mahdi's (Muslim) revolt in the Sudan, in the House of Commons, 12 May 1884

Think well, think wisely, think not for the moment but for the years that are to come, before you reject this Bill.

On the introduction of the Government of Ireland Home Rule Bill, 1886, cited in D. Brack et al. (eds), *Dictionary of Liberal Biography* (1998)

This, if I understand it, is one of those golden moments of our history, one of those opportunities which may come and may go, but which rarely returns.

Winding up the debate on the second reading of the Home Rule Bill, in the House of Commons, 7 June 1886; the Bill was defeated by thirty votes, with ninety-three Liberals voting against

I will venture to say, that upon the one great class of subjects, the largest and the most weighty of them all, where the leading and determining considerations that ought to lead to a conclusion are truth, justice, and humanity – upon these, gentlemen, all the world over, I will back the masses against the classes.

At Liverpool, 28 June 1886

One prayer absorbs all others: Ireland, Ireland, Ireland.

Diary, 10 April 1887

We are part of the community of Europe, and must do our duty as such.

At Caernarvon, 10 April 1888

I do not like changes for their own sake, I only like a change when it is needful to alter something bad into something good, or something which is good into something which is better.

At Norwich, 16 May 1890

But the basis of my Liberalism is this ... I am a lover of liberty; and that liberty which I value for myself, I value for every human being in proportion to his means and opportunities.

At Norwich, 16 May 1890

But what is a leader good for, if he dare not tell his party that ... they are wrong?

On Northcote's leadership of the Tories in the fight to keep the atheist Bradlaugh out of the House of Commons, letter to J. Morley, 17 December 1891, cited in A. Briggs (ed.), *Gladstone's Boswell* (1984)

It will stand bare naked with no shelter or shield, only endured as the better of two evils.

On the monarchy if the Lords was abolished, letter to J. Morley, 22 December 1891, cited in A. Briggs (ed.), *Gladstone's Boswell* (1984)

Unless a man has a considerable gift for taking things as they come, he may make up his mind that political life will be sheer torment to him. He must meet fortune in all its moods.

Letter to J. Morley, 4 January 1892, cited in A. Briggs (ed.), *Gladstone's Boswell* (1984)

The great fact is that liberty is a great and precious gift of God, and that human excellence cannot grow up in a nation without it.

Memorandum, 12 July 1892, cited in J. Brooke & M. Sorensen (eds), *The Prime Minister's Papers: W. E. Gladstone* (1971)

My name stands in Europe as a symbol of the policy of peace, moderation and non-aggression. What would be said of my active participation in a policy that will be taken as plunging England into the whirlpool of militarism?

Commenting on his resignation as Prime Minister in 1894, which was triggered by his failure to persuade colleagues not to increase the naval estimate

The blubbering Cabinet.

Of the colleagues who wept at his final Cabinet meeting, *Diary*, 1 March 1894

To emancipate is comparatively easy. It is simple to remove restrictions, to allow natural forces free play. We have to face the problem of constructive legislation ... I am thankful I have borne a great part in the emancipating labours of the last sixty years, but entirely uncertain how, had I now to begin my life, I could face the very different problems of the next sixty years. Of one thing I am, and always have been, convinced – it is not by the state that man can be regenerated and the terrible woes of the darkened world effectively dealt with.

Letter to J. Cowan, 17 March 1894, cited in J. Morley, *The Life of William Ewart Gladstone*, Vol. 2 (1903)

I can say three things of him:
1) He is one of the ablest men I have ever known;
2) He is of the highest honour and probity;
3) I do not know whether he really has any common sense.

On the Earl of Rosebery, 1895, cited in D. Englefield, J. Seaton & I. White, *Facts About the British Prime Ministers* (1996)

Be inspired with the belief that life is a great and noble calling, not a mean and grovelling thing that we are to shuffle through as best we can, but an elevated and lofty destiny.

Cited in J. Morley, *The Life of W. E. Gladstone* (1903)

Men have no business to talk of disenchantment. Ideals are never realised.

> Cited in J. Morley, *The Life of W. E. Gladstone* (1903)

All excess in the public expenditure beyond the legitimate wants of the country is not only a pecuniary waste, but a great political, and above all, a great moral evil.

> Cited in J. Morley, *The Life of W. E. Gladstone* (1903)

A man not born a Liberal may become a Liberal, but to be a Whig he must be a born Whig.

> Cited in G. W. E. Russell, *Social Silhouettes* (1906)

I absorb the vapour and return it as a flood.

> On public speaking, cited in Lord Riddell (ed.), *Some Things That Matter* (1927)

We are bound to lose Ireland in consequence of years of cruelty, stupidity and misgovernment and I would rather lose her as a friend than as a foe.

> Cited in M. Asquith, *More Memories* (1933)

For me, Socialism has no attractions: nothing but disappointment awaits the working classes if they yield to the exaggerated anticipations which are held out to them by the Labour Party.

> At All Souls' College, Oxford, cited in A. Briggs (ed.), *Gladstone's Boswell* (1984)

I was brought up to distrust and dislike liberty, I learned to believe in it. That is the key to all my changes.

> To John Morley, cited in A. Briggs (ed.), *Gladstone's Boswell* (1984)

What, because a man is what is called a leader to a party, does that constitute him a censor and a judge of faith and morals? I will not accept it. It would make life intolerable.

On being asked to condemn Parnell publicly after the divorce case, cited by R. Blake, in P. Jagger (ed.), *Gladstone: Politics and Religion* (1985)

[Money should] fructify in the pockets of the people.

Cited in H. C. G. Matthew, *Gladstone 1809–1874* (1986)

No man connected with the City can make a good Chancellor.

Cited in R. Jenkins, *The Chancellors* (1998)

Standing up to one's enemies is commendable, but give me the man who can stand up to his friends.

Cited in G. Knight, *Honourable Insults* (1990)

He is like a minute insect which bites without being felt.

On Randolph Churchill, cited in G. Knight, *Honourable Insults* (1990)

To the actual, as distinct from the reported, strength of the Empire, India adds nothing. She immensely adds to the responsibility of Government.

Cited in H. C. G. Matthew, *Gladstone 1875–98* (1995)

An account book to God for the all-precious gift of time.

His description of his diary, cited in R. Jenkins, 'Gladstone: The Colossus of the Nineteenth Century – Politics Then and Now', *Journal of Liberal Democrat History*, No. 12, September 1996

Gunpowder and glory.

Characterising Palmerston's foreign policy, cited in A. Howard, *Sunday Times*, 4 July 1999

A radical is a Liberal who is in earnest.

Attributed

Johann Wolfgang von Goethe

1749–1832; German poet, playwright, bon viveur

He only earns his freedom and existence who daily conquers
them anew.

Faust (1832)

Which government is best? That which teaches us to govern
ourselves.

Attributed

None are more hopelessly enslaved than those who falsely
believe they are free.

Attributed

Edward Goodman

1915–96; founder, Acton Society Trust, 1946; trustee, Joseph Rowntree
Social Service Trust, 1946–86

The association of freedom and justice, as well as of morality
and all the other values thrown into prominence by conscience,
was the habit of political expression shared in reality by a very
much greater number of people than [Lord] Acton implied
when he referred to them as 'sincere friends of freedom'
who 'have at all times been rare'. It was this large class of
people who in the nineteenth century was responsible for the
achievements of freedom and justice on a considerable scale.

A Study of Liberty and Revolution (1975)

It has always to be remembered that ... authority is founded
in and sanctioned by popular consent. For public opinion to
be informed and zealous, alert and resolute is immensely
important; there can be no revolutions of liberty without public
opinion being won over to its side.

A Study of Liberty and Revolution (1975)

Frank Gray
1880–1935; MP (Liberal) Oxford 1922–24

The goods side and drivers and firemen not brought into touch with the public are Radicals, passenger guards and porters who are also underpaid but with funds augmented by tips and the patronage of the rich are Conservative.
Confessions of a Candidate (1925)

Gilbert Gray QC
1928–2011; Liberal activist and candidate

I'm a Liberal – I don't just believe in miracles, I rely on them.
Leeds Chamber of Commerce dinner, February 1986

Richard S. Grayson
b. 1969; academic and Liberal Democrat activist

His style is more chairman than leader.
On Charles Kennedy as leader, BBC Radio, *Today* programme, 19 September 2005

Bernard Greaves and Gordon Lishman
Greaves: b. 1942; Lishman: b. 1947; Liberal activists and writers

Liberty is the end product of politics and not its starting point.
The Theory and Practice of Community Politics (1980)

The Liberal view is based on the moral imperative that all people have an equal right to take part in the process by which decisions that affect their lives are taken. The greatest threat to that right is the concentration of power. Democracy is dependent as much on the dissemination, distribution and control of power as it is upon the ballot.

The Theory and Practice of Community Politics (1980)

The objective of community politics is not the welfare of communities themselves. Communities are not in themselves an end. The end is the quality of the experience of each individual within them. The justification for community politics lies in the belief that the key to releasing the potential of each person as a unique individual lies in bringing together all individuals in voluntary, mutual and cooperative enterprise within relevant communities.

The Theory and Practice of Community Politics (1980)

We are concerned with the distribution and control of power within communities and with the manner in which decisions, attitudes and priorities emerge from the full range of smaller communities to govern larger and larger communities. That process of confrontation, conflict, negotiation, cooperation, change and law-making is the way in which societies should be run. The concept of pluralism is central to our view of politics, just as the concepts of free choice and diversity are central to our view of personal development. Pluralism is not a neat prescription or an easy concept; it is, however, essential to the alternative society which we are advocating.

The Theory and Practice of Community Politics (1980)

Tony Greaves

b. 1942; Liberal activist, councillor and bookseller; created Baron Greaves of Pendle 2000

The whole document has the stench of Thatcherism about it, and ill-thought out Thatcherism at that.

On the policy declaration, abortively launched before the merger of the Liberal Party and SDP, *The Guardian*, 15 January 1988

T. H. Green

1836–82; philosopher and political theorist

By freedom he meant every man to make the most of himself, to turn to the best account all the talents and capabilities God had given him. Only in that sense was freedom worth having.

The Oxford Chronicle, 13 March 1875

Our modern legislation, then, with reference to labour, and education, and health, involving as it does manifold interference with freedom of contract, is justified on the ground that it is the business of the state, not indeed directly to promote moral goodness, for that, from the very nature of moral goodness, it cannot do, but to maintain the conditions without which a free exercise of the human faculties is impossible.

Lecture on Liberal Legislation and Freedom of Contract (1881)

If there are such things as rights at all, then, there must be a right to life and liberty, or, to put it more properly, to free life. No distinction can be made between the right to life and the right to liberty, for there can be no right to mere life – no right to life on the part of a being that has not also the right to direct the life according to the motions of his own will.

Lectures on the Principles of Political Obligation (1886)

When we speak of freedom, we do not mean merely freedom to do as we like irrespective of what it is we like. We mean the greatest power on the part of the citizens as a body to make the most and best of themselves.

Cited in R. L. Nettleship (ed.), *The Works of Thomas Hill Green*, Vol. 3 (1888)

The nature of the political reformer is always the same. The passion for improving mankind, in its ultimate object, does not vary.

Cited in R. L. Nettleship (ed.), *The Works of Thomas Hill Green*, Vol. 3 (1888)

George Grenville

1712–70; MP (Whig) Buckingham 1741–70; Prime Minister and
Chancellor of the Exchequer 1763–65

It is the common artifice of the false patriot to use the people
as a scaling ladder to preferment and, when they are firmly
seated on the pinnacle of power, they spurn the means of their
promotion.

In the House of Commons, 24 January 1758

A wise government knows how to enforce with temper, or
conciliate with dignity.

In the House of Commons, in the debate on the expulsion of John
Wilkes, 3 February 1769

The account of the Cabinet Council meeting being put off, first
for a match at Newmarket and secondly because the Duke of
Grafton had company at his house, exhibits a lively picture of
the present administration.

1768, cited in D. Englefield, J. Seaton & I. White, *Facts About the British
Prime Ministers* (1996)

William Wyndham Grenville

1759–1834; MP (Whig) Buckingham 1782–84, Buckinghamshire
1784–90; created Baron Grenville of Wooton-under-Bernewood 1790;
Home Secretary 1789–91, Foreign Secretary 1791–1801, Prime Minister
1806–07

I can hardly keep wondering at my own folly in thinking it
worthwhile to leave my books and garden, even for one day's
attendance in the House of Commons.

1803, cited in D. Englefield, J. Seaton & I. White, *Facts About the British
Prime Ministers* (1996)

Charles Grey

1764–1845; MP (Whig) Northumberland 1786–1807, Appleby 1807;
became 2nd Earl Grey 1807; Prime Minister 1830–34

No man can subscribe more cordially than I do to the maxim
that in government practical good is infinitely preferable to
speculative perfection.

In the House of Commons, 25 April 1800

We shall have the satisfaction of making what are called good
divisions, when the more important business of Fox-hunting
etc. does not prevent.

Letter to Lord Holland on the forthcoming parliamentary session,
1807

The principle of my reform is to prevent the necessity for
revolution.

In the House of Lords on the Great Reform Bill, 1831

Reforming to preserve and not to overthrow.

In the House of Lords on the Great Reform Bill, 1831

Mark my words, within two years you will find that we have
become unpopular, for having brought forward the most
aristocratic measure that ever was proposed in Parliament.

To Lord Sidmouth, about the Great Reform Bill, April 1832

Edward Grey

1862–1933; MP (Liberal) Berwick-upon-Tweed 1885–1916; created
Viscount Grey of Falloden 1916; Foreign Secretary 1905–16, leader of
the Liberal peers 1923–24

There is one great abiding cause of satisfaction in having been in
this Cabinet – we have been in it 7½ years and I believe it can

be said with truth that the personal relations of all of us have not only stood the long strain but have gained in attachment.

Letter to D. Lloyd George, June 1913, on the Liberal Cabinet, cited in P. Rowland, *The Last Liberal Governments: Unfinished Business 1911–14* (1971)

The lamps are going out all over Europe; we shall not see them lit again in our lifetime.

On the imminent outbreak of war, in the Foreign Office, 3 August 1914, quoted in *Twenty-Five Years*, Vol. 2 (1925)

He is using the machine of a great political brain to rearrange old ideas.

On Asquith as Liberal leader in the 1920s, cited in T. Wilson, *The Downfall of the Liberal Party 1914–35* (1966)

Wulff Henry Grey

1876–1961; soldier; treasurer, Liberal Party, 1950–58

We do not need a new Research Department to discover a new Liberal creed. The one of Peace, Retrenchment and Reform, including Free Trade and a recovery of our civil liberties, is good enough for any Liberal.

Resigning as treasurer in 1958 on the creation of new research department under Harry Cowie

Jo Grimond

1913–93; MP (Liberal) Orkney and Shetland 1950–83; Liberal Chief Whip 1950–56, leader of the Liberal Party 1956–67; created Baron Grimond of Firth 1983

It is the best thing that has happened in politics ... for years, at any rate since the National Government took office in the bad days which have continued so long ... You are a household word, and one that will not easily be forgotten. For years pessimism has reigned and the Labour Party has whined. Your plan fitted in with a new mood ... You have said that you want from the Liberals a policy far more radical than Socialism. I agree entirely and it wants to be an immediate programme.

Letter to Sir William Beveridge MP, 21 October 1944

For more than twenty years, it has limped at the heels of world events; they led the path to Munich, they fumbled feebly with unemployment, they fostered no enterprise, private or public, they sheltered monopoly, they lit no beacon for the young, they offered no hope to the old.

On the Conservative Party, *The Orcadian*, 3 July 1945

It was not strong government we needed, but less government, better government and government nearer home.

The Orcadian, 2 March 1950

The working class will disappear with universal education, television, cars and a middle-class wage.

1951, cited in W. Wallace in V. Bogdanor (ed.), *Liberal Party Politics* (1983)

Liberalism to me is the political philosophy of British empiricism. It springs from the philosophy of Locke and Hume. A philosophy based on the individual and his experience. A philosophy profoundly suspicious of deities, innate ideas and dogma. A philosophy which finds that all our knowledge comes from experience.

'The Principles of Liberalism,' *Political Quarterly*, Vol. 24, No. 3, 1953

I for my part am not interested in causes which are perpetually lost. I am not attracted by the wistful glamour of defeat ... We shall get neither [converts or allies] by hugging our own private crosses.

The Guardian, 18 April 1955

I stand here not as the White Hope of the Liberal Party, but as the White Hope of Kingston, Malden and Coombe.

When introduced as the 'the Great White Hope of the Liberal Party' at the Liberal assembly, Folkestone, 1956 (Grimond was a member of Kingston, Malden & Coombe Liberal Association)

In the next ten years it is a question of get on or get out.

At the Liberal assembly, Southport, 21 September 1957

[It should not be] a brains' trust standing on the side lines of politics shouting advice to Tories and Socialists alike. It would not survive if it was content merely to write in the margins of politics.

On the future role of the Liberal Party, *Liberal News*, 27 September 1957

The Liberals had to try to blow some of the cobwebs out of politics in this country. They had to be actively seeking out new ideas, as too many of the old arguments were dead, and the old Socialist answers had a strong whiff of the grave.

Cited in T. Joyce & F. Ware, *What Liberals Mean by Opportunity* (1957)

It was lunacy for each country to collect its own nuclear weapons. It means three or six or twenty triggers, each one if pulled will mean doom for all. If the West must have nuclear weapons, it should be under joint control.

Orkney Herald, 10 June 1958

A socialist way of life embalmed under a Tory government.

On the post-war consensus, at Taunton, 14 June 1958

Liberals must give up being so excessively respectable. We have got to have some bloody noses in the party.

At the Royal Albert Hall, 10 November 1958

The long-term objective is clear; to replace the Labour Party as the progressive wing of politics in this country, to sweep in

not only Liberals but Liberal-Socialists and Liberal-Tories. It is
certain that in the sixties a fresh tide will flow with new ideas
and new leaders. I say to you that has got to be a Liberal tide.

At the Royal Albert Hall, 10 November 1958

The Liberal Party should be the party to which people look for
reforms which affect their daily lives ... let us get things done
and let us start in local government.

Liberal News, 7 May 1959

Every summer when I go back to Orkney I feel the immense
well-being of people free from the jealousies, stresses and
antagonisms of industrial life.

Bulletin, 21 August 1959

The chance of getting new thought through the Liberal Party
is infinitely greater than through the Labour Party ... I do
suggest that the Left must not get bogged down in a theological
discussion about nationalisation which is like stoking up a
hangover by further draughts of alcohol already taken to excess.

At the National Liberal Club, 14 November 1959

Now it may be strange in a Liberal politician, but I don't enjoy
being in a minority. I don't want the trappings of politics
without some power.

Liberal News, 19 November 1959

We say quite openly to Liberally-minded socialists and to
liberals of all varieties who at present spell their names with a
small 'l' come in and help us. Play your own part in moulding
a new progressive party which will not be preoccupied with its
own feuds nor trussed up in its own constitution ... I remain
convinced that there is a progressive majority in this country if
it can be mobilised.

At Aberdeen University, 11 December 1959

To take the word society first. It emphasises the individual but the individual in conjunction with other men and women.

The Liberal Future (1959)

If you believe that people might freely choose such things as the legalisation of indiscriminate murder of one's children, then there really is no basis for Liberalism at all.

The Liberal Future (1959)

The possession of some property widens a man's choice and gives him more scope to exercise his talents. Personal ownership is the badge of a citizen as against a proletarian. It is a shield against petty tyranny.

The Liberal Future (1959)

'The poorest he that is in England hath a life to live, as the greatest he ...' (Colonel Thomas Rainborough, Putney Debates, 1647). This is one Liberal Text. And it is more distinctive than may at first appear. It asserts the individual and the value of any individual – even the poorest He. But it asserts it without envy. It does not demand that the rich be made poor – nor even claim that the poor are more deserving than the rich. It demands equality in one thing only, the right to live one's own life.

The Liberal Future (1959)

A Liberal Government must not be frightened to take positive action to promote Liberal conditions. Defence of the weak, help for the poor, eradication of evils, guardianship of scarce resources, maintenance of the coherence of society, the setting of an agenda in those fields where the Government acts, all these are part of its legitimate duties.

The Liberal Future (1959)

Every time a local Liberal councillor gets a bus stop moved to a better place he strikes a blow for the Liberal Party.

The Guardian, 3 October 1960

For too long, Liberal MPs have been acting like an overworked and rather ragged repertory company insisting on putting up a spokesman in every major debate. Suffering too from a sad case of under-rehearsal. One day it is *East Lynne*, the next *Hamlet* or *Waiting for Godot*.

Daily Mail, 8 December 1960

In international affairs it is the attempt to keep up outworn ideas of national prestige which leads to insecurity. Keeping out of Europe won't make us secure. Suez didn't make us secure. To work for practical steps in international cooperation — that makes for security. If we could show that the West could reconcile its internal stresses, that would make us more secure because more sure of ourselves. The piling up of weapons is the business of the war ministries. It is unfair to blame them for this futile exercise. It is fair to blame the politicians for failing to canalise the very obvious desire, as evidenced by the Aldermaston marchers for instance, to try other ways of achieving security.

Let's Get On With It (1960)

Many Liberals don't want to be radical, they are comfortable, not very political, middle of the road people ... It makes nonsense of nine-tenths of what the group at the top of the party are trying to say or do.

Memorandum to L. Behrens, 13 April 1961

Boards can give up using directorships as well-paid retirement work for the exhausted members of the Establishment. Workers would have to take responsibility right up to the boardroom. If industry won't give workers proper status, it is up to a Liberal government to change the company law to see that their status is recognised. Liberals want to break down the devilish British class structure. The workers should feel that ultimately they employed the managers and were consulted at every stage of the industrial process.

At the Liberal assembly, Edinburgh, 1961

It is no good just giving the workers a share in the profits, especially if this is to be at the expense of their getting a fair wage. Liberals want to give them a share in the running of the industry.

At Central Hall, London, 2 March 1961

I am not interested in a political debating society. I am interested in power. I am interested in power because I am interested in getting some things done.

At Central Hall, London, 2 March 1961

My God ... an incredible result.

Reaction to the Liberal victory in the Orpington by-election, 14 March 1962

I can see — we've done rather disgustingly well.

Telephone comment to Michael Meadowcroft in Orpington, having seen the TV coverage of the by-election count, 14 March 1962

In bygone days, commanders were taught that, when in doubt, they should march their troops towards the sound of gunfire. I intend to march my troops towards the sound of gunfire. Politics are a confused affair and the fog of political controversy can obscure many issues. But we will march towards the sound of the guns.

At the Liberal assembly, Brighton, 15 September 1963

There are enemies, there are difficulties to be faced. There are decisions to be made. There is passion to be generated. The enemy is complacency and wrong values and inertia in the face of incompetence and injustice. It is against this enemy that we march.

At the Liberal assembly, Brighton, 15 September 1963

The need for publicity corrupts as much or more than power.

The Liberal Challenge (1963)

It has been said that Socialism is about Equality. If you ask for an equivalent shorthand description of Liberalism I should say that it is about Freedom and Participation.

The Liberal Challenge (1963)

Those who went into the Tory Party to make it a party of progress and reform have had no more success than most wives who marry debauched husbands hoping to reclaim them.

The Liberal Challenge (1963)

If there had been no First World War, if there had been a synthesis of Liberals and Labour in 1929, if Guild Socialism or Syndicalism had not been rejected, we might have had a continuation of the main flood of progressive radical thought. But we did not. Belief in the state and state Socialism dominated politics between the wars. This was to be the main road forward for the Left.

The Liberal Challenge (1963)

The socialist heritage of the Labour Party is not fire in its belly but dead weight in its luggage. It prevents the party from setting about the reform of the private enterprise system – but it provides no alternative inspiration.

At Beckenham, 20 March 1964

You must have some touch of idealism in politics.

On television during the 1964 election campaign, cited in D. Butler & D. King, *The British General Election of 1964*

It was surely inconceivable that we should plunge again into a long dark tunnel of Tory government, with no light at the end. Our parliamentary system could not stand it. The country could not afford it. Millions of people would simply contract out of public affairs.

Bolton Evening News, 3 October 1964

The presence of three million Liberal voters in the country has muted any triumphant call for Socialism. This is a position which the Liberal Party has not occupied for many years. Our teeth are in the real meat and our muscles exerted in the real power struggle of politics. It has been my aim to get the Liberals into the middle of the field of play. We are in it.

At the Liberal assembly, 1965

The trouble with the Labour Party is that they don't really believe in socialism, but they cannot wholeheartedly approve of private enterprise either.

1965, attributed

The slogan 'Let's Go with Labour' should be replaced with 'Let's Go to Sleep with Labour'.

Shetland Times, 25 March 1966

Political power should reside in the individual. The individual does not live in isolation but in a community. All political institutions must be viewed as the means by which the individual in the community can realise his or her full potential, exercise as much freedom as is consonant with the freedom of others, and be able to lead a full and secure life under the law.

A Roar for the Lion (1976)

The reason the Scots have voted against devolution is that, given a choice, they would prefer to be ruled by Westminster than by trade unionists from Glasgow and lawyers from Edinburgh.

At the London Book Fair, March 1979

Our strategy depended upon the Labour Party or some part of it being convinced that, as a socialist party committed to public ownership of all the means of production, distribution and exchange, it had a poor future. The state of public opinion pointed to realignment. There was a hope that the full-blooded socialists would split off to the Left leaving a radical party on the left of centre of British politics but free of socialist dogma.

Memoirs (1979)

I was right, I believe, in telling the Party that it could not by some miracle of parthogenesis spring from six MPs to a majority in the House of Commons. It would have to go through a period of coalition.

Memoirs (1979)

A leader who had grasped more firmly the 'schwerpunkt' of politics could perhaps have achieved more; a leader perhaps who had more confidence in his and the party's destiny ... The power of the leader is overestimated, yet, in the short term, the leader is pre-eminent.

Memoirs (1979)

Cooperatives ... can ... give the individual a framework in which he feels himself to be one of a team, in which he will be guaranteed some security, some help in trouble, but he will also have an opportunity to take part in decision making.

Inaugural Eighty Club Lecture, National Liberal Club, 29 October 1980

Only the actions and states of mind of individuals voluntarily arrived at can have value: what we do or what is done to us at the orders of others – however materially beneficial or indeed necessary – has no value.

Inaugural Eighty Club Lecture, National Liberal Club, 29 October 1980

I do not believe that a new centrist group, whether supported by a new 'wet' party or by a coalition of compromise, will have much future. The voter of the floating centre should be offered not conservatism with a socialist tinge but a new radicalism.

A Personal Manifesto (1983)

A party of radical change ... required three essentials: a new
political philosophy, a leader who would inspire confidence, and
a political base. The coalition lacked all three.

On the Lloyd George coalition, 1918–22; *Daily Telegraph*, 1983

It is time for the new party to offer a third way.

Foreword to P. Ashdown, *Citizen's Britain* (1989)

What should alarm us about politicians is not that they break
their promises but that they frequently keep them.

Cited in R. Ingrams, *Quips and Quotes* (2012)

The Guardian

The Liberals have kept public interest alive since 1945 in the
critical question of the place of the individual in an increasingly
complex society.

21 April 1964

The Liberal Democrat essay far out-distances its competitors
with a fizz of ideas and an absence of fudge.

On the 1992 election manifesto, 19 March 1992

The Ashdown strategy of cooperation where possible,
obstruction where necessary has already borne more fruit
for the Lib Dems in a year than they gathered in decades of
struggle.

April 1998

H

Peter Hain

b. 1950; Chairman of the National League of Young Liberals 1971–73; MP (Labour) Neath 1991–; Secretary of State for Northern Ireland 2005–07, Secretary of State for Work and Pensions and Secretary of State for Wales 2007–08, Secretary of State for Wales 2009–10

The party leadership does not understand what community politics is all about, and if they did they wouldn't like it.

> 1970, cited in R. Ingham & D. Brack (eds), *Peace, Reform and Liberation* (2011)

Community politics is a style of political action through which people gain the confidence to agitate for their rights and the ability to control their own destinies. It involves cultivating in each individual the *habit* of participation. It also involves a willingness to take direct action. It is essentially an alternative form of politics, bursting out from within the community and involving people in the experience of taking and using power on their own behalf and on their community's behalf.

> *Community Politics* (1976)

There is a great reservoir of radicals throughout the country who share a common disenfranchisement with conventional party politics, an estrangement from the system and yet a suspicion of sectarian left-wing groups. They could come together to form a new radical movement committed to community politics. Such a realignment of radicals is different in kind and in ideological stamp from the much canvassed realignment of parliamentary social democrats … the revolution will not be brought about through a series of ad hoc, one-off pressure pricks on the system.

> *Community Politics* (1976)

R. B. Haldane
1856–1928; MP (Liberal) Haddingtonshire 1885–1911; created Viscount
Haldane of Cloan 1911; Secretary of State for War 1905–12, Lord
Chancellor 1912–15, 1924; leader of the Labour peers 1924–28

Mr G. thoroughly demoralised the Liberal Party by the policy of
sop-throwing in the two years before 1892.

> Letter to Lord Rosebery, 24 April 1895, cited in M. Pugh, *The Making
> of Modern British Politics 1867–1939* (1982)

Today it is not for individual freedom that we have to struggle
against classes and privilege; we have to win a yet harder fight,
a fight for emancipation from conditions which deny fair play to
the collective energy for the good of society as a whole.

> *Progressive Review* 1 (November 1896)

George Savile, 1st Marquis Halifax
1633–95; created Viscount Halifax 1668, Marquis Halifax 1682; Lord
Privy Seal and Lord President of the Council throughout 1670s and 1680s

When the people contend for their liberty, they seldom get
anything by their victory but new masters.

> 'Of Prerogative, Power and Liberty', *Political, Moral, and Miscellaneous
> Thoughts and Reflections* (1750)

Power is so apt to be insolent and Liberty to be saucy, that they
are very seldom upon good terms.

> 'Of Prerogative, Power and Liberty', *Political, Moral, and Miscellaneous
> Thoughts and Reflections* (1750)

If none were to have liberty but those who understand what it
is, there would not be many freed men in the world.

> 'Of Prerogative, Power and Liberty', *Political, Moral, and Miscellaneous
> Thoughts and Reflections* (1750)

In parliaments, men wrangle in behalf of liberty, that do as little care for it, as they deserve it.

'Of Parliaments', *Political, Moral, and Miscellaneous Thoughts and Reflections* (1750)

Alexander Hamilton
1757–1804; American politician and contributor to the *Federalist Papers*

In a government framed for durable liberty, not less regard must be paid to giving the magistrate a proper degree of authority to make and execute the laws with rigour, than to guard against encroachments upon the rights of the community; as too much power leads to despotism, too little leads to anarchy, and both eventually to the ruin of the people.

Cited in F. S. Oliver, *Alexander Hamilton* (1906)

Learned Hand
1872–1961; American jurist and judge

Liberty is so much latitude as the powerful choose to accord to the weak.

At the University of Pennsylvania Law School, June 1930

The spirit of liberty is the spirit which is not too sure it is right.

At New York City, 21 May 1944

William Harcourt
1827–1904; MP (Liberal) Oxford 1868–80, Derby 1880–95, West Monmouthshire 1895–1904; Home Secretary 1880–85, Chancellor of the Exchequer 1886, 1892–94; leader of the Liberal Party 1896–98

The last Doge of Whiggism.

On Lord John Russell, *Saturday Review*, 17 November 1885

We are all socialists now.

> 1888, cited in G. B. Shaw, *Fabian Essays in Socialism* (1889)

Like the Kingdom of Heaven, the Liberal Party is a house of many mansions.

> Letter to John Morley, 1891, cited in D. A. Hamer, *Liberal Politics in the Age of Gladstone and Rosebery* (1972)

Once pay a Member for his votes collectively and he will very soon make a market for his individual votes.

> 1892, cited in M. Pugh, *The Making of Modern British Politics 1867–1939* (1982)

It is no good committing suicide when one is dying. It is only the addition of an unnecessary crime.

> When John Morley suggested resigning in 1895 as the Rosebery government neared its end, cited in A. G. Gardiner, *The Life of Sir William Harcourt* (1923)

The value of the political heads of departments is to tell the permanent officials what the public will not stand.

> Cited in A. G. Gardiner, *The Life of Sir William Harcourt* (1923)

Mary Hardcastle, Lady Monkswell

1849–1930; diarist, wife of 2nd Baron Monkswell, Progressive Chairman of London County Council 1903–07, and junior minister in the 1892 government

It was announced yesterday in *The Times* that Lord Rosebery had resigned the leadership of the Opposition because he could not agree with his colleagues on the Armenian question. As nobody yet knows what they want on that question he might have found another excuse.

> 9 October 1896, cited in E. C. F. Collier, *A Victorian Diarist: Later Extracts* (1946)

Percy Harris

1876–1952; MP (Liberal) Market Harborough 1916–18, Bethnal Green
South West 1922–45; Liberal Chief Whip 1935–45

I compared the pygmies now sitting on the Treasury Bench with
the great figures of past Liberal governments, Mr Asquith, Sir
Edward Grey, Lord Haldane and Lloyd George. These names
are remembered but who will know the names of the present
government twenty years hence? I have omitted the name of
your own member [Sir Winston Churchill] ... he is quite the
greatest Parliamentarian we have got, but I sometimes think that
patriotic as our Ministers are, they would rather lose a war than
have him as a colleague. These Lilliputians don't like Gulliver; he
makes them feel small.

To Epping Liberal Association, 22 November 1938

Robert Harris

b. 1957; journalist

One should never forget the Liberals' immense capacity for
survival. They are like an ancient tribe whose watering hole
dried up seventy years ago. Ever since they have been on a trek
through the wilderness to find a fresh spring, led in recent times
by a succession of gesticulating prophets: the white-haired sage
Grimond; the suave princeling Thorpe; the boy David; and now
the warrior Ashdown.

Sunday Times conference sketch, September 1991

Frederic Harrison

1831–1923; barrister and academic

Any Liberal Ministry must be pledged to deal with
redistribution in this house. Unless this is done, there will be a
swinging back again some day, and in 1886 the old trick of 1874
will be played over again. The Tory is only stunned, he must be

killed. And not only killed, but put in his coffin, and not only
put in his coffin, but screwed down, and a brass plate nailed on
the top. The only way to screw him down is redistribution.

Letter to Sir Charles Dilke, 5 April 1880, cited in T. A. Jenkins,
Parliament, Party and Politics in Victorian Britain (1996); as part of the
Third Reform Act of 1884, redistribution of seats was achieved but
with heavy Tory input

Richard Harrison

1960s Young Liberal

We are radicals, not disillusioned Tories who retain the vestiges
of a Sunday School education. We aim to make clear the basically
anti-capitalist nature of Liberal economic proposals. Capital is
the servant of labour and not vice-versa.

New Outlook, No. 31, May 1964

Spencer Compton Cavendish, Marquis of Hartington

1833–1908; MP (Liberal) Lancashire North 1857–68, Radnor Boroughs
1869–80, Lancashire North East 1880–85, (Liberal, Liberal Unionist)
Rossendale 1885–91; leader of the Liberal Party 1875–80; created
Marquis of Hartington 1858, 8th Duke of Devonshire 1891; Lord
President of the Council 1895–1903; broke with Gladstone over Home
Rule 1886

Let me remind you that a political party is an engine not merely
for the carrying of this or that reform – not merely for the
removal of this or that abuse; it is an engine the object of which
is to form the opinion and guide the destinies of the nation.

Speech at Keighley, quoted in *Manchester Guardian*, 4 November 1876

A defeated and discredited statesman.

Describing Gladstone following the 'Hawarden kite' and the split in
the Liberal Party over Home Rule, 1886

Roy Hattersley

b. 1932; MP (Labour) Birmingham Sparkbrook 1964–97; Secretary of
State for Prices and Consumer Protection 1976–79; deputy leader of the
Labour Party 1983–92; created Baron Hattersley of Sparkbrook 1993

Most important of all, he was a genuine radical. On each of
the defining issues of the day he passed the progressive test. He
supported women's suffrage, trade union rights, freedom from
censorship and the great social reforms for which his successor
took credit. He did so with the apparent certainty that common
sense commended each reform. And that is the mark of the true
radical – the certainty that the changes he proposed in society
were reasonable as well as right.

Campbell-Bannerman (2006)

William Hazlitt

1778–1830; Romantic author and essayist

The love of liberty is the love of others; the love of power is the
love of ourselves.

Political Essays, quoted in the *Oxford Dictionary of Quotations* (1996)

Liberty is the only true riches: of all the rest we are at once the
masters and the slaves.

The Round Table (1817)

Denis Healey

b. 1917; MP (Labour) Leeds South East, later East 1952–92; Chancellor
of the Exchequer 1974–79; deputy leader of the Labour Party 1980–83;
created Baron Healey of Riddlesden 1992

He was not well suited to the politics of class and ideology
which played so large a role in the Labour Party. His natural
environment was the Edwardian age on which he wrote so
well. He saw politics very much like Trollope, as the interplay

of personalities seeking preferment, rather than, like me, as a conflict of principles and programmes about social and economic change.

On Roy Jenkins, *The Time of My Life* (1989)

It was never easy working with the Liberals, since David Steel was unable to control his tiny flock. I found it particularly difficult working with their economic spokesman, John Pardoe; he was robust and intelligent enough, but sometimes I felt he was simply Denis Healey with no redeeming features. More than once Joel Barnett had to pick up the pieces after we had sent the crockery flying.

On the Lib–Lab Pact, *The Time of My Life* (1989)

The lamentable history of the SDP bore out all the warnings I had given. Its most important effect was to delay the Labour Party's recovery by nearly ten years, and to guarantee Mrs Thatcher two more terms in office. Another effect was to weaken and fragment the centre in British politics, though this was due largely to David Owen's rebarbative personality ... Like all right-wing breakaways from left-wing parties, the SDP achieved nothing significant on its own account, but did grievous damage to those who shared many of its views in the party it deserted.

The Time of My Life (1989)

When we returned to the Embassy to change out of our winter clothing, I opened a door to find David Owen and David Steel clinging to one another in their long-johns as they tried to take off their boots. I made a rapid departure, murmuring 'I've heard of the Alliance, but this is going too far'.

Relating events on a trip to the Soviet Union, February 1984, *The Time of My Life* (1989)

The good fairies gave the young doctor almost everything: thick dark locks, matinee idol features, a lightning intelligence – unfortunately the bad fairy made him a shit.

On David Owen, cited in David Owen, *Time to Declare* (1992)

Georg Wilhelm Friedrich Hegel
1770–1831; German philosopher

The history of the world is none other than the progress of the consciousness of freedom.

Philosophy of History (1832)

Hubert Henderson
1890–1952; economist, associated with the Liberal Summer Schools and the 'Yellow Book'

We are the manufacturing establishment of politics and, if we are compelled for a time to let others do the retailing, we must not try to deprive them of good salesmen and handsome shop-walkers.

On the state of the Liberal Party in the 1920s, cited in R. Ingham & D. Brack (eds), *Peace, Reform and Liberation* (2011)

Patrick Henry
1736–99; American politician; Governor of Virginia, 1776–77, 1784–86

Is life so dear or peace so sweet, as to be purchased at the price of chains and slavery? Forbid it, Almighty God! I know not what course others may take, but as for me, give me liberty or give me death!

At the Virginia Convention, 23 March 1775

A. P. Herbert
1890–1971; author; MP (Independent) Oxford University 1935–50

No, no, there is not so much fun in the world that we can do without a Liberal Party. No, no, let them march on, two or three hearts that beat as one though they vote as three or four.

1929

Aleksandr Herzen
1812–70; Russian political thinker and writer

The world will not know liberty until all that is religious or political is transformed into something simple and human, is made susceptible to criticism and denial.

   1849

Emily Hobhouse
1860–1926; welfare campaigner

Of all whom I saw at that time … he alone … seemed to have the leisure and the determination to hear and understand everything … As I dwelt upon the wholesale burning of farms and villages, the deportations, the desperate condition of a burnt-out population brought in by hundreds in convoys, the people deprived of clothes, bedding, utensils and necessities, the semi-starvation in the camps, the fever-stricken children lying … upon the bare earth … the appalling mortality …
– he was deeply moved – and now and again muttered sotto voce 'methods of barbarism, methods of barbarism'. He was right.

   On her meeting with Campbell-Bannerman after her trip to South Africa on behalf of the South African Women and Children Distress Fund, 1901, cited in J. Wilson, *CB: A Life of Sir Henry Campbell-Bannerman* (1973)

John Cam Hobhouse
1786–1869; MP (Whig) Westminster 1820–33, Nottingham 1834–47, Harwich 1848–51; President of the Board of Control 1835–41, 1846–52; created Baron Broughton 1851

Thus ends this great national exploit. The deed is done. It is difficult to believe that it is done.

   On the Reform Act receiving Royal Assent, 7 June 1832, cited in A. Fraser, *Perilous Question: the Drama of the Great Reform Bill 1832* (2013)

L.T. Hobhouse

1864–1929; political theorist and journalist

An ideal is as necessary to the reformer as the established fact
is to the conservative ... A progressive movement ... must
have an ideal, and an ethical ideal for the future must be in
so far abstract as it is not yet realised and embodied in social
institutions.

'The Ethical Basis of Collectivism', *International Journal of Ethics*, Vol. 8
(1898)

We do not love principles, as such, in England. We distrust the
abstract, and pride ourselves upon holding by hard facts. Yet it
is these same hard facts themselves that are at last teaching us
to see that men like Cobden and Bright, or, again, like Bentham
and Mill, who had principles and knew how to apply them,
were the real spiritual leaders who moved the masses of social
prejudice and political obstruction and made the way plain
for reform. The truth is forced upon us that it is precisely the
absence of clearly thought-out principles, such as these men
understood and applied, that has destroyed the nerve and
paralysed the efforts of Liberalism in our own day. The hope for
the future of the party of progress must largely depend upon the
efforts of thinkers – not thinkers of the study, but thinkers in
close contact with the concrete necessities of national life – to
restate the fundamental principles of Liberalism in the form
which modern circumstances require.

'England, A Nation', leader, *Manchester Guardian*, 17 December 1904

The road to political democracy in England lies through what,
in a broader sense than is usually given to the term, we may call
Social Democracy.

1907, cited in V. Bogdanor (ed.), *Liberal Party Politics* (1983)

The ideas of Socialism, when translated into practical terms,
coincide with the ideas to which Liberals are led when they seek

to apply their principles of Liberty, Equality and the Common Good to the industrial life of our time.

'The Prospects of Liberalism', *Contemporary Review*, Vol. 93 (1908)

Liberalism is the belief that society can safety be founded on [the] self-directing power of personality, that it is only on this foundation that a true community can be built, and that so established its foundations are so deep and so wide that there is no limit that we can place to the extent of the building. Liberty then becomes not so much a right of the individual as a necessity of society. It rests not on the claim of A to be let alone by B, but on the duty of B to treat A as a rational being.

Liberalism (1911)

There is somewhere a defect in the social system, a hitch in the economic machine. Now, the individual workman cannot put the machine straight. He is the last person to have any say in the control of the market ... He does not direct or regulate industry. He is not responsible for its ups and downs, but he has to pay for them. That is why it is not charity but justice for which he is asking.

Liberalism (1911)

The struggle for liberty is also, when pushed through, a struggle for equality. Freedom to choose and follow an occupation, if it is to become fully effective, means equality with others in the opportunities for following such an occupation. This is, in fact, one among the various considerations which leads Liberalism to support a national system of free education and will lead it further on the same lines.

Liberalism (1911)

Liberty without equality is a name of noble sound and squalid meaning.

Liberalism (1911)

Amid all differences and conflicts one idea is common to the modern democratic movement, whether it takes the shape of revolution or reform, of Liberalism or Socialism. The political order must conform to the ethical ideal of what is just.

Cited in R. Rae, *Social Reform Versus Socialism* (1912)

I am sorry that the Liberals did not get more seats, as I think (I know it's blasphemy) they carry more brains to the square inch than Labour, most of whose men are merely dull and terribly afraid of their permanent officials.

On the 1929 election; cited in D. Brack & E. Randall (eds), *Dictionary of Liberal Thought* (2007)

Every liberty depends on a corresponding act of control.

Attributed

J. A. Hobson

1858–1940; economic writer and radical journalist

Liberalism is now formally committed to a task which certainly involves a new conception of the State in its relation to the individual life and to private enterprise ... From the standpoint which best presents its continuity with earlier Liberalism, it appears as a fuller appreciation and realisation of individual liberty contained in the provision of equal opportunities for self-development. But to this individual standpoint must be joined a just apprehension of the social, viz., the insistence that these claims or rights of self-development be adjusted to the sovereignty of social welfare.

The Crisis of Liberalism: new issues of democracy (1909)

Liberals must ever insist that each enlargement of the authority and functions of the State must justify itself as an enlargement of personal liberty, interfering with individuals only in order to set free new and larger opportunities.

The Crisis of Liberalism: new issues of democracy (1909)

Liberalism will probably retain its distinction from Socialism, in taking for its chief test of policy the freedom of the individual citizen rather than the strength of the State.

The Crisis of Liberalism: new issues of democracy (1909)

The audacity of the Budget has put a new spirit into English politics. The nature and magnitude of its financial proposals have come upon our people as a surprise ... To such an extent has blind, short-range opportunism become the ruling principle of English politics that any measure which, like this Budget, brings into the foreground of debate vital issues of political theory is staggering to the intelligence.

On the People's Budget, 'The Significance of the Budget', *English Review*, Vol. 2 (1909)

The tendency of all strong governments has always been to suppress liberty, partly in order to ease the processes of rule, partly from sheer disbelief in innovation.

Attributed

Simon Hoggart

b. 1946; journalist

Basically the Liberal Party is divided between wispy beards and others. Wispy beards ... wear T-shirts with slogans on, usually faintly dated, e.g.: 'The Only Safe Fast Breeder is a Rabbit'. They tend to have ill-fitting jeans, and those heavy shoes which look like Cornish pasties. They have briefcases stuffed with documents, chiefly about community politics, nuclear power and ecology. They drink real ale.

On the House (1981)

Richard Holme

1936–2008; politician and businessman; created Baron Holme of
Cheltenham 1990

[Mrs Thatcher] is the Enid Blyton of economics. Nothing must
be allowed to spoil her simple plots.

    At the Liberal Party assembly, Blackpool, 1980

If knowledge is power, then ignorance must be powerlessness,
and that is the condition of too many people in modern Britain.

    The People's Kingdom (1987)

Ah, the books! Do we choose them or do they choose us?
Suffice it to say that if I ever thought I could escape from
liberalism, the books stand around me in a tall circle telling me
to stay. From the pages of Bunyan to Blake, from Milton and
Mill, Paine and Popper, and from many, many others, the sprite
of freedom dances before my eyes.

    Cited in D. Brack (ed.), *Why I am a Liberal Democrat* (1996)

You must not get carried away with the film script you have
written in your head – two strong people standing up and
shaping history.

    Warning to Paddy Ashdown over his talks with Tony Blair, cited in *The
    Ashdown Diaries*, Vol. 1 1988–1997, entry for 17 July 1996 (2000)

Anyone who campaigns for proportional representation but
rules out a coalition in any circumstances is suffering from a
serious logic deficit.

    At the Liberal Democrat conference, Eastbourne, 21 September 1997

Oliver Wendell Holmes

1809–94; American physician and writer

The very aim and end of our institutions is just this: that we may
think what we like and say what we think.

The Professor at the Breakfast Table (1860)

Arthur Holt

1914–95; MP (Liberal) Bolton West 1951–64; Liberal Chief Whip 1962–
63; President, Liberal Party 1974–75

South Africa is a typical example of how the true voice of
Liberalism is eventually unheard if its expression is left in the
unsafe keeping of other political parties.

Political Quarterly, Vol. 24, No. 3

George Jacob Holyoake

1817–1906; publisher and radical leader

A Whig is to be preferred to a Tory ... because he professes
liberality, and the profession of it is an advantage. It makes liberality
fashionable, and encourages the imitation of it and at last
the real thing springs up. The Whigs made freedom possible
among us.

Reasoner, 1852, cited in L. E. Grugel, *George Jacob Holyoake* (1976)

I maintain always and everywhere that the people should keep
the state and not the state the people.

On the offer of a pension, letter to W. E. Gladstone, 11 March 1881

[Serious difficulties arose] when Liberals publicly contend that
coercion in defence of order was alien to Liberalism, which
meant that a Liberal is a sentimental fool who is prevented by
his principles from coercing the man who would cut his throat.

Deliberate Liberalism (1886)

If it comes to be understood that freedom paralyses the hand of order, it would be a more serious argument against Liberty than tyranny ever invented.

Deliberate Liberalism (1886)

An intelligent Liberal is one who is for liberty of discussion till a question has been fully debated – then he comes to action.

Deliberate Liberalism (1886)

A Liberal is one who seeks to secure for everyone the same rights, political, social or religious, which he claims for himself.

Undated, Holyoake Collection, Manchester, cited in I. Bradley, *The Optimists* (1980)

Emlyn Hooson

1925–2012; MP (Liberal) Montgomeryshire 1962–79; created Baron Hooson of Montgomery 1979

We should soldier on in complete independence.

Rejecting Jo Grimond's realignment strategy, cited in D. Butler & D. King, *The British General Election of 1966*

Thomas Horabin

1896–1956; MP (Liberal, Independent, Labour) North Cornwall 1939–50

The duty of Radical Liberals ... is to fight Tory despotism with all [their] strength so that the power of the State is used to build a Britain fit for ordinary decent people to live in by ensuring jobs for all, the end of poverty, equality of opportunity, decent houses for all, and the end of war.

Politics Made Plain (1944)

John Horam

b. 1939; MP (Labour, SDP) Gateshead West 1970–83; (Conservative)
Orpington 1992–2010

I believe that the Social Democrats should have freedom as their
main aim, while appreciating that more freedom does involve
at least a minimum of equality … that the State should lean
towards greater equality, but that if it intervenes oppressively it
will damage individual liberty and diminish the nation's wealth.

Journal of Economic Affairs, July 1981, cited in D. Eden, *The Future of
Social Democracy* (1983)

Anyone who knows anything about general elections knows
local campaigning isn't worth a damn. It is all about the
package you present. Either you sweep in on a tide of support,
or you don't.

The Guardian, January 1982

Peter Howard

1908–65; 'Crossbencher' in the *Sunday Express*; writer

Dry as dust the pair of them. Without the Feet, I think the next
Parliament should be able to move forward a good deal faster.

On Isaac and Dingle Foot, in the *Sunday Express*, autumn 1935, cited in
S. Hoggart & D. Leigh, *Michael Foot: a Portrait* (1981)

David Howarth

b. 1958; academic; MP (Liberal Democrat) Cambridge 2005–10

Ultimately, one can divide political ideologies into those that
appeal to fantasies of control and those that appeal to fantasies
of liberation. Socialism appeals to people offended by the
disorganisation of markets and by apparently never-ending

political debate. Liberalism, in contrast, appeals to those who wish themselves and others to be free.

Cited in D. Brack (ed.), *Why I am a Liberal Democrat* (1996)

The ... version of 'economic liberalism' used within British liberalism is a preference for market mechanisms not in opposition to redistribution but as a method to be used in the detailed design of mechanism for it. For all social liberals, whenever the use of the market might undermine the central aim of social liberalism – namely a society that protects effective freedom for all and which thus can generate and recognise a legitimate form of government – the market has to give way. The political goals of liberalism are always more important than any particular method of achieving them.

'What is Social Liberalism?' cited in D. Brack, R. Grayson & D. Howarth (eds), *Reinventing the State: Social Liberalism for the 21ˢᵗ Century* (2007)

Simon Hughes

b. 1951; MP (Liberal, Liberal Democrat) Bermondsey, later Southwark North & Bermondsey 1983–; deputy leader of the Liberal Democrats 2010–

My politics are to be those politics of liberation. I am anxious to liberate our people – those whom I can help – in little ways as we are allowed to do, from enforced idleness, unjustified discrimination and harmful dogma.

Maiden speech in the House of Commons, 21 March 1983

I hope we wouldn't wish to see other countries developing a membership of the nuclear arsenal – a Euro-nuclear bomb mountain, twelve fingers on the button.

In the defence debate at the Liberal assembly, Eastbourne, 23 September 1986

We must be determined that our young people, our children and our grandchildren, have a non-nuclear world to inherit. We

are on the verge of responsibility. There's no more important
subject – the battle is not between us, that battle is for our
future.

In the defence debate at the Liberal assembly, Eastbourne, 23
September 1986

This liberal will be a Liberal Democrat for as long as the party
of the same name preaches – and more importantly, practices –
liberal democracy to empower people. The test of our success is
how well we overcome the poverty, ignorance and conformity
which it is the duty of radical politicians to challenge.

Cited in D. Brack (ed.), *Why I am a Liberal Democrat* (1996)

Of course in a coalition there will be compromise. But as we
campaign in our democracy we must pursue the clearest of
goals. Towards the goal of a more equal society we must never
waver. Towards the goal of a more green and sustainable society
we must never waver. Towards the goal of global peace and
security we must never waver. Towards the goal of full electoral
and political reform we must never waver.

Arguing the case for coalition, at the Liberal Democrat special
conference, 16 May 2010

Last Wednesday morning, we made a decision to go over the
top. We must now go forward, to capture new ground, to win a
succession of new victories for liberalism and liberal democracy.
The banner of liberal democracy has flown too long from the
lines of defeated armies.

Arguing the case for coalition, at the Liberal Democrat special
conference, 16 May 2010

Remember as liberals what our core values are: a passionate
commitment to the rule of law, equally applied to all, the
powerful and the weak, the rich and poor; a passionate
commitment to the rights of all human beings to freedom of

expression; and a passionate commitment to economic and social justice.

Speech at the closing ceremony of the Liberal International Congress, Abidjan, 21 October 2012

Seventeenthly...

In a House of Commons debate, cited in D. Brack et al. (eds), *Dictionary of Liberal Biography* (1998)

David Hume

1711–76; philosopher

That policy is violent, which aggrandises the public by the poverty of individuals.

'Of Money', *Essays: Moral and Political* (1741–42)

In all ages of the world, priests have been enemies of liberty.

'Of the Parties of Great Britain', *Essays: Moral and Political* (1741–42)

Nothing appears more surprising to those who consider human affairs with a philosophical eye, than the ease with which the many are governed by the few and the implicit submission with which men resign their own sentiments and passions to those of their rulers.

The First Principles of Government (1742)

Should it be said, that, by living under the dominion of a prince, which one might leave, every individual has given a tacit assent to his authority ... We may as well assert, that a man by remaining in a vessel, freely consents to the dominion of the master; though he was carried on board while asleep, and must leap into the ocean, and perish, the moment he leaves her.

Of the Original Contract (1748)

It is just a political maxim, that every man must be supposed a knave.

Political Discourses (1751)

Will Hutton

b. 1950; editor of *The Observer* 1996–1998; writer

Suddenly a new idea is abroad; an idea with the power to divide one political party, unite another and dissolve the dilemmas of a third. Owenites claim it as their true credo; Conservatives as the faith they have always professed, if sometimes unknowingly; Liberals define themselves as its oldest British guardian, while even one or two luminaries in the Labour Party see it as the route to modernising socialism. What can this androgynous, all-purpose, elastic idea be? Why, the social market economy, of course; the idea, that if only one knew what it was, as the SDP delegate said in their debate on the matter, one would be bound to endorse it.

'Stalking the social market', *The Listener*, 10 September 1987

I

Ivan Illich
1926–2002; Austrian philosopher and social critic

The celebration of man's humanity through joining together in
the healing expression of one's relationships with others, and
one's growing acceptance of one's own nature and needs, will
clearly create major confrontations with existing values and
systems. The expanding dignity of each man and each human
relationship must necessarily challenge existing systems. The call
is to live the future. Let us join together joyfully to celebrate
our awareness that we can make our life today the shape of
tomorrow's future.

Celebration of Awareness (1971)

James Ings
c. 1785–1820; butcher, coffee-shop owner and conspirator

Oh, give me liberty or give me death.

Before his execution for his part in the Cato Street Conspiracy, 1820

J

Andrew Jackson

1767–1845; American President 1829–37

It is to be regretted that the rich and powerful too often bend the acts of government to their selfish purposes ... when the laws undertake ... to make the rich richer and the potent more powerful, the humble members of society have a right to complain of the injustice of their government.

 1832

Thomas Jefferson

1743–1826; American President 1801–09

Under the law of nature, all men are born free, every one comes into the world with a right to his own person, which includes the liberty of moving and using it at his own will. This is what is called personal liberty, and is given him by the Author of nature, because it is necessary for his own sustenance.

 Legal Argument (1770)

We hold these truths to be self-evident, that all men are created equal; that they are endowed by their Creator with inherent and inalienable rights; that among these, are life, liberty, and the pursuit of happiness; that to secure these rights, governments are instituted among men, deriving their just powers from the consent of the governed; that whenever any form of government becomes destructive of these ends, it is the right of the people to alter or abolish it, and to institute new government, laying its foundation on such principles, and organising its powers in such form, as to them shall seem most likely to effect their safety and happiness.

US Declaration of Independence, original draft (1776)

Prudence, indeed, will dictate that governments long established, should not be changed for light and transient causes ... But, when a long train of abuses and usurpations, pursuing invariably the same object, evinces a design to reduce them under absolute despotism, it is [the people's] right, it is their duty, to throw off such government, and to provide new guards for their future security.

US Declaration of Independence, original draft (1776)

I hold it that a little rebellion, now and then, is a good thing, and as necessary in the political world as storms are in the physical. Unsuccessful rebellions, indeed, generally establish the encroachments on the rights of the people which have produced them. An observation of this truth should render honest republican governors so mild in their punishment of rebellions, as not to discourage them too much. It is medicine necessary for the sound health of government.

Letter to James Madison, 30 January 1787

I am convinced that, on the good sense of the people, we may rely with the most security for the preservation of a due degree of liberty.

Letter to James Madison, 30 January 1787

Were it left to me to decide whether we should have a government without newspapers or newspapers without a government, I should not hesitate a moment to prefer the latter.

Letter to Edward Carrington, 1787

What country can preserve its liberties if its rulers are not warned from time to time that their people preserve the spirit of resistance? The tree of liberty must be refreshed from time to time with the blood of patriots and tyrants. It is its natural manure.

Letter to William Stephens Smith, 1787

Liberty is the great parent of science and of virtue; and a nation will be great in both in proportion as it is free.

Letter to Joseph Willard, 1789

The republican is the only form of government which is not eternally at open or secret war with the rights of mankind.

Reply to Address (1790)

The ground of liberty is to be gained by inches, and we must be contented to secure what we can get from time to time and eternally press forward for what is yet to get. It takes time to persuade men to do even what is for their own good.

Letter to Charles Clay, 1790

It had become an universal and almost uncontroverted position in the several States, that the purposes of society do not require a surrender of all our rights to our ordinary governors; that there are certain portions of right not necessary to enable them to carry on an effective government, and which experience has nevertheless proved they will be constantly encroaching on, if submitted to them; that there are also certain fences which experience has proved peculiarly efficacious against wrong, and rarely obstructive of right, which yet the governing powers have ever shown a disposition to weaken and remove. Of the first kind, for instance, is freedom of religion; of the second, trial by jury, habeas corpus laws, free presses.

Letter to Noah Webster, 1790

I would rather be exposed to the inconveniences attending too much liberty than to those attending too small a degree of it.

Letter to Archibald Stuart, 1791

Whenever a man has cast a longing eye on [offices] a rottenness begins in his conduct.

Letter to Tench Coxe, 1799

In every country where man is free to think and to speak,
differences of opinion will arise from difference of perception,
and the imperfection of reason; but these differences when
permitted, as in this happy country, to purify themselves by
free discussion, are but as passing clouds overspreading our land
transiently and leaving our horizon more bright and serene.

Letter to Benjamin Waring, 1801

Bear in mind this sacred principle, that though the will of
the majority is in all cases to prevail, that will, to be rightful,
must be reasonable; that the minority possess their equal
rights, which equal laws must protect, and to violate would be
oppression.

Inaugural message to Congress, 1801

Sometimes it is said that man cannot be trusted with the
government of himself. Can he, then, be trusted with
the government of others? Or have we found angels in the
form of kings to govern him? Let history answer this question.

Inaugural message to Congress, 1801

Peace, commerce and honest friendship with all nations;
entangling alliances with none.

Inaugural message to Congress, 1801

The voluntary support of laws, formed by persons of their
own choice, distinguishes peculiarly the minds capable of self-
government. The contrary spirit is anarchy, which of necessity
produces despotism.

To Philadelphia citizens, 1809

I have never been able to conceive how any rational being could
propose happiness to himself from the exercise of power over
others.

Letter to A. L. C. Destutt de Tracy, 1811

In every country, and in every age, the priest has been hostile
to liberty. He is always in alliance with the despot, abetting his
abuses in return for protection to his own.

Letter to Horatio G. Spafford, 1814

The idea is quite unfounded that on entering into society we
give up any natural rights. No man has a natural right to commit
aggression on the equal rights of another, and this is all from
which the laws ought to restrain him.

Letter to Francis Gilmer, 1816

I am not among those who fear the people. They, and not the
rich, are our dependence for continued freedom.

Letter to Samuel Kercheval, 1816

Where the press is free, and every man able to read, all is safe.

Letter to Charles Yancey, 1816

Ignorance and bigotry, like other insanities, are incapable of self-
government.

Letter to Lafayette, 1817

If the condition of man is to be progressively ameliorated, as we
fondly hope and believe, education is to be the chief instrument
in effecting it.

Letter to M. A. Jullien, 1818

The equal rights of man, and the happiness of every individual,
are now acknowledged to be the only legitimate objects of
government. Modern times have the signal advantage, too, of
having discovered the only device by which these rights can
be secured, to wit: government by the people, acting not in
person, but by representatives chosen by themselves, that is to
say, by every man of ripe years and sane mind, who contributes
either by his purse or person to the support of his country.

Letter to A. Coray, 1823

Men by their constitutions are naturally divided into two parties: 1. Those who fear and distrust the people, and wish to draw all powers from them into the hands of the higher classes. 2. Those who identify themselves with the people, have confidence in them, cherish and consider them as the most honest and safe, although not the most wise depositary of the public interests. In every country these two parties exist, and in every one where they are free to think, speak, and write, they will declare themselves.

Letter to Henry Lee, 1824

Equal rights for all, special privileges for none.

Attributed

Peter Jenkins

1934–92; journalist

The fights within the Alliance are fights about nothing. The protagonists are engaged in tearing apart the stuff of a dead dream.

On the merger negotiations, *The Independent*, 22 December 1987

Roy Jenkins

1920–2003; MP (Labour) Southwark Central 1948–50, Birmingham Stechford 1950–77, (SDP) Glasgow Hillhead 1982–87; President of the European Commission 1977–80; leader of the SDP 1982–83; created Lord Jenkins of Hillhead 1987; leader of the Liberal Democrat peers 1987–97

Paisley was a false dawn, both for Asquith and the Liberal Party. At best, it was the equivalent of some later winter daybreak on the fringes of the Arctic circle.

On Asquith's victory in the Paisley by-election, 1920, *Asquith* (1964)

189

We must break loose from the present political strait-
jacket ... But I don't intend to do a Ramsay MacDonald. I must
have a substantial part of the Party with me.

> To Christopher Mayhew, late 1960s, cited in C. Mayhew, *Time to
> Explain* (1987)

We cannot successfully survive unless we can make our society
more adaptable; and an unadaptable political system works
heavily against this. Politicians cannot cling defensively to their
present somewhat ossified party and political system while
convincingly advocating acceptance of change everywhere else
in industry and society. 'Everybody change but us' is never a
good slogan.

> Dimbleby Lecture, 29 November 1979

I think we could escape from what I increasingly regard as the
constricting rigidity – almost the tyranny – of the present party
system.

> Dimbleby Lecture, 29 November 1979

A strengthening of the radical centre.

> Dimbleby Lecture, 29 November 1979

The politics of the left and centre of this country are frozen
in an out-of-date mould which is bad for the political and
economic health of Britain and increasingly inhibiting for those
who live within the mould. Can it be broken?

> Speech to the parliamentary press gallery, 9 June 1980

[There is] mounting evidence from all over the world that full-
scale state ownership is more successful in producing tyranny
than in producing goods.

> Speech to the parliamentary press gallery, 9 June 1980

The likelihood before the start of most adventures is that of
failure. The experimental plane may well finish up a few fields
from the end of the runway. If this is so, the voluntary occupants

will have only inflicted bruises or worse upon themselves. But the reverse could occur and the experimental plane soar into the sky.

Speech to the parliamentary press gallery, 9 June 1980

There was once a book more famous for its title than for its contents called *The Strange Death of Liberal England*. That death caught many people rather unawares. Do not discount the possibility that in a few years' time someone may be able to write at least equally convincingly of the strange and rapid revival of Liberal and Social Democratic Britain.

Speech to the parliamentary press gallery, 9 June 1980

I haven't used that word in years.

On 'socialism', *Sunday Times*, 15 February 1981

We are saying that the rules of the game itself, with its unfair electoral system, big minorities almost unrepresented in the House of Commons, people feeling that they have to choose between two rigid party machines neither of which they like very much, violent swings of policy based on small shifts of opinion, have damaged British industry, destroyed British jobs and undermined the prosperity and influence of this country. We offer not so much a new party – although it is that – as a new approach to politics.

At the press conference launching the SDP, Connaught Rooms, London, 26 March 1981

I have taken part in twelve elections. This is the first I have lost in thirty-five years, but it is by far the greatest victory in which I have ever participated.

On the Warrington by-election, the first contested by the SDP, where Jenkins came within 1,759 votes of victory, 16 July 1981

Is the Alliance credible? Is it honest? Again I answer unswervingly 'yes' … We can therefore honourably achieve not a marriage of convenience but a partnership of principle. I would go further and say that it can be still more. To use an old Gladstonian phrase, it can be a union of hearts. Of course we can let it all slip. You can fall back on your ancient purity and we can console ourselves with our exciting novelty. But what fools we would be if we did ... Still more important, a great part of public opinion would experience a sense of disappointment and let-down. The duopoly would survive, unloved, uncreative, but almost unscarred. This must not happen. We have jointly made an unprecedented opportunity. Let us seize it together in an Alliance of mutual respect and mutual trust.

> To a fringe meeting at the Liberal assembly, Llandudno, on the proposed Liberal–SDP Alliance, September 1981

The Liberal Party has hope but no sense.

> At the Liberal assembly, Bournemouth, 25 September 1982

Our sights are firmly on 1983, be it June, be it October, be it any month. And we intend that to be the beginning, not merely of a new Government, but of a new period of politics, innovative, libertarian, close to the people, but above all based on reconciliation rather than digging deeper and deeper into the divide of politics.

> At Central Hall, 20 January 1983, in *The Social Democrat*, special pre-election issue

Budgets are not nearly as important as Chancellors think they are. Nor are they mostly quite as awful as Shadow Chancellors say they are.

> On the 1984 Budget, in the House of Commons

The spirit of the SDP was to some substantial extent a revolt against the meaningless hyperbole of language which adversarial politics had encouraged.

> Tawney Society Lecture, Bedford College, London, 11 July 1984

I suppose we've always had different approaches to the party. Owen disapproved of my Dimbleby Lecture. He was not ready for it. He is not as radical as I am ... I made the first radical move. It's a paradox, isn't it? – that people should consider Owen the radical. Well, there are a great many paradoxes in politics.

1984, cited in P. Lee Sykes, *Losing from the Inside: The Cost of Conflict in the British SDP* (1990)

We would make a great mistake if we gave the impression that our marriage with the Liberals was one of short-term convenience, and that if we ever felt free and strong enough to do so we would be off on our own. The Alliance in my view is 'for better or for worse'. There can be no SDP triumphs or defeats which are not Liberal triumphs or defeats and vice versa. Nor can one party effectively immunise itself from weakness or instability of the other. Foolish policies adopted by one are a noose around the neck of the other. This will be even more true if we get to the threshold of winning a general election and have a sharper light of public scrutiny turned upon us. The way to avoid danger here is to work out a sensible joint policy together, and not to believe that one party can deny the sins of the other.

Tawney Society Lecture, 1986

A dead or dying beast lying across a railway line and preventing other trains from getting through.

On the Labour Party, *The Guardian*, 16 May 1987

Like the fabulous Upas tree, which destroys all life for miles around it.

On David Owen, cited in D. Healey, *The Time of My Life* (1989), but attributed to Healey in G. Knight, *Honourable Insults* (1990)

A First Minister whose self-righteous stubbornness has not been equalled, save briefly by Neville Chamberlain, since Lord North.

On Margaret Thatcher, *The Observer*, 11 March 1990

A great lighthouse which stands there, flashing out beams of light, indifferent to the waves which beat against him.

On Edward Heath, *The Independent*, 22 September 1990

He had a dazzling charm saved from ever being cloying because he could not see a balloon with even a touch of pomposity in it – his own as much as anyone else's – without desiring to prick it.

On Jo Grimond, *The Orcadian*, 28 June 1993

It was received rather negatively in that debate in the House of Commons. There were some people who made good speeches, but the majority were on the whole know-nothing, do-nothing, think-nothing.

On the Commons debate on Lord Jenkins' report on electoral reform, interview on BBC Online, 14 January 1999

The government has been doing rather a lot of kicking into the long grass recently. I am beginning to feel a bit sorry for the grasshoppers, which must find things rather overcrowded in their territory.

On the failure of the Labour government to implement the Jenkins report on reform of the voting system, BBC Radio, *Today* programme, 26 June 2001

David Steel and I always got on very well, but then some people said: 'they would, wouldn't they, because David Steel was one of nature's Social Democrats and Roy Jenkins was one of nature's Liberals'.

Interview, November 2002; *Journal of Liberal History*, issue 38, spring 2003

For managing, and it is an increasingly rare thing in British politics, to combine being a fairly major politician with many outside interests, without being dominated by them.

On how he would like to be remembered, interview, November 2002; *Journal of Liberal History*, issue 38, spring 2003

I rather think I would have liked being Prime Minister in retrospect, rather more than I would have enjoyed it at the time.

Conversation with Robert Harris, cited in A. Adonis & K. Thomas, *Roy Jenkins: A Retrospective* (2004)

With David Owen, Bill Rodgers and Shirley Williams

Our intention is to rally all those who are committed to the values, principles and policies of Social Democracy. We seek to reverse Britain's economic decline. We want to create an open, classless and more equal society, one which rejects ugly prejudices based upon sex, race or religion.

Limehouse Declaration, 25 January 1981

Breaking the mould of British politics.

Often used to describe the aim of the SDP; attributed to David Marquand, as well as to Roy Jenkins in *What Matters Now* (1972)

Samuel Johnson

1709–84; poet, critic and lexicographer

I have always said, the first Whig was the devil.

28 April 1778, cited in J. Boswell, *Life of Samuel Johnson* (1791)

A wise Tory and a wise Whig, I believe, will agree. Their principles are the same, though their modes of thinking are different.

May 1781, cited in J. Boswell, *The Life of Samuel Johnson* (1791)

Nothing will be attempted if all possible objections must be overcome first.

Attributed

William Johnson

Rosebery's school master

He is one of those who like the palm without the dust.

Referring to Lord Rosebery, *Letters and Journals* (1897)

Russell Johnston

1932–2008; MP (Liberal, Liberal Democrat) Inverness 1964–97; created Baron Russell-Johnston of Minginish 1997

Liberalism is an attitude. While recognising interests it refuses to base its approach upon them (as do the Labour and Conservative Parties). It is a never-to-be-completed effort, to build a community, not of communally imposed standards (Socialism) or endlessly in-built conflicts between the haves and the have-nots (Conservatism) … but a lively, individualistic community of free persons, pushing for achievement, but conscious of the responsibility their talents lay upon them and ever anxious to reconcile. Reconciliation on the basis of radical reform. This, for me, is what Liberalism is about.

At the Scottish Liberal Party conference, Perth, 19 June 1976

I became a Liberal at university because I agreed with the writings of a Yorkshire Liberal, Elliot Dodds, who, in trying the impossible, to sum up Liberalism, settled upon three words: Liberty, Welfare and Responsibility. I have never been able to do better.

At the Scottish Liberal Party conference, Perth, 19 June 1976

Liberals who cry for slogans and simplicity, cry in ignorance of the cause they espouse but yet barely comprehend. A credo with a valid claim to provide the basic rules for human society cannot be other than complex and full of ifs and buts and perhaps.

Introduction to collected Scottish Liberal Party conference speeches 1971–78 (1979)

Liberalism does not live long if it allows itself to be absorbed into a non-Liberal organisation.

Introduction to collected Scottish Liberal Party conference speeches 1971–78 (1979)

My political mentor was a Scot of untidy kindness called John Bannerman who once said to me: 'I really don't understand why everyone isn't a Liberal'. Neither really do I. But I believe that if we persist, in time they will be.

At the Liberal Democrat conference, 1989

He taught me that politics was not only about devising rules, but enabling exceptions. And that the openness and cooperation, which an individual-based philosophy required, could only work with compassion.

On John Bannerman, cited in D. Brack (ed.), *Why I Am A Liberal Democrat* (1996)

There are certain words which have a liberal resonance, not exclusively but predominantly … fairness, openness, tolerance, compassion; I do not find them so well represented in other political philosophies.

Cited in D. Brack (ed.), *Why I Am A Liberal Democrat* (1996)

Harcourt Johnstone

1895–1945; MP (Liberal) Willesden East 1923–24, South Shields 1931–35, Middlesbrough West 1940–45

Mr Lloyd George seems to have but few of the virtues with which he is popularly credited and all the vices which his political record only too amply displays.

Letter to *The Wiltshire Times*, June 1926

Those of us who are free traders feel more confidence in Messrs Snowden and Graham than in Mr Lloyd George, with his patchy fiscal history and his roving political eye.

Letter to *The Times*, 16 January 1930

We must keep up the bluff until the last moment or decide here and now to disband the Liberal Party as an organised political entity.

Letter to Lord Lothian, 19 November 1934

Mervyn Jones
1922–2010; writer

[Clement Davies] tended to agree with the last person who had put a strong argument to him.

A Radical Life: The Biography of Megan Lloyd George (1991)

Trevor Jones
b. 1927; Liverpool councillor and political strategist; President, Liberal Party 1972–73; 'Jones the Vote'

But the votes, fellow Liberals … I love the votes!

At the Liberal assembly, 1973

The object of the exercise in any election campaign is to find out the issues on people's minds and to deal with those issues.

Attributed

Benjamin Jowett
1817–93; Master of Balliol College, Oxford 1870–93

[He is] very able, shy, sensitive, ambitious, the last two qualities rather at war with each other – very likely a future PM.

On Lord Rosebery, letter to M. Tennant, March 1890

K

Richard Kemp

Liberal Democrat activist and Liverpool councillor

Liberalism inherently believes that almost everyone has the capacity to run their own lives and should be given the freedom to do it. It also believes that, given the freedom, most people will act responsibly and not become too greedy and try to take out more than their due.

Cited in D. Brack (ed.), *Why I Am A Liberal Democrat* (1996)

[The Liberal Democrats] are unique in devising a political system which links the concept of fairness to an ideology which says not that: 'Jack is as good as his master,' but rather: 'Jack should be his own master'.

Cited in D. Brack (ed.), *Why I Am A Liberal Democrat* (1996)

Charles Kennedy

b. 1959; MP (SDP, Liberal Democrat) Ross Cromarty & Skye, later Ross, Skye & Inverness West, then Ross, Skye & Lochaber 1983–; President, Liberal Democrats 1990–94; leader of the Liberal Democrats 1999–2006

Paddy Ashdown is the only party leader who's a trained killer. Although, to be fair, Mrs Thatcher was self-taught.

1998, though said originally by Gilbert Archer, President, Edinburgh Chamber of Commerce, 1992

I have been a long-standing advocate of cross-party cooperation. When I was party president, I was saying, before it became fashionable, that if we were going to advance the constitutional agenda the only party that we could work with was self-evidently the Labour Party.

The Observer, 7 March 1999

The tide of history is in favour of European integration – but we must ensure that it is diverted down the right channels to ensure that British interests and democratic values are not drowned. Only by taking a lead in Europe can we achieve our worthy goal.

Speech at European Movement Conference, 11 March 1999

Leaders have to lead, but they also have to listen.

Leadership hustings, Llanwrst, 8 July 1999

What a sight it was, on the night of the first benefits vote in this Parliament, to see ministers supping champagne at No. 10 with their celebrity friends. It was the clearest sign that we have of the divisions in Britain, and of the priorities of New Labour.

Shelter Lecture, 19 July 1999

We need a liberal agenda in which government resists the temptation to interfere in the lives of individuals, but equally is determined to play an active role where creative action can advance the liberties of all.

'Escape into Freedom', *The Guardian*, 5 August 1999

From here on it's downhill all the way.

Leadership acceptance speech, 9 August 1999

There are not enough people in politics who are actually normal members of the human race. If that is the charge against me I'm happy to plead guilty.

Cited in *The Guardian*, 10 August 1999

That's enough health, I need a fag.

After posing for photographers at a Glasgow supermarket to promote healthy food, 1999, cited in *The Times*, 10 August 1999

Oh come on now, he's the leader of the Liberal Democrats.

Asked whether, as leader of a 'major political party', Paddy Ashdown should be 'yomping' around the country, cited in *The Times*, 10 August 1999

I believe in being serious about politics, though not in taking myself too seriously.

Cited in *The Times*, 10 August 1999

Being in the SDP was rather like having your first motor car – it may now be sitting on bricks, completely clapped out, but it still has a special place in your heart.

Cited in *The Times*, 10 August 1999

There is a curious assumption that individual freedom means the withdrawal of the state, and that taxation is a form of state control. The opposite should be the case. Taxation, efficiently gathered and efficiently spent, is not a curb on personal freedom – it is the means to achieve it.

The Observer, 17 September 2000

It is desperately important, for the government in Britain, for our public services such as health and education, and for the have-nots in society, that our representation should increase. That will overcome the complacency and timidity of Labour and provide the leadership that cannot come from the divided and distracted Conservatives.

General election speech, 5 June 2001

Make no mistake: Liberalism and fundamentalism are fearsome enemies. As Liberals, we do not ask, nor necessarily want, people to be like us. We ask only for the freedom to be ourselves. And, in return, to guarantee others that self-same freedom.

At the Liberal Democrat conference, Bournemouth, 27 September 2001

Moderately, socially.

In answer to Jeremy Paxman's question 'How much do you drink?',
BBC TV, *Newsnight*, 17 July 2002

I don't say that everything should be done through the public
sector. I have no ideological hang-ups between public and
private. What I do say is that there shouldn't be an automatic
American-style assumption that the private sector is always
better.

At the TUC conference, Blackpool, 11 September 2002

All other options must be exhausted before there is any
recourse to force. I join with you today because I have yet to
be persuaded as to the case for war against Iraq ... without
a second UN resolution, there is no way that the Liberal
Democrats could or should support war.

At Hyde Park, 15 February 2003, cited in G. Hurst, *Charles Kennedy: A
Tragic Flaw* (2006)

While some competing political creeds look tired and outdated,
the extent to which the principles of Liberalism have stood the
test of time is striking. Liberalism is as compelling at the
beginning of the 21st century as it was two hundred years ago.

Foreword to *The Orange Book* (2004)

Being a Liberal is not about spin and presentation, as the
Conservatives seem to believe. It's not about just taking off your
tie. It's about taking the tough decisions on climate change – not
talking the talk. It's about policies to tackle unfairness at the
heart of our tax system, where poor people pay proportionately
more than the rich. It's about tackling inequalities in education
and the NHS – not setting up an escape route for the wealthy.
It's about standing up for international law and rebuilding
Britain's reputation after the horror of Iraq – not voting with
Labour, as David Cameron did, for a war that has been the worst
foreign-policy mistake since Suez.

The Observer, 18 December 2005

With uncharacteristic understatement, Paddy Ashdown
described last week's events as 'a rather unexpected moment'.
Certainly, they drive a strategic coach and horses through the
long-nurtured 'realignment of the centre-left' to which leaders
in the Liberal tradition, this one included, have all subscribed
since the Jo Grimond era. It is hardly surprising that, for some
of us at least, our political compass currently feels confused.

On the formation of the coalition government, *The Observer*, 16 May
2010

Thatcher never understood why the Scots despised her. We
reckoned it was because we understood her only too well.

The Guardian, 9 April 2013

John F. Kennedy
1917–63; American President 1961–63

The most powerful single force in the world today is neither
Communism nor capitalism, neither the H-bomb nor the guided
missile – it is man's eternal desire to be free and independent.

At Washington DC, 2 July 1957

Political action is the highest responsibility of a citizen.

At New York, 20 October 1960

My fellow citizens of the world: ask not what America will do
for you, but what together we can do for the freedom of man.

Inaugural address to Congress, 20 January 1961

Let every nation know, whether it wishes us well or ill, that we
shall pay any price, bear any burden, meet any hardship, support
any friend, oppose any foe, in order to assure the survival and
success of liberty.

Inaugural address to Congress, 20 January 1961

If the self-discipline of the free cannot match the iron discipline of the mailed fist, in economic, political, scientific, and all of the other kinds of struggles, as well as the military, then the peril to freedom will continue to rise.

Address to the American Society of Newspaper Editors, 20 April 1961

We stand for freedom. That is our conviction for ourselves; that is our only commitment to others.

Message to Congress, 25 May 1961

If a free society cannot help the many who are poor, it cannot save the few who are rich.

Vital Speeches (1961)

Robert Kennedy
1925–68; American Democratic politician

The free way of life proposes ends, but it does not prescribe means.

The Pursuit of Justice (1964)

Whenever men take the law into their own hands, the loser is the law. And when the law loses, freedom languishes.

Attributed

John Maynard Keynes
1883–1946; economist; created Baron Keynes of Tilton 1942

I work for a Government I despise for ends I think criminal.

Letter to D. Grant, 15 December 1917

In the long run we are all dead.

A Tract on Monetary Reform (1923)

I believe in Free Trade because, in the long run and in general, it is the only policy which is technically sound and intellectually tight.

'Am I a Liberal?', Liberal Summer School, Cambridge, 1 August 1925

Half the copy-book wisdom of our statesmen is based on assumptions which were at one time true or partly true, but are now less and less true day by day. We have to invent new wisdom for a new age. And in the meantime we must, if we are to do any good, appear unorthodox, troublesome, dangerous, disobedient to them that begat us.

'Am I a Liberal?', Liberal Summer School, Cambridge, 1 August 1925

A Whig is a perfectly sensible Conservative.
A Radical is a perfectly sensible Labourite.
A Liberal is anyone who is perfectly sensible.

1926

It is the task of Liberals, as I conceive it, to guide the aspirations of the masses for social justice along channels which will not be inconsistent with social efficiency; and a party which pursues that task with sincerity and devotion will exercise an influence over the future of this country altogether disproportionate to its numerical strength or to its parliamentary position.

The End of Laissez-Faire (1926)

I think that Capitalism, wisely managed, can probably be made more efficient for attaining economic ends than any alternative system yet in sight, but that in itself is in many ways extremely objectionable.

The End of Laissez-Faire (1926)

Marxian Socialism must always remain a portent to the historians of Opinion – how a doctrine so illogical and so dull can have exercised so powerful and enduring an influence over the minds of men, and, through them, the events of history.

The End of Laissez-Faire (1926)

I do not know which makes a man more conservative – to know nothing but the present, or nothing but the past.

The End of Laissez-Faire (1926)

The important thing for Government is not to do things which individuals are doing already, and to do them a little better or a little worse; but to do those things which at present are not done at all.

The End of Laissez-Faire (1926)

Possibly the Liberal Party cannot serve the state in any better way than by supplying Conservative Governments with Cabinets and Labour Governments with ideas.

'Liberalism and Labour' (1926), reprinted in *Essays in Persuasion* (1931)

The syren, this goat-footed bard, this half-human visitor to our age from the hag-ridden magic and enchanted woods of Celtic antiquity.

Describing David Lloyd George, *Essays and Sketches in Biography* (1933)

Who shall paint the chameleon, who can tether a broomstick?

On David Lloyd George, *Essays and Sketches in Biography* (1933)

The ideas of economists and political philosophers, both when they are right and when they are wrong, are more powerful than is commonly understood ... Practical men, who believe themselves to be quite exempt from any intellectual influences, are usually the slaves of some defunct economist. Madmen in authority, who hear voices in the air, are distilling their frenzy from some academic scribbler of a few years back.

A General Theory of Employment, Interest and Money (1936)

Why cannot they face the fact that they are not sectaries of an outworn creed mumbling moss-grown demi-semi Fabian Marxism, but heirs of eternal liberalism?

On the Labour Party, cited in V. Bogdanor (ed.), *Liberal Party Politics* (1983)

I evidently knew more about economics than they did.

Explaining his poor result in the Civil Service exam, cited in
R. Harrod, *Life of John Maynard Keynes* (1951)

We threw good house-keeping to the winds. But we saved
ourselves and helped save the world.

On the Lend-Lease scheme and the Marshall Plan, cited in
A. J. P. Taylor, *English History 1914–45* (1965)

When he is alone in the room there is nobody there.

When Lady Violet Bonham Carter asked 'What do you think happens
to Mr Lloyd George when he is alone in the room?', cited during Lady
Bonham Carter's Romanes Lecture, 1963

[I look for] the development of new methods and new ideas
for effecting the transition from the economic anarchy of the
individualistic capitalism which rules today in Western Europe
towards a regime which will deliberately aim at controlling and
directing economic forces in the interests of social justice and
social stability. I still have enough optimism to believe that to
effect this tradition may be the true destiny of the new Liberalism.

Cited in V. Bogdanor (ed.), *Liberal Party Politics* (1983)

[Liberals] are inclined to sympathise with Labour about what
is just, but to suspect that in their blind ignorant striving after
justice Labour may destroy what is at least as important and
is a necessary condition of any social progress at all – namely,
efficiency.

Cited in V. Bogdanor (ed.), *Liberal Party Politics* (1983)

Søren Kierkegaard

1813–55; Danish philosopher

People demand freedom of speech as a compensation for the
freedom of thought which they seldom use.

Attributed

John Wodehouse, 1st Earl of Kimberley

1826–1902; diplomat; became Earl Kimberley 1866; Foreign Secretary 1894–95; leader of the Liberal peers 1891–94 and 1896–1902

Hartington's appointment is chiefly notable as showing that, tho' a young man may spend his time in riot and debauchery, yet if he shows a spark of ability & is connected with one of the great aristocratic families, he has the door always open to political office. Ld Hartington it is said has abilities, but above all he is the son of the D. of Devonshire. Bow down ye ignoble hard-working members!

20 April 1863, cited in A. Hawkins & J. Powell (eds), *The Journal of John Wodehouse First Earl of Kimberley 1862–1902* (1997)

Notwithstanding his great abilities in debate I believe it would be a real blessing to the Liberal party if he disappeared altogether from the political stage. Utterly without principle, an arrant coward & a blustering bully, he combines every quality which unfits a man for the conduct of the affairs of a nation.

Of cabinet colleague Sir William Harcourt, 21 July 1895, cited in A. Hawkins & J. Powell (eds), *The Journal of John Wodehouse First Earl of Kimberley 1862–1902* (1997)

Ld Kimberley told Margot Asquith that he once received a letter which began: 'My Lord, Tomorrow we intend to kill you at the corner of Kildare Street; but we would like you to know that there is nothing personal in it!'

Kimberley was Lord Lieutenant of Ireland during the 1860s Fenian outrages; cited in J. Powell (ed.), *Liberal by Principle* (1996)

It is strange that Englishmen can never be convinced that it is worse than useless to force English ideas on Ireland. They expect too that the habits and temper of a nation are to be changed at once by Acts of Parliament. Laws, however good, can only very slowly mould national character. It is idle to expect much change in less than a generation.

15 April 1870, cited in J. Powell (ed.), *Liberal by Principle* (1996)

Edward King

1829–1910; clergyman; Oxford Professor of Pastoral Theology

I have been voting against Gladstone all my life, and now he makes me a bishop.

> On King's appointment as Bishop of Lincoln, 1885, in his entry to the *Dictionary of National Biography*

Martin Luther King

1929–68; American civil rights leader

I have a dream that one day on the red hills of Georgia the sons of former slaves and the sons of former slave-owners will be able to sit down together at the table of brotherhood ... I have a dream that my four little children will one day live in a nation where they will not be judged by the colour of their skin but by the content of their character.

> At Washington DC, 15 June 1963

Injustice anywhere is a threat to justice everywhere.

> *Atlanta Monthly*, 1963

One of the great tragedies of man's long trek along the highway of history has been the limiting of neighbourly concern to tribe, race, class or nation.

> *Strength to Love* (1963)

We must learn to live together as brothers or perish together as fools.

> *St Louis Post-Dispatch*, 1964

Neil Kinnock

b. 1942; MP (Labour) Bedwellty, later Islwyn 1970–95; leader of the
Labour Party 1983–92; European Commissioner 1995–2004

They have policies like liquid grease.

On the SDP, cited in G. Knight, *Honourable Insults* (1990)

He possesses an ego fat on arrogance and drunk on ambition.

On David Owen, cited in G. Knight, *Honourable Insults* (1990)

Horatio Kitchener

1850–1916; soldier; created Baron Kitchener of Khartoum 1898, Viscount
Kitchener 1902, Earl Kitchener 1914; Secretary of State for War 1914–16

My colleagues tell military secrets to their wives, except X, who
tells them to other people's wives.

X was H. H. Asquith; cited in P. Magnus, *Kitchener* (1958)

Irving Kristol

1920–2009; American journalist and academic

A liberal is one who says it's all right for an eighteen-year-old
girl to perform in a pornographic movie as long as she gets paid
minimum wage.

Two Cheers for Capitalism (1979)

L

Henry Labouchère
1831–1912; MP (Liberal) Windsor 1865–66, Middlesex 1867–89,
Northampton 1880–1906

That grand old man.
> On Gladstone, at Northampton in 1881, cited in A. Thorold, *The Life
> of Henry Labouchère* (1913); the phrase has also been attributed to Sir
> William Harcourt

I do not object to the old man always having a card up his sleeve,
but I do object to his insinuating that the almighty placed it
there.
> On W. E. Gladstone, cited in G. Curzon, *Modern Parliamentary Eloquence*
> (1913)

Justice to Ireland does not arouse enthusiasm, unless it be
wrapped up in what they regard as justice to themselves.
> On Unionists, cited in D. A. Hamer, *John Morley* (1968)

Enid Lakeman
1903–95; Liberal politician and electoral reformer

Liberals believe in the rights of men as persons. They are less
concerned with the rights of men as Britons, Americans or
Russians, as labourers, officials or company directors. Liberals
are accustomed to look beyond the conflicts of groups to the
common interests that can reconcile those conflicts. Therefore
they are better qualified to build peace than can be any party
that habitually looks first at sectional interest and only later at
our common humanity.
> *When Labour Fails* (1946)

Each of us who feels himself to be a person, each one who wants the chance to develop his personality, must put that personality into the fight. He who believes in the rights of men as personas has responsibilities as a person. His will be the blame if we sink into a regimented world of eclipsed personality; his will be the credit if we climb towards a less depressing prospect.

When Labour Fails (1946)

George Lambert

1866–1958; MP (Liberal, Liberal National) South Molton 1891–1924, 1929–45; created Viscount Lambert 1945

The future of the old party hardly bears thinking about.

After the 1929 election, cited in T. Wilson, *The Downfall of the Liberal Party 1914–35* (1966)

Wilfrid Laurier

1841–1919; Liberal Prime Minister of Canada 1896–1911

Toryism … like the serpent, sheds its skin but ever remains the same reptile.

Letter to Sir Allen Aylesworth, 15 May 1917

David Laws

b. 1965; MP (Liberal Democrat) Yeovil 2001–; Chief Secretary to the Treasury 2010, Minister of State, Department for Education and Cabinet Office 2012–

Over the past few decades, we have also seen, alongside the strong, overarching commitment to personal liberalism, the development of a well-meaning 'nanny-state liberalism', in which respect for personal rights and freedoms has at times been compromised by the pursuit of other, no doubt well-intentioned, objectives.

'Reclaiming Liberalism', in P. Marshall & D. Laws (eds), *The Orange Book: Reclaiming Liberalism* (2004)

How did it come about that over the decades up to the 1980s the Liberal belief in economic Liberalism was progressively eroded by forms of soggy socialism and corporatism, which have too often been falsely perceived as a necessary corollary of social liberalism?

'Reclaiming Liberalism', in P. Marshall & D. Laws (eds), *The Orange Book: Reclaiming Liberalism* (2004)

In the *Orange Book* I argued that the Liberal Democrats need to reclaim our economic liberal heritage. This was misunderstood, or even misrepresented, as implying a downgraded commitment to the party's social liberal roots. But the *Orange Book* argued for a synthesis of economic and social liberalism, and for a clearer distinction between social liberalism and socialism.

'Size isn't Everything', in J. Margo (ed.), *Beyond Liberty* (2007)

The early liberal vision of the state was a minimal vision, with the state as protector of basic personal and political freedoms. Today's liberal and Liberal Democratic vision of the state is still a much more limited vision than often associated with the centre-left of British politics, but it includes the same aspiration for social liberalism that has been at the centre of the party's values for over 100 years.

'Size isn't Everything', in J. Margo (ed.), *Beyond Liberty* (2007)

The liberal state encourages personal responsibility and freedom … seeks to secure a stable environment for wealth creation, but does not interfere in this process itself. [Indeed] … on economic management, the role of the state in business, and in micro-economic interventionism, the liberal view of the state's role is a strictly limited one. [The liberal state also] … ensures that basic services are available to every citizen, but does not

213

need to provide all of these itself, and devolves as much power
to the social level as possible.

'Size isn't Everything', in J. Margo (ed.), *Beyond Liberty* (2007)

Nigel Lawson

b. 1932; MP (Conservative) Blaby 1974–92; Chancellor of the Exchequer
1983–89; created Baron Lawson of Newnham 1992

It is the only time in history that rats have been known to join a
sinking ship.

On the Lib–Lab Pact, cited in G. Knight, *Honourable Insults* (1990)

Wilfrid Lawson

1829–1906; MP (Liberal) Carlisle 1859–65, 1868–85, Cockermouth
1886–1900, 1906, Camborne 1903–06

Politics is not a pastime, but … a perpetual contest with wrong.

The Times, 9 September 1879

My recipe for getting the Liberals back to power is for them to
declare a crusade against drinking and fighting … and counter
the Tory arguments in favour of gin and glory.

Cited in A. Reid (ed.), *The New Liberal Programme* (1886)

Walter Layton

1884–1966; economist, newspaper owner and politician; created Baron
Layton of Danehill 1947

Liberals have never believed that an economic and social system
is an end in itself. We are concerned simply with creating the
conditions in which the human personality can most easily
develop and expand.

Broadcast, 'Why Britain needs a Liberal Party', BBC, 7 July 1950

Vladimir Ilyich Ulyanov, Lenin

1870–1924; founder of the Soviet Union and Chairman of the Council of People's Commissars 1917–24

When a liberal is abused, he says: thank God they didn't beat me. When he is beaten he thanks God they didn't kill him. When he is killed he will thank God that his immortal soul has been delivered from its mortal clay.

'The Government's Falsification of the Duma and the Tasks of the Social-Democrats', *Proletary*, December 1906

Bernard Levin

1928–2004; writer and journalist

An aimless, all-purpose, wish-fulfilment machine.

On the Liberal Party, cited in I. Crewe & A. King, *SDP* (1995)

Liberal Commission

Experience has shown that a Liberal Party is essential if Liberalism is to be effectively promoted and the Liberal influence in British politics maintained and strengthened. There will, of course, be room for cooperation with sympathetic groups, with other parties on particular issues; but such cooperation must not compromise our long-term objectives.

Liberals Look Ahead, the Report of the Liberal Commission (1969)

Liberal Democrats

The Liberal Democrats exist to build and safeguard a fair, free and open society in which we seek to balance the fundamental values of liberty, equality and community, and in which no one shall be enslaved by poverty, ignorance or conformity. We champion the freedom, dignity and well-being of individuals we acknowledge and respect their right to freedom of conscience and their right to develop their talents to the full. We aim to disperse power, to foster diversity and to nurture creativity. We believe that the role of the state is to enable all citizens to attain these ideals, to contribute fully to their communities and to take part in the decisions which affect their lives.

First paragraph of the preamble to the constitution of the Liberal Democrats, written 1988, amended 1993

Liberal Party

Liberalism stands for liberty; but it is an error to think that a policy of liberty must always be negative, that the state can help liberty only by abstaining from action ... often more law may mean more liberty.

Britain's Industrial Future (the 'Yellow Book') (1928)

The measures we advocate in relation to all these things spring from one clear purpose. We believe with a passionate faith that the end of all political and economic action is not the perfecting of this or that piece of mechanism or organisation but that individual men and women may have life and that they have it more abundantly.

Britain's Industrial Future (the 'Yellow Book') (1928)

The remedy [to the contemporary order] in our view is not concentration in the hands of the State but the diffusion of ownership throughout the community. We stand not for public ownership but for popular ownership. The aim must be not to destroy the owner-class, but to enlarge it.

Britain's Industrial Future (the 'Yellow Book') (1928)

We can conquer unemployment.

1929 election slogan

Now that the party machines have crushed the independent, protection of the rights of minorities rest solely in the hands of Liberal Members of Parliament.

Statement from the Liberal Party Organisation following the 1950 general election, cited in H. G. Nicholas, *The British General Election of 1950*

A hard core of Liberalism will remain in this country.

Statement from the Liberal Party Organisation following the 1951 general election, cited in D. Butler, *The British General Election of 1951*

Crisis unresolved.

Title of the Liberal Party's 1955 manifesto — commentators suggested this applied more to the state of the party than of the nation

We must have more Liberals to save us from Tory or Labour reactionaries.

People Count, 1959 general election manifesto

Liberals fight to give back power to the people, to take it out of the hands of the big party machines supported by patronage and vested interests.

The Party for You (1962)

If you think like a Liberal, vote like a Liberal.

1964 election slogan

The Liberal Party exists to build a Liberal society in which every citizen shall possess liberty, property and security, and none shall be enslaved by poverty, ignorance and conformity. Its chief care is for the rights and opportunities of the individual and in all spheres it sets freedom first.

Liberal Party's Constitution, first paragraph, as amended in 1969

Our role as political activists is to help and organise people in communities to take and use power; to use our political skills to

redress grievances; and to represent people at all levels of the
political structure.

Extract from Liberal assembly 'community politics' resolution,
September 1970

One more heave!

Attributed to Adrian Slade, October 1974 election slogan

Once the basic needs of food and shelter are met, man's greatest
satisfactions are to be found in love, trust and friendship, in
beauty, art and music and in learning, none of which are served
by the mythology of growth for its own sake.

The Environment, Liberal Party Report (1974)

Roger Liddle

b. 1947; political adviser; Labour activist who joined the SDP, then
returned to Labour; created Baron Liddle of Carlisle 2010

Six months' membership of Lambeth Council has convinced me
of two political facts: the ferocity of the struggle the SDP faces
in replacing the Labour Party on the left of British politics and
the inevitability of our ultimate victory.

The Social Democrat, 3 December 1982

Abraham Lincoln

1809–65; American President 1861–65

The party lash and the fear of ridicule will overawe justice and
liberty.

At Bloomington, 1856

As I would not be a slave, so I would not be a master. This
expresses my idea of democracy.

1858

Must a government of necessity be too strong for the liberties of its own people, or too weak to maintain its own existence?

First message to Congress, 1861

That this nation, under God, shall have a new birth of freedom; and that government of the people, by the people and for the people, shall not perish from the earth.

At the consecration of the National Cemetery, Gettysburg, 19 November1863

I see in the near future a crisis approaching that unnerves me and causes me to tremble for the safety of my country ... Corporations have been enthroned, an era of corruption in high places will follow, and the money power of the country will endeavour to prolong its reign by working upon the prejudices of the people until the wealth is aggregated in a few hands and the Republic is destroyed.

Attributed

The shepherd drives the wolf from the sheep's throat, for which the sheep thanks the shepherd as his liberator, while the wolf denounces him for the same act as the destroyer of liberty.

Attributed

The ballot is stronger than the bullet.

Attributed

Ken Livingstone

b. 1945; leader of the Greater London Council 1981–86; MP (Labour) Brent East 1987–2001; Mayor of London 2000–08

We may be about to enter a period of transition, as in the Twenties when Labour replaced the Liberals as one of the major parties. But, this time, it is the Liberals who have their chance to displace the Tories, who seem destined to split into two.

The Independent, 5 May 1999

Humankind owes him a debt of gratitude for destroying the SDP.

> On the death of Screaming Lord Sutch, leader of the Monster Raving Loony Party, whose defeat of the Owenite 'continuing SDP' candidate at the Bootle by-election in 1990 presaged the winding-up of the party, *The Independent*, 17 June 1999

David Lloyd George

1863–1945; MP (Liberal) Caernarvon Boroughs 1890–1945; Chancellor of the Exchequer 1908–15, Prime Minister 1916–22, leader of the Liberal Party 1926–31; created Earl Lloyd-George of Dwyfor and Viscount Gwynedd 1945

They died with their drawn salaries in their hands.

> On the 1905 Conservative government, cited in G. Knight, *Honourable Insults* (1990)

The lean and trusty mastiff which is to watch over our interests, but which runs away at the first snarl of the trade unions ... A mastiff? It is the right honourable gentleman's poodle. It fetches and carries for him. It barks for him. It bites anybody that he sets it on to.

> On the Conservative leader Arthur Balfour's relationship with the House of Lords, in the House of Commons, 26 June 1907

British Liberalism is not going to repeat the errors of Continental Liberalism ... Let Liberalism proceed with its glorious work of building up the temple of liberty in this country, but let it also bear in mind that the worshippers at the shrine have to live.

> At Swansea, 1 October 1908

The old Liberals used the natural discontent of the people with the poverty and precariousness of the means of subsistence as a motive power to win for them a better, more influential, and more honourable status in the citizenship of their native land.

The new Liberalism, while pursuing this great political ideal with unflinching energy, devotes a part of its endeavour also to the removing of the immediate causes of discontent. It is true that man cannot live by bread alone. It is equally true that a man cannot live without bread.

> 1908, on the distinction between the old and the new Liberalism, cited in A. Bullock & M. Shock (eds), *The Liberal Tradition from Fox to Keynes* (1966)

I have no nest-eggs. I am looking for someone else's hen-roost to rob next year.

> 1908, when Chancellor of the Exchequer, cited in F. Owen, *Tempestuous Journey* (1954)

The ownership of land is not merely an enjoyment, it is a stewardship.

> On the 1909 Budget, at Limehouse, 30 July 1909

A fully-equipped duke costs as much to keep up as two Dreadnoughts; and they are just as great a terror and they last longer.

> In response to criticism of the 1909 Budget from the Duke of Buccleuch, at Newcastle, 9 October 1909

A body of five hundred men chosen at random from amongst the unemployed.

> On the House of Lords, at Newcastle, 9 October 1909

On the spur of the moment I can think of no better example of the unearned increment than the hyphen in the Honourable Member's name.

> 1909, in response to the Conservative William Joynson-Hicks' attack on the proposal in the Budget to tax the 'unearned increment' of land values – the impecunious Joynson-Hicks had added his (rich) wife's surname to his own on marriage; attributed

You cannot trust the interests of any class entirely to another class; and you cannot trust the interests of any sex entirely to another sex.

On women's suffrage, 1911

We have been living in a sheltered valley for generations. We have been too comfortable and indulgent – many, perhaps, too selfish – and the stern hand of fate has scourged us to an elevation where we can see the everlasting things that matter for a nation – the high peaks we had forgotten of honour, duty, patriotism, and clad in glittering white, the great pinnacle of sacrifice, pointing like a rugged finger to heaven. We shall descend into the valleys again; but as long as the men and women of this generation last, they will carry in their hearts the image of those great mountain peaks whose foundations are not shaken, though Europe rock and sway in the convulsions of a great war.

At Queen's Hall, London, 19 September 1914

We are putting more capital into this branch of the national business – putting it in freely and confidently, knowing that it will in time yield an abundant return not only in the increased welfare and happiness of the workers but in larger material gain for the whole nation.

On the benefits of Liberal health and social reform policies, introduction to H. A. Walter, *Die neue englische Sozialpolitik* (1914)

Too late in moving here. Too late in arriving there. Too late in coming to this decision. Too late in starting with enterprises. Too late in preparing. In this war the footsteps of the Allied forces have been dogged by the mocking spectre of 'too late'; and unless we quicken our movements, damnation will fall on the sacred cause for which so much gallant blood has flowed.

Implied criticism of the Liberal government of which he was a member, in the House of Commons, 20 December 1915

Asquith worries too much about small points. If you were buying a large mansion he would come to you and say 'have you thought there is no accommodation for the cat?'

Letter to Lord Riddell, 1915

I hate fences, I always feel like knocking down every fence I come across.

1915

I wonder if I can do it? On becoming Prime Minister, December 1916, Frances Stevenson's *Diary* (1971)

I would as soon go for a sunny evening stroll around Walton Heath with a grasshopper, as try to work with Northcliffe.

On Lord Northcliffe, 1916, cited in F. Owen, *Tempestuous Journey* (1954)

At eleven o'clock this morning came to an end the cruellest and most terrible war that has ever scourged mankind. I hope we may say that thus, this fateful morning, came to an end all wars.

In the House of Commons, 11 November 1918

Revolution I am not afraid of. Bolshevism I am not afraid of. It is reaction I am afraid of.

To Liberal MPs, when announcing his decision to call a general election, Downing Street, 12 November 1918

What is our task? To make Britain a fit country for heroes to live in.

At Wolverhampton, 23 November 1918

Would you take sandwiches to a banquet?

On being asked whether he was taking his wife to the Paris Peace Conference, 1919, cited in A. Roberts, *The Holy Fox: a Life of Lord Halifax* (1991)

Wild men screaming through the keyholes.

> On the Paris Peace Conference, in the House of Commons, 16 April
> 1919

If you want to succeed in politics, you must keep your
conscience well under control.

> 23 April 1919, cited in Baron Riddell, *Lord Riddell's Intimate Diary of the
> Peace Conference and After (1918–23)* (1933)

We want a peace which will be just, but not vindictive ... We
want a stern peace, because the occasion demands it. The crime
demands it.

> In the House of Commons, April 1919, cited in *The Truth About the Peace
> Treaties*, Vol. 1 (1938)

The terms are in many respects terrible terms to impose on a
country. Terrible were the deeds which it requites.

> July 1919, cited in *The Truth About the Peace Treaties*, Vol. 1 (1938)

It is no more than the whiff of scent on a lady's handkerchief.

> An assessment of Arthur Balfour's historical impact, 9 June 1922, cited
> in T. J. Jones, *Whitehall Diary* (1969–71)

Bonar Law ought to take a drink. Failing drink, the only remedy
for Bonar is a wife.

> Referring to Andrew Bonar Law's illness, brought on by over-work,
> cited in *The Independent on Sunday*, 18 April 1999

A second-rate brewer.

> Referring to Sir George Younger, the Conservative Party manager
> whose opposition to the Lloyd George government precipitated its
> break-up and the 1922 general election

The world is becoming like a lunatic asylum run by lunatics.

> *The Observer*, 8 January 1923

Of all the bigotries that savage the human temper there is none so stupid as the anti-Semitic.

Is It Peace? (1923)

Liberals are to be the oxen to drag the Labour wain over the rough roads of Parliament ... and ... when there is no further use for them, they are to be slaughtered. That is the Labour idea of cooperation.

On the experience of supporting the minority Labour government of 1924, cited in John Campbell, *Lloyd George: The Goat in the Wilderness* (1977)

I am convinced ... that the nation will return to its Liberal allegiance, for Liberalism, after all, is the basic faith of the people of this country. They are repelled by the pretentiousness of Conservatism; they want, not subservience to high-sounding phrases, but the exercise of vision and the driving power of proved ideas. They are repelled by the sterility and artificiality of Socialism; they seek a Government which offers them progress, but not a permanent whirligig of change. They desire, within the limits that statecraft must necessarily set, to live their lives in their own way. But they recognise that, with the growing complexity of social organisation and social needs, the responsibilities of government have steadily increased, and the Government they will choose is the Government which offers them, in the fullest measure, the means to peace, to progress, prosperity.

Introduction to *The Liberal Outlook* (1929)

I do object to this intolerable self-righteousness ... Greater men ... have done it in the past, but ... they, at any rate, did not leave behind them the slime of hypocrisy in passing from one side to another.

On Sir John Simon, in the House of Commons, 1931

Death is the most convenient time to tax rich people.

Cited in Baron Riddell, *Lord Riddell's Intimate Diary of the Peace Conference and After (1918–23)* (1933)

I never believed in costly frontal attacks, either in war or politics, if there were a way round.

War Memoirs (1934)

A politician was a person with whose politics you did not agree. When you did agree, he was a statesman.

At Central Hall, Westminster, 2 July 1935

Neville has a retail mind in a wholesale business.

On Neville Chamberlain, 1935, cited in D. Dilks, *Neville Chamberlain* (1984)

Winston would go up to his Creator and say that he would very much like to meet His Son, of Whom he had heard a great deal and, if possible, would like to call on the Holy Ghost. Winston *loves* meeting people.

On Winston Churchill, 2 January 1937, cited in A. J. Sylvester, *Life with Lloyd George: The Diary of A. J. Sylvester 1931–45* (1975)

The Government are behaving like a bevy of maiden aunts who have fallen among buccaneers.

During the Spanish Civil War, when Merchant Navy ships had been bombed off Spain, 21 June 1938, cited in P. Rowland, *Lloyd George* (1975)

He has sufficient conscience to bother him – but not enough to keep him straight.

On Ramsay Macdonald, 1938, cited in A. J. Sylvester, *Life with Lloyd George: The Diary of A. J. Sylvester 1931–45* (1975)

The Right Honourable Gentleman must not allow himself to be converted into an air raid shelter to keep the splinters from hitting his colleagues.

After Winston Churchill had defended the conduct of the Norway campaign, in the House of Commons, 8 May 1940

The nation is prepared for every sacrifice so long as it has leadership ... I say solemnly that the Prime Minister should give an example of sacrifice, because there is nothing which can contribute more to victory in this war than that he should sacrifice the seals of office.

To Neville Chamberlain, in the House of Commons, 8 May 1940

Negotiating with de Valera ... is like trying to pick up mercury with a fork.

De Valera responded: 'Why doesn't he use a spoon?'; cited in M. J. McManus, *Eamon de Valera* (1944)

There is no friendship at the top.

Cited in A. J. P. Taylor, *Lloyd George: Rise and Fall* (1961)

Truth against the world.

Motto taken on his elevation to the peerage, cited in D. McCormick, *The Mask of Merlin* (1963)

He saw foreign policy through the wrong end of a municipal drainpipe.

On Neville Chamberlain, cited in L. A. Harris, *The Fine Art of Political Wit* (1964)

He would make a drum out of the skin of his mother in order to sound his own praises.

On Winston Churchill, cited in P. Rowland, *Lloyd George* (1975)

Now my War Cabinet was different. They were all big men. I was never able to treat *any* of my colleagues the way Churchill treats *all* of his. Oh yes, there was one I treated that way – Curzon.

Discussing Churchill's War Cabinet with Michael Foot and Frank Owen, cited in M. Foot, *Loyalists and Loners* (1986)

Simon has sat on the fence for so long that the iron has entered into his soul.

Attributed to Lloyd George, perhaps inaccurately, by P. Johnson, *The Oxford Book of Political Anecdotes* (1989)

When they circumcised him they threw away the wrong bit.
> On Herbert Samuel, cited in G. Knight, *Honourable Insults* (1990)

One of those revolving lighthouses which radiate momentary gleams of revealing light and then suddenly relapse into complete darkness. There are no intermediate stages.
> On Lord Kitchener, cited in G. Knight, *Honourable Insults* (1990)

He has half a dozen solutions to any problem and one of them is right – but the trouble is he does not know which it is.
> On Winston Churchill, cited in G. Knight, *Honourable Insults* (1990)

The best living embodiment of the Liberal doctrine that quality is not hereditary.
> On Herbert Gladstone, cited in G. Knight, *Honourable Insults* (1990)

A volatile creature, so prone to hop from one political position to another that he could rightly be compared to a flea.
> On Lord Northcliffe, cited in G. Knight, *Honourable Insults* (1990)

To anyone with politics in his blood, this place is like a pub to a drunkard.
> On the House of Commons, cited in G. Knight, *Honourable Insults* (1990)

Ah, on the water, I presume.
> On being told that Lord Beaverbrook was out for a walk, cited in Lord Cudlipp, *Daily Telegraph*, 13 September 1993

Every man has a House of Lords in his own head. Fears, prejudices, misconceptions – those are the peers, and they are hereditary.
> Cited in J. Green, *Dictionary of Insulting Quotations* (1996)

Don't be afraid to take a big step. You can't cross a chasm in two small jumps.
> Attributed

Gwilym Lloyd George

1894–1967; MP (National Liberal) Pembrokeshire 1922–24, (Liberal, Liberal and Conservative) 1929–50, (Conservative) Newcastle North 1951–57; Minister for Food 1951–54, Home Secretary and Minister for Welsh Affairs 1954–57; created Viscount Tenby 1957

He's been waiting thirty years to make that one.

> When asked by Isaac Foot how long David Lloyd George had waited to make his 'slime of hypocrisy' speech about John Simon, 1931, cited in M. Foot, *Loyalists and Loners* (1986)

Politicians are like monkeys. The higher they climb, the more revolting are the parts they expose.

> 1954, attributed

Megan Lloyd George

1902–66; MP (Liberal) Anglesey 1929–51, (Labour) Carmarthen 1957–66

I have always supported and will always support every measure brought before the House by the Labour government to raise the standard of living of ordinary people.

> At Anglesey, during the 1951 election, cited in M. Jones, *A Radical Life: The Biography of Megan Lloyd George* (1991)

I am a Radical, I was born a Radical and I'll be a Radical as long as I live.

> At Anglesey, during the 1951 election, cited in M. Jones, *A Radical Life: The Biography of Megan Lloyd George* (1991)

Any colour will do, except for violet.

> On discussing a national campaigning colour for the Liberal Party, referring to her well-known antipathy towards Lady Violet Bonham Carter; attributed (but attributed to Violet Bonham Carter herself by M. Tester, *Wit of The Asquiths* (1974))

The official Liberal Party seems to me to have lost all touch
with the Radical tradition that inspired it ... there is a common
attitude of mind and thought between Radicals and Labour.

Statement on resigning from the Liberal Party, 26 April 1955

Richard Lloyd George

1889–1968; engineer; became 2nd Earl Lloyd George of Dwyfor 1945

My father was probably the greatest natural Don Juan in the
history of British politics.

Lloyd George (1960)

John Locke

1632–1704; philosopher

New opinions are always suspected and usually opposed, without
any other reason but because they are not already common.

An Essay on Human Understanding (1690)

To understand political power right and derive it from its
original, we must consider what state all men are naturally
in, and that is a state of perfect freedom to order their actions
and dispose of their possessions and persons as they think fit,
within the bounds of the law of nature, without asking leave
or depending upon the will of any other man. A state also of
equality, wherein all the power and jurisdiction is reciprocal, no
one having more than another; though this be a state of liberty,
yet it is not a state of licence, though man in that state has an
uncontrollable liberty to dispose of his person or possessions,
yet he has not liberty to destroy himself or so much as any
creature in his possession but where some nobler use than its
bare preservation calls for it. The state of nature has a law of
nature to govern it which obliges everyone; and reason, which
is that law, teaches all mankind, who will but consult it, that
being all equal and independent, no one ought to harm another

in his life, health, liberty, or possessions ... Everyone, as he is bound to preserve himself ... so by like reason, when his own preservation comes not in competition, ought he, as much as he can, to preserve the rest of mankind and may not, unless it be to do justice to an offender, take away or impair the life, or what tends to the preservation of life, the liberty, health, limb, or goods of another.

'Of Civil Government', *Two Treatises on Governance* (1690)

The only way, whereby any one divests himself of his natural liberty and puts on the bonds of civil society is by agreeing with other men to join and unite into a community for their comfortable, safe and peaceable living amongst one another, in a secure enjoyment of their properties and a greater security against any that are not of it. This any number of men may do because it injures not the freedom of the rest; they are left as they were in the liberty of the state of nature. When any number of men have so consented to make one community or government, they are thereby presently incorporated and make one body politic, wherein the majority have a right to act and include the rest.

'Of Civil Government', *Two Treatises on Governance* (1690)

Man being ... by nature all free, equal, and independent, no once can be put out of this estate, and subjected to the political power of another, without his consent.

'Of Civil Government', *Two Treatises on Government* (1690)

Absolute Liberty, equal and impartial Liberty, is the thing that we stand in need of.

A letter concerning toleration, undated

There being nothing more evident than that creatures of the same species ... should be equal amongst one another without subordination or subjection.

Attributed

In all states of created being capable of Laws, where there is no Law there is no Freedom. For Liberty is to be free from restraint and violence from others which cannot be, where there is no Law.

Attributed

Philip Henry Kerr, Lord Lothian

1882–1940; diplomat, expert on foreign affairs, Chancellor of the Duchy of Lancaster, 1931; Ambassador to the US 1939–40

The only body capable of establishing a really scientific communism in the West, and this aim must carry it to the Left of the Labour Party as a new factor in British politics.

On the Liberal Party, to Stalin in 1931, cited in T. Horabin, *Politics Made Plain* (1944)

It may prove to be the best, perhaps the only course, for Liberals to join one or other of the two main parties and liberalise from within.

After the 1935 general election

Robert Lowe

1811–1892; MP (Liberal) Kidderminster 1852–59, Calne 1859–68, London University 1868–80; created Viscount Sherbrooke 1880; Chancellor of the Exchequer 1868–73, Home Secretary 1873–74

I believe it will be absolutely necessary that you should prevail on our future masters to learn their lessons.

In the House of Commons, 15 July 1867; Lowe successfully opposed the 1866 Reform Bill, but could not stop Disraeli's more democratic 1867 Reform Bill from being enacted

The Chancellor of the Exchequer is a man whose duties make him more or less of a taxing machine. He is entrusted with a

certain amount of misery which it is his duty to distribute as
fairly as he can.

In the House of Commons, 11 April 1870

Henry Lucy

1842–1924; journalist, humourist and parliamentary sketch-writer

Mr Asquith picked up the glove and vigorously flung it back in
the face of the challenger. Now the hot bloods of the party are
for war to the knife – and fork.

Satirising a series of dinners held by different factions within the
Liberal Party, *The Balfourian Parliament* (1906)

Sarah Ludford

b. 1951; Islington councillor; created Baroness Ludford of Clerkenwell
1997; MEP (Liberal Democrat) London 1999–

The biggest and most important challenge for Liberal
Democrats is to stop concentrations and abuses of power. We
are the only major party for whom this is a prime determinant
of policy, the others being driven mainly by economic analysis.
That is why we do not fit the classic left-right linear spread, and
prefer our own conservative-radical spectrum, on which Tories
and Labour are closer to each other than either is to us.

Cited in D. Brack (ed.), *Why I am a Liberal Democrat* (1996)

Henry Lunn

1859–1939; travel agent

[As a young man, I used] to calculate the number of Liberals
present at a political meeting by looking at the hats on the pegs
outside. The big hats belonged to Liberals, because Liberals had
big brains; the small hats to the unintelligent Tories.

Cited in A. Lunn, *Come What May* (1940)

M

Thomas Babington Macaulay

1800–59; historian; MP (Whig, Liberal) Calne 1830–32, Leeds 1832–34,
Edinburgh 1839–47, 1852–56; Secretary at War 1839–41, Paymaster-
General 1846–48; created Baron Macaulay 1857

Many politicians of our time are in the habit of laying it down
as a self-evident proposition that no people ought to be free till
they are fit to use their freedom. The maxim is worthy of the
fool in the old story, who resolved not to go into the water till
he had learnt to swim. If men are to wait for liberty till they
became wise and good in slavery, they may indeed wait for ever.

Edinburgh Review, August 1825

Nothing is so galling to a people not broken in from the birth as a
paternal, or in other words a meddling government, a government
which tells them what to read and say and eat and drink and wear.

Edinburgh Review, January 1830

Turn where we may – within, around – the voice of great events
is proclaiming to us, 'Reform that you may preserve'.

On parliamentary reform, in the House of Commons, 2 March 1831

All great revolutions have been produced by a disproportion
between society and its institutions.

On parliamentary reform, in the House of Commons, 5 July 1831

I detest him more than cold boiled veal.

About the Tory John Wilson Croker, letter, 5 August 1831

It has always been the trick of bigots … to divide society, and to
wonder that it is not united.

On Jewish disabilities, in the House of Commons, 17 April 1833

We must at present do our best to form a class who may be interpreters between us and the millions whom we govern; a class of persons, Indian in blood and colour, but English in taste, in opinions, in morals, and in intellect.

> Minute written as a member of the Supreme Council of India, 2 February 1835

Then none was for a party;
Then all were for the state;
Then the great man helped the poor,
And the poor man loved the great:
Then lands were fairly portioned;
Then spoils were fairly sold:
The Romans were like brothers
In the brave days of old.

> 'Horatius', *Lays of Ancient Rome* (1842)

The business of everybody is the business of nobody.

> 'Hallam', *Edinburgh Review*, 1843

The gallery in which the reporters sit has become a fourth estate of the realm.

> Referring to the press gallery in the House of Commons, 'Hallam', *Edinburgh Review* 1843

We know no spectacle so ridiculous as the British public in one of its periodical fits of morality.

> 'Moore's Life of Lord Byron', *Edinburgh Review*, 1843

The rising hope of those stern and unbending Tories.

> Referring to Gladstone, 'Gladstone on Church and State', *Edinburgh Review*, 1843

The highest intellects, like the tops of mountains, are the first to catch and to reflect the dawn.

> 'Sir James Mackintosh', *Edinburgh Review*, 1843

The history of England is emphatically the history of progress.

'Sir James Mackintosh', *Edinburgh Review*, 1843

On the day of the accession of George the Third, the ascendancy of the Whig party terminated; and on that day the purification of the Whig party began.

'William Pitt, Earl of Chatham', *Edinburgh Review*, 1843

The reluctant obedience of distant provinces generally costs more than it is worth.

'The War of Succession in Spain, *Edinburgh Review*, 1843

I believe, Sir, that it is the right and the duty of the state to provide means of education for the common people. This proposition seems to me to be implied in every definition that has ever yet been given of the functions of a government.

In the House of Commons, 18 April 1847

It is because we had a preserving revolution in the seventeenth century that we have not had a destroying revolution in the nineteenth.

History of England (1848)

Thus our democracy was, from an early period, the most aristocratic, and our aristocracy the most democratic in the world.

History of England (1848)

No man is fit to govern great societies who hesitates about disobliging the few who have access to him for the sake of the many he will never see.

History of England (1848)

It has often been found that profuse expenditure, heavy taxation, absurd commercial restrictions, corrupt tribunals, disastrous wars, seditions, persecutions, conflagrations, inundations, have not been able to destroy capital so fast as the exertions of private citizens have been able to create it.

History of England (1848)

Everywhere there is a class of men who cling with fondness to whatever is ancient, and who, even when convinced by overpowering reasons that innovation would be beneficial, consent to it with many misgivings and forebodings. We find also everywhere another class of men, sanguine in hope, bold in speculation, always pressing forward, quick to discern the imperfections in whatever exists, disposed to think lightly of the risks and inconveniences which attend improvements, and disposed to give every change credit for being an improvement.

History of England (1848)

Economic growth is not worth the cost of imposing economic misery on the population at large.

Cited in A. Cyr, *Liberal Politics in Britain* (1988)

Ronald Buchanan McCallum

1898–1973; Master of Pembroke College, Oxford

At the last election some of us felt that we were voting Liberal for the last time. That feeling has vanished. In Mr Grimond we have found a leader who is giving us new life.

The Observer, 4 October 1959

Eugene McCarthy

1916–2005; American politician; Democratic Senator, Minnesota, 1958–70

The only thing that saves us from the bureaucracy is inefficiency. An efficient bureaucracy is the greatest threat to liberty.

Attributed

Norman McCord

b. 1930; historian

[They] seemed to start from the prejudice that anything done by their fellow countrymen abroad was likely to be evil, while conversely they were ever ready to accord to headhunters in Borneo or to a Burmese King the attributes of the noble savage.

On Cobden and Bright, 'Cobden and Bright 1846–57' in R. Robson (ed.), *Ideas and Institutions in Britain: Essays in Honour of George Kitson Clark* (1967)

Albert McElroy

1915–75; Minister of the Non-Subscribing Presbyterian Church of Ireland; President, Ulster Liberal Party 1956–75

What we are dealing with in the north of Ireland is not a rational body of political thought, what we are dealing with is a state of mind, something bordering on psychosis.

At the Liberal assembly, 1969

To secure, maintain and extend a liberal and humane civilisation the existence of a strong political Liberal Party is a necessity. To keep such a party in existence demands standards of single-mindedness, of purpose, self-sacrifice, intellectual discipline and moral courage of a very high order. No medals, let alone political careers are to be offered. However, if you think and feel as a Liberal you stick and hold your corner and don't count the cost. Of course it is desperately frustrating at times. As a consequence the weaker brethren give up the ghost and settle for cultivating their gardens or else they go for rides on other people's political tigers.

General election message for the four Liberal candidates in Northern Ireland, *Northern Radical* 24 June 1970

Andrew McFadyean

1887–1974; international civil servant and politician; President, Liberal
Party 1949–50

If Liberalism has seemed at times to its opponents to make an
undue display of its breastplate of righteousness – for the word
has been debased and the thing in mortal men may be perverted
into self-righteousness – it has never thrown away the sword of
the spirit and thought to fight with an empty scabbard.

The Liberal Case, general election 1950

Reginald McKenna

1863–1943; banker; MP (Liberal) Monmouth 1895–1918; Home
Secretary 1911–15, Chancellor of the Exchequer 1915–16

If you want to ruin a man send him to the Home Office.

September 1913, cited in M. Farr, *Reginald McKenna: Financier among
Statesmen 1863–1916* (2008)

Anti-Germanism and the desire for revenge were strong
amongst large masses of the people … the Liberals are not
thought as a party to be sufficiently venomous.

Explaining the results of the 1918 general election in a letter to
A. G. Gardiner, 29 December 1918

Robert McKenzie

1917–81; Canadian political scientist and broadcaster

The Labour Party, I suspect, would never have got off the
ground in 1900–06 unless Herbert Gladstone had said, 'look
boys, you give us these, we'll give you those', and that's how it
happened.

On Herbert Gladstone's 1900s Lib–Lab Pact, BBC 2
TV series *The Pursuit of Power* (1981)

Robert Maclennan

b. 1936; MP (Labour, SDP, Liberal Democrat) Caithness & Sutherland
1966–2001; leader of the SDP 1987–88, President, Liberal Democrats
1994–98; created Baron Maclennan of Rogart 2001

Today the raging must stop. The realism starts here.

> On the splits within the SDP over merger with the Liberal, at the SDP
> conference, 1 September 1987

I've never seen vagueness done with such brilliance. Labour
offered a sort of bravura vacuum. Everything was 'new',
'exciting', 'challenging' and 'modern'. Four adjectives in search
of a noun. Four attitudes looking for substance.

> On the Labour Party's election campaign, at the Liberal Democrat
> conference, Eastbourne, 21 September 1997

We are the party of the pamphlet, the working party, the
report, the debate on the report. If you prick us we bleed ink –
ink and ideas.

> At the Liberal Democrat conference, Eastbourne, 23 September 1997

Recently there has been much talk of the 'third way'. May I let
you into a rather open secret? The third way doesn't need to be
looked for in tomes on political economy or plucked out of the
air. It is embodied, and is increasingly seen to be embodied, in
the Liberal Democrats.

> To Liberal Democrats, London Region conference, February 1998

This is the party at whose conferences you get argument,
the party which couldn't be on-message if it tried, the party
which can't afford consultants and can't stand focus groups, the
party which says: 'Go on, persuade me.' For all the clever and
worthwhile people you find in the Labour and Conservative
ranks, those parties are entering a plastic age of frozen debate,
control culture, submission to the snappish and imperial
message and, around the spotlit leaderships, a chorus of mimic
extras wrapped in affirmation. We can't ever be like that. Which

is why 'radical' is the word for us. Fellow Liberal Democrats, fellow radicals – uncontrolled, off-message, non-plastic, thinking the next ideas – this is what we are for.

At the Liberal Democrat conference, Southport, 14 March 1998

Harold Macmillan

1894–1986; MP (Conservative) Stockton-on-Tees 1924–29, 1931–45, Bromley 1945–64; Prime Minister 1957–63; created Earl Macmillan of Stockton 1984

As usual the Liberals offer a mixture of sound and original ideas. Unfortunately none of the sound ideas is original and none of the original ideas is sound.

To London Conservatives, 7 March 1961

We have been swept off our feet by the Liberal revival and made the world safe for Liberalism.

In his *Diary* following the Orpington by-election, 1962, cited in
R. Lamb, Introduction to J. Thorpe, *In My Own Time* (1999)

Tom McNally

b. 1943; MP (Labour, SDP) Stockport South 1979–83; created Baron McNally of Blackpool 1995; leader of the Liberal Democrat peers 2004–; Minister of State for Justice 2010–

A negative Midas: everything he touches turns to dross … Mrs Thatcher's self-beheading boomerang.

On Trade Secretary Lord Cockfield, who subsequently became a
member of the European Commission, cited in *The Social Democrat*, 14
January 1983

T. J. Macnamara

1861–1931; MP (Liberal) Camberwell North, later North West 1900–24;
Minister of Labour 1920–22

All this sounds terribly like rank Socialism. I'm afraid it is; but I
am not in the least dismayed. Because I know it also to be first-
class Imperialism. Because I know Empire cannot be built on
rickety and flat-chested citizens.

> On the benefits of free school meals, 'In Corpore Sano', *Contemporary
> Review*, Vol. 87 (1905)

Salvador de Madariaga

1886–1978; Spanish writer and diplomat

The freedom to think is the freedom to communicate one's
thought.

> Cited in E. M. Forster, *Nordic Twilight* (1940)

James Madison

1751–1836; American President 1809–17

It is a universal truth that the loss of liberty will be charged to
dangers, real or imagined, from abroad.

> Attributed

John Major

b. 1943; MP (Conservative) Huntingdon 1979–2001; Foreign Secretary
1989, Chancellor of the Exchequer 1989–90, Prime Minister 1990–97

You end as pious and pompous as you have been throughout this
Parliament.

> To Paddy Ashdown at the last Prime Minister's Question Time of the
> 1992–97 Parliament, 20 March 1997

Edwin Malindine

1909–93; President, Liberal Party 1961–62

MPs … are certainly not to be dictated to by the party
conference. That is a cardinal principle of our Liberal activities.

Cited in J. Rasmussen, *The Liberal Party: A Study of Retrenchment and
Revival* (1965)

Nelson Mandela

b. 1918; African National Congress activist; President of South Africa
1994–99

During my lifetime I have dedicated myself to this struggle of
the African people. I have fought against white domination, and
I have fought against black domination. I have cherished the
ideal of a democratic and free society in which all persons live
together in harmony and with equal opportunities. It is an ideal
which I hope to live for and to achieve. But if needs be, it is an
ideal for which I am prepared to die.

Rivonia trial, 20 April 1964

We have, at last, achieved our political emancipation. We
pledge ourselves to liberate all our people from the continuing
bondage of poverty, deprivation, suffering, gender and other
discrimination. Never, never, and never again shall it be that
this beautiful land will again experience the oppression of one
by another … The sun shall never set on so glorious a human
achievement. Let freedom reign. God bless Africa!

On his inauguration as President of South Africa, 10 May 1994

No one is born hating another person because of the colour of
his skin, or his background, or his religion. People must learn to
hate, and if they can learn to hate, they can be taught to love, for
love comes more naturally to the human heart than its opposite.

Long Walk to Freedom (1994)

A man who takes away another man's freedom is a prisoner of hatred, he is locked behind the bars of prejudice and narrow-mindedness. I am not truly free if I am taking away someone else's freedom, just as surely as I am not free when my freedom is taken from me. The oppressed and the oppressor alike are robbed of their humanity.

Long Walk to Freedom (1994)

Your freedom and mine cannot be separated.

Attributed

Geoffrey Mander

1882–1962; MP (Liberal) Wolverhampton East 1929–45

We were *not* all wrong.

Title of Mander's book on Liberal opposition to appeasement (1941)

David John Manning

Academic

Liberals have never seen the threats to the way of life of which they approve as being a purely national concern. Although there is no such thing as universal liberalism, in the sense that it has one theme throughout, it is an internationalist and international doctrine.

Liberalism (1976)

Mao Zedong

1893–1976; Chinese communist revolutionary, founder of the People's Republic of China

Liberalism is extremely harmful in a revolutionary collective. It is a corrosive which eats away unity, undermines cohesion, causes apathy and creates dissension. It robs the revolutionary ranks of compact organisation and strict discipline, prevent policies from being carried through and alienates the Party organisation from the masses which the Party leads. It is an extremely bad tendency.

'Combat Liberalism', 7 September 1937

Gregorio Marañón

1887–1960; Spanish doctor, intellectual and politician

It is easier to die for an idea, and I would add that it is less heroic, than to try to understand the ideas of others.

Speech at the Royal Academy of History, Madrid, 8 June 1958

Jean-Paul Marat

1743–93; French radical politician

Of what use is political liberty to those who have no bread? It is of value only to ambitious theorists and politicians.

Attributed

Princess Marie-Louise

1872–1956; grand-daughter of Queen Victoria

When I left the dining room after sitting next to Mr Gladstone I thought he was the cleverest man in England. But after sitting next to Mr Disraeli I thought I was the cleverest woman in England.

Story related about a young lady dining with Disraeli and Gladstone, cited in D. Englefield, J. Seaton & I. White, *Facts About the British Prime Ministers* (1996)

David Marquand

b. 1934; MP (Labour) Ashfield 1966–77; later joined SDP; academic

There was no Social Democratic Party as such, indeed, there was not even a recognised Social Democratic leader or social democratic text. Social democracy was difficult to define – Tony Crosland had once described the term as 'historically inaccurate and philosophically vacuous'.

> Report of a dialogue with Michael Meadowcroft, at a Liberal assembly
> fringe meeting organised by a Liberal discussion group, *Arena*, 9
> September 1980

Social Democrats are the heirs of the New Liberals at the turn of the century, such as Hobhouse and Clarke; the heirs of the Fabians who sought to work through the ballot box and persuasion, not by violence; and the heir of Keynesian economics without total transfer of ownership.

> Report of a dialogue with Michael Meadowcroft, at a Liberal assembly
> fringe meeting organised by a Liberal discussion group, *Arena*, 9
> September 1980

The city, the *polis*, belongs to and is fashioned by its citizens; they must not hand over their obligation to honour and defend it to some charismatic leader or remote bureaucracy.

> *The Guardian*, 16 August 1990

Edward Martell

1909–89; publisher; organiser of Liberal election campaigns in 1950 and 1951; later, founder of the Freedom Movement

Her blatant pro-Tory attitude dismayed many in the party who had hitherto held her in the highest respect, and destroyed the public belief in our independence.

> On Lady Bonham Carter, who stood as a Liberal with Conservative
> support at Colne Valley in 1951, cited in M. Jones, *A Radical Life: A
> Biography of Megan Lloyd George* (1991)

José Martí

1853–95; Cuban writer

The dagger plunged in the name of Freedom is plunged into the breast of Freedom.

Granos de Oro: Pensamientos Seleccionados en las Obras de José Martí (1942)

Karl Marx

1818–83; German philosopher

Gladstone's eloquence ... Polished blandness, empty profundity, unction not without poisonous ingredients, the velvet paw not without the claws, scholastic distinctions both grandiose and petty, *quaestiones* and *quaestiuniculae* [minor questions], the entire arsenal of probabilism with its casuistic scruples and unscrupulous reservations, its hesitating motives and motivated hesitation, its humble pretensions of superiority, virtuous intrigue, intricate simplicity, Byzantium and Liverpool.

On Gladstone in 1855, cited in A. Adonis, 'Gladstone, Marx and Modern Progressives', *Journal of Liberal Democrat History* No. 8, September 1995

The arch-philistine Jeremy Bentham was the insipid, pedantic, leather-tongued oracle of the bourgeois intelligence of the nineteenth century.

Das Kapital (1867)

H.W. Massingham

1860–1924; journalist

Liberalism is not a revolutionary force, and it cannot dispense with middle-class brains and management.

'Mr Churchill's Career', *Nation*, 13 January 1912

To me there are few spectacles more melancholy than that of dear old C. P. Scott wearily dredging in a foul pool for the soul of Lloyd George.

> Commenting on Scott's efforts to defend Lloyd George during the death throes of the 1918 government, cited in V. Phillipps, *My Days and Ways* (1943)

Charles Masterman

1873–1927; MP (Liberal) West Ham North 1906–11, Bethnal Green South West 1911–14, Manchester Rusholme 1923–24; Chancellor of the Duchy of Lancaster 1914–15

The first task of Liberalism is … to champion Liberty for all nations, classes, creeds and persons who compose this variegated family of mankind. In so far as it works against it, it is false to its tradition and has gone astray down hazardous ways.

The New Liberalism (1920)

Liberalism in practice … has always refused to be bound by the hard logical doctrines of complete individualistic philosophy on the one hand, or collectivist philosophy on the other. It sees unchecked private enterprise, protected by instruments of order and the law of inheritance of man's making, if not creating, yet acquiescing in the creation of, a population so driven against the boundaries of decent existence, as to possess neither time, wages, leisure nor security adequate to make them free. It is determined that freedom for these classes shall be attained; that such inequality in the presence of such fortune is incompatible with the ultimate principles and traditions. It is determined to build a platform of minimum subsidence and comfort, below which no man or woman shall be allowed to fall, except by deliberate choice.

The New Liberalism (1920)

Liberalism is not a compromise between two extremes of opinion. It is not a 'Middle Party'. It is not a combination of compromises, stratagems and make-beliefs. It does not appeal for recruits among Tories who are a little sentimental, and Socialists who are a little timid. It has a solution of its own for the ills which scourge humanity. It is not a 'half-way house' between Conservatism and Revolution.

The New Liberalism (1920)

I've fought him as hard as anyone else, but I have to confess, when Lloyd George came back to the party, ideas came back to the party.

Cited in L. Masterman, *C. F. G. Masterman* (1939)

John Shackleton Mathers

1844–99; Leeds Liberal organiser and councillor

There are questions ... coming on in leaps and bounds ... To use the broadest terms, I mean Socialism and by that I mean immediately all the questions which concern capital and labour; all that which concerns the very direct interests and comforts of the toilers. For over five years I have been warning friends that, unless the Liberal Party took up and considered these questions and dealt with them, a great Labour Party would spring up and sweep aside both Tories and Liberals as such and govern for themselves. You may think this Utopian, it only remains so until the hour, and not a moment beyond, when the masses have accumulated funds to sustain their men for their cause.

Letter to Herbert Gladstone MP, 23 March 1890

Francis Maude

b. 1953; MP (Conservative) Warwickshire North 1983–92, Horsham 1997–; Minister for the Cabinet Office and Paymaster General 2010–

The Liberal Democrats are so far in bed with Tony Blair that they're just a hideous lump under the duvet.

Cited in *The Independent*, 29 April 1999

Christopher Mayhew

1915–97; MP (Labour) Norfolk South 1945–50, (Labour, Liberal) Woolwich East 1951–74; created Baron Mayhew of Wimbledon 1981

The role of the Labour moderates has been ignominious for years: now it has become discreditable. They neither reform the Labour Party nor leave it. Instead, they go through the motions of revolt and then stay in, giving an air of democratic respectability to political elements which they themselves deeply and rightly distrust.

At Dorking, 14 June 1980, cited in *Time to Explain* (1987)

Liberal supporters of CND proved to be no less active and enthusiastic, and a good deal less ill-natured, than their left-wing predecessors of the early sixties. But they had no leaders to compare with Nye Began, Bertrand Russell and Michael Foot. Our debates were conducted in a more civilised manner but at a lower political and intellectual level.

Time to Explain (1987)

Giuseppe Mazzini

1805–72; Italian politician, activist for the unification of Italy

God has created you social and progressive beings. It is therefore your duty to associate yourselves, and to progress as far as the sphere of activity in which circumstances have placed you will permit. You have a right to demand that the society to which you belong shall in no way impede your work of association and progress, but, on the contrary, shall assist you, and furnish you with the means of association and of progress of which you stand in need.

The Duties of Man (1844–58)

Michael Meadowcroft

b. 1942; MP (Liberal) Leeds West 1983–87

Realignment on the Left of politics has been our aim for twenty-five years and we need to ensure that an alliance [with the SDP] is a realignment of the Left and not the Centre.

Social Democracy: Barrier or Bridge (1981)

Liberals, who see the key political spectrum running from diffusion of power to corporatism – public or private – always have difficulty in relating to parties who perceive themselves along a different spectrum, from public ownership to private ownership.

Social Democracy: Barrier or Bridge (1981)

For the Liberal there are certain constant beliefs. The Liberal is committed to liberty, participation, partnership, and diversity and to a belief in the value of human personality.

Liberal Values for a New Decade, second edition (1981)

Liberalism is not an abstract political theory existing to provide mental stimulus for a handful of philosophers; it is a basis for political action. Its values are guidelines for a practical programme which entails grappling with the problems of government.

Liberal Values for a New Decade, second edition (1981)

Liberals sometimes request a snappy phrase to encapsulate liberalism in the way that it is thought that 'public ownership' and 'private enterprise' sum up Labour and Conservative attitudes respectively. Quite apart from the fact that such over-simplifications are harmful to political discussion, it is particularly futile to reduce liberalism to a single phrase because it is more an attitude of mind and a way of life than a political system. It is because of this crucial fact that an understanding of Liberal *philosophy* is vital to Liberals.

Liberal Values for a New Decade, second edition (1981)

For the Liberal there are aspects of equality that are absolute. These include equality of esteem and equality of treatment. There can be no compromise with the view that each individual whatever his failings and weaknesses, is intrinsically worthy of respect – by virtue of his humanity if not his deeds.

Liberalism and the Left (1982)

There are so few wealthy individuals – relatively – that even to confiscate a substantial 'excess' would only generate a tiny sum for everyone else. In other words, to achieve by force the liberal end of equality would require such illiberal means as to render the eventual achievement more destructive than the inequality it replaced.

Liberalism and the Left (1982)

It was lack of intellectual rigour that appalled me and which I hoped to diminish by writing and speaking. I failed, and superficialism, as practised by Steel and the SDP, won.

Cited in D. Brack and E. Randall (eds), *Dictionary of Liberal Thought* (2007)

Liberalism has the necessary beliefs and arguments; all it requires is Liberals with confidence to deploy them.

Liberalism Today and Tomorrow (1989)

Occasionally in politics there appears a party leader able not only to ride the tide of public opinion but also able to accelerate it. Jo Grimond personified the '60s disaffection with staid tradition; the electorate was ready to be seduced.

Liberator, September 1994

We believe that in the Liberal philosophy alone lies the vision to enable our world to guarantee its future and the potential to make it happen. We are not so naïve as to believe that human nature can be changed but we do believe that individuals do not necessarily choose narrow self-interest if the broader case for stability, security and sensitivity is argued persuasively. It is not that the case for Liberalism has been rejected but that it has hardly had a hearing at all. There may be few 'natural' Liberals, but there are many more will support Liberal solutions. If, as the merest observation makes all too evident, human beings are a combination of altruism and selfishness, then the politician's task is not to ignore reality, but to provide cogent reasons to enhance altruism and to diminish selfishness.

Focus on Freedom (2001)

In an increasing number of places the Liberal society is threatened by religious fundamentalism which would seek, in effect to impose a form of theocratic rule. Such fundamentalists ... wish to force the whole of society to adopt that which otherwise they are otherwise they are perfectly at liberty to persuade the individual to accept ... It is, however, illegitimate and counterproductive to seek to impose by force what one cannot gain by argument ... The inevitable consequence is a recourse to repression and force. Consent is essential to the survival of democracy and can only be sustained within a civil society based on rational debate and democratic decision making.

Focus on Freedom (2001)

A regular call to politicians is 'less talk and more action.' I profoundly disagree. Much of post-war public policy that it currently, and rightly, under serious criticism is the consequence of conscientious men and women producing immediate responses to perceived needs, under the pressure of an inexorable electoral timetable, without the benefit of thorough analysis and assessment of alternatives and their consequences.

Diversity in Danger – Pluralism and Policy Development (2009)

Liberals are anarchists by nature and constitutionalists by necessity.

Attributed

William Lamb, Lord Melbourne

1779–1848; MP (Whig) Leominster 1806, Haddington Burghs 1806–07, Portarlington 1807–16, Peterborough 1816–19, Hertfordshire 1819–26, Newport, Isle of Wight 1827, Bletchingley 1827–28; became 2nd Viscount Melbourne 1828; Home Secretary 1830–34, Prime Minister 1834, 1835–41

It is impossible that anybody can feel the being out of parliament more keenly for me than I feel it for myself. It is actually cutting my throat. It is depriving me of the great object of my life.

1812, cited in D. Englefield, J. Seaton & I. White, *Facts About The British Prime Ministers* (1996)

My principles are, I believe, the Whig principles of the Revolution; the main foundation of these is the irresponsibility of the crown, the consequent responsibility of Ministers, the preservation of the power and dignity of Parliament as constituted by Law and Custom.

Letter to Lord Holland, 1815, cited in D. Cecil, *Melbourne* (1955)

A Cabinet is a delicate and fragile machine, this is still more the case when it has recently been shaken and broken, and repaired with new materials. Those who remain are anxious not to have to concede anything to their new allies; those who join are equally desirous of obtaining as much concession as possible, in order to justify themselves for having accepted office.

1834, cited in D. Cecil, *Melbourne* (1955)

I have always thought complaints of ill-usage contemptible, whether from a seduced disappointed girl or a turned-out Prime Minister.

To Emily Eden after being dismissed by William IV, letter to Mrs Lister, 23 November 1834, cited in D. Cecil, *Melbourne* (1955)

If left out he would be dangerous, but if taken in, he would be simply destructive.

1835; Melbourne omitted the former Lord Chancellor, Lord Brougham, from his second administration, cited in D. Cecil, *Melbourne* (1955)

Now, is it to lower the price of corn, or isn't it? It is not much matter which we say, but mind, we must all say the same.

At the end of a Cabinet meeting to agree a fixed tariff for corn, cited in W. Bagehot, *The English Constitution* (1867)

Nobody ever did anything very foolish except from some strong principle.

Cited in D. Cecil, *Melbourne* (1955)

'I will support you as long as you are in the right,' said a politician to him on one occasion. 'That is no use at all,' replied Melbourne; 'What I want is men who will support me when I am in the wrong.'

D. Cecil, *Melbourne* (1955)

When in doubt about what should be done, do nothing.

Cited in D. Cecil, *Melbourne* (1955)

The whole duty of government is to prevent crime and to preserve contracts.

Cited in D. Cecil, *Melbourne* (1955)

I don't know, Ma'am, why they make all this fuss about education; none of the Pagets can read, or write, and they get on well enough.

To Queen Victoria, cited in D. Cecil, *Melbourne* (1955)

A doctrinaire is a fool but an honest man.

Cited in D. Cecil, *Melbourne* (1955)

My esoteric doctrine is that if you entertain any doubt, it is safest to take the unpopular side in the first instance. Transit from the unpopular, is easy ... but from the popular to the unpopular the ascent is so steep and rugged that it is impossible to maintain it.

Cited in D. Cecil, *Melbourne* (1955)

Friends are generally more troublesome and often more hostile than adversaries.

To Lord Palmerston, about Lord John Russell and Lord Holland, cited in D. Cecil, *Melbourne* (1955)

No woman should touch pen and ink ... they have too much passion and too little sense.

To Queen Victoria, cited in D. Englefield, J. Seaton & I. White, *Facts About The British Prime Ministers* (1996)

If a thing is very urgent you can always find time for it; but if a thing can be put off, why then you put it off.

Cited in D. Englefield, J. Seaton & I. White, *Facts About The British Prime Ministers* (1996)

George Meredith
1828–1909; writer

[An ill-assorted collection of] stranded Whigs; crotchety manufacturers; dissentient religionists; the half-minded and the hare-hearted.

Dr Shrapnel describing the Liberal Party, cited in G. Meredith, *Beauchamp's Career*, Vol. 1 (1910)

The greatness of England has been built up by the Tories ... They have the honour and safety of the country at heart. They do not play disgracefully at reductions of taxes, as the Liberals do.

Cecilia Halkett, cited in *Beauchamp's Career* (1910)

Edward Miall

1809–81; MP (Liberal) Rochdale 1852–57, Bradford 1869–74;
established *Nonconformist* journal 1841

It is one thing to recognise a right; it is another and much
more difficult one to give to that right a complete practical
expression.

Reconciliation Between the Middle and Labouring Classes (1842)

Perhaps the greatest peril to which our social organisation
exposes us is the temptation it offers to shift from ourselves
to our rulers all active care for the myriads around us, and to
condense our whole duty into the payment of the Queen's
taxes.

Views of Voluntary Principle (1845)

Nathaniel Micklem

1888–1976; Principal, Mansfield College, Oxford 1932–53; President,
Liberal Party 1957–58

Liberalism aims at the moralising of power through the
enlargement of liberty.

The Theology of Politics (1941)

It is not possible to demonstrate the truth of one's convictions
or intuitions. I believe, though I should never claim to
demonstrate, that the spiritual presuppositions of liberal
democracy correspond with the nature of reality. That is to say,
I believe it to be true that man is a spiritual being, and therefore
he must be free, that is in fact he is also a 'fallen' or very
imperfect and often very selfish being and therefore law and
order must be enforced.

The Idea of Liberal Democracy (1957)

Harriet Taylor Mill
1807–58; writer, philosopher and women's rights activist; wife of John Stuart Mill

Concerning the fitness, then, of women for politics there can be no question, but the dispute is more likely to turn upon the fitness of politics for women.

> 'Enfranchisement of Women', cited in A. S. Rossi, *Essays on Sex Equality by John Stuart Mill and Harriet Taylor* (1970)

John Stuart Mill
1806–73; MP (Liberal) Westminster 1865–68; writer and philosopher

High wages and universal reading are the two elements of democracy; where they coexist, all government, except the government of public opinion, is impossible.

> *The State of Society in America* (1836)

The motto of a radical politician should be government by means of the middle for the working classes.

> 'The Reorganisation of the Reform Party', *London and Westminster Review* XXXII (1839)

People understand their own business, and their own interests better, and care for them more, than the government does or can be expected to do.

> *Principles of Political Economy* (1848)

Laissez-faire, in short, should be the general practice: every departure from it, unless required by some great good, is a certain evil.

> *Principles of Political Economy* (1848)

It must always have been seen ... by political economists, that the increase in wealth is not boundless: that at the end of what they term the progressive state lies the stationary state, that all progress in wealth is but a postponement of this, and that each step in advance is an approach to it.

Principles of Political Economy (1848)

It is scarcely necessary to remark that a stationary condition of capital and population implies no stationary state of human improvement. There would be as much scope as ever for all kinds of mental culture, and moral and social progress, as much room for improving the art of living, and much more likelihood of it being improved, when minds ceased to be engrossed by the art of getting on.

Principles of Political Economy (1848)

The liberty of the individual must be thus far limited: he must not make himself a nuisance to other people.

On Liberty (1859)

The worth of a state, in the long run, is the worth of the individuals comprising it.

On Liberty (1859)

If all mankind, minus one, were of one opinion, and only one person were of the contrary opinion, mankind would be no more justified in silencing that one person, than he, if he had the power, would be justified in silencing mankind.

On Liberty (1859)

Precisely because the tyranny of opinion is such as to make eccentricity a reproach, it is desirable, in order to break through that tyranny, that people should be eccentric.

On Liberty (1859)

The spirit of improvement is not always a spirit of liberty, for it may aim at forcing improvements on an unwilling people.

On Liberty (1859)

The only part of the conduct of any one for which he is amenable to society is that which concerns others. In the part which merely concerns himself, his independence is, of right, absolute. Over himself, over his own body and mind, the individual is sovereign.

On Liberty (1859)

A government cannot have too much of the kind of activity which does not impede, but aids and stimulates, individual exertion and development. The mischief begins when, instead of calling forth the activity and powers of individuals and bodies, it substitutes its own activity for theirs.

On Liberty (1859)

The only purpose for which power can be rightfully exercised over any member of a civilised community, against his will, is to prevent harm to others. His own good, either physical or moral, is not a sufficient warrant.

On Liberty (1859)

He who knows only his own side of the case knows little of that.

On Liberty (1859)

The only freedom that deserves the name is that of pursuing our own good in our own way, so long as we do not attempt to deprive others of theirs, or impede their efforts to attain it.

On Liberty (1859)

We can never be sure that the opinion we are endeavouring to stifle is a false opinion.

On Liberty (1859)

It is better to be a human dissatisfied than a pig satisfied; better to be a Socrates dissatisfied than a fool satisfied. And if the fool or the pig are of a different opinion, it is because they only know their own side of the question.

On Liberty (1859)

A party of order or stability, and a party of progress or reform, are both necessary elements of a healthy state of political life.

On Liberty (1859)

A State which dwarfs its men, in order that they may be more docile instruments in its hands even for beneficial purposes, will find that with small men no great thing can really be accomplished.

On Liberty (1859)

Persons of genius, it is true, are, and are always likely to be, a small minority; but in order to have them, it is necessary to preserve the soil in which they grow. Genius can only breathe freely in an *atmosphere* of freedom.

On Liberty (1859)

Despotism is a legitimate mode of government in dealing with barbarians, provided that the end be their improvement.

On Liberty (1859)

I am not aware that any community has a right to force another to be civilised.

On Liberty (1859)

The peculiar evil of silencing the expression of an opinion is, that it is robbing the human race; posterity as well as the existing generation; those who dissent from the opinion, still more than those who hold it. If the opinion is right, they are deprived of the opportunity of exchanging error for truth: if wrong, they lose, what is almost as great a benefit, the clearer perception and livelier impression of truth, produced by its collision with error.

On Liberty (1859)

When society requires to be rebuilt, there is no use in attempting to rebuild it on the old plan.

Dissertations and Discussions, Political, Philosophical and Historical, Vol. 1 (1859)

[The duty of every Liberal government or people is] to assist struggling liberalism, by mediation, by money, or by arms, wherever it can prudently do so; as every despotic government, when its aid is needed or asked for, never scruples to aid despotic governments.

Dissertations and Discussions, Political, Philosophical and Historical, Vol. 2 (1859)

What I stated was that the Conservative Party was by the law of its constitution necessarily the stupidest party. Now, I do not retract this assertion, but I did not mean that Conservatives are generally stupid; I meant that stupid persons are generally Conservative ... I do not see why honourable gentlemen should feel that position at all offensive to them, for it ensures their always being an extremely powerful party. There is a dead solid force in sheer stupidity such that a few able men, with that force pressing behind them, are assured of victory in many a struggle; and many a victory the Conservative Party have indeed owed to that force.

Also quoted as 'Conservatives are not necessarily stupid, but most stupid people are conservatives' and often cited as a description of the Conservative Party as 'the stupid party'; *Considerations on Representative Government* (1861)

Most of the great positive evils of the world are in themselves removable, and will, if human affairs continue to improve, be in the end reduced to within narrow limits. Poverty, in any sense implying suffering, may be completely extinguished by the wisdom of society, combined with the good sense and providence of individuals. Even that most intractable of enemies, disease, may be indefinitely reduced in dimensions by good physical and moral education, and proper control of noxious influences, while the progress of science holds out a promise for the future of still more direct conquests over this detestable foe ... As for vicissitudes of fortune, and other disappointments connected with worldly circumstances, these are principally the effect either of gross imprudence, or ill-regulated desires, or of bad and imperfect social institutions. All the grand sources, in short, of human suffering are in a great degree, many of them almost entirely, conquerable by human care and effort.

Utilitarianism (1863)

A Liberal is he who looks forward for his principles of government, a Tory looks backward.

Morning Star, 6 July 1865

We ought not to deny to them, what we are conceding to everybody else – a right to be consulted; the ordinary chance of placing in the great Council of the nation a few organs of their sentiments – of having, what every petty trade or profession has, a few members who feel specially called on to attend to their interests, and to point out how those interests are affected by the law, or by any proposed changes in it.

Arguing the case for votes for women, in the House of Commons, 20 May 1867

The principle which regulates the existing social relations between the two sexes – the legal subordination of one sex to the other – is wrong in itself and ought to be replaced by a principle of perfect equality, admitting no power or privilege on the one side, nor disability on the other.

The Subjection of Women (1869)

Everyone who desires power, desires it most over those who are nearest to him, with whom his life is passed, with whom he has most concerns in common, and in whom any independence of his authority is oftenest likely to interfere with his individual preferences.

The Subjection of Women (1869)

In every respect the burthen is hard on those who attack an almost universal opinion.

The Subjection of Women (1869)

Any limitation on the field of selection deprives society of some chances of being served by the competent, without ever saving it from the incompetent.

The Subjection of Women (1869)

What is now called the nature of women is an eminently artificial thing – the result of forced repression in some directions, unnatural stimulation in others.

The Subjection of Women (1869)

In the present day, power holds a smoother language, and, whomsoever it oppresses, always pretends to do so for their own good.

The Subjection of Women (1869)

If no one could vote for a member of Parliament who was not fit to be a candidate, the government would be a narrow oligarchy indeed.

The Subjection of Women (1869)

To have a voice in choosing those by whom one is to be governed is a means of self-protection due to every one.

The Subjection of Women (1869)

Marriage is the only actual bondage known to our law.

The Subjection of Women (1869)

He found it impossible to believe that a world so full of evil was the work of an Author combining infinite power with perfect goodness and righteousness.

On his father, James Mill, *Autobiography* (1873)

I thought the predominance of the aristocratic classes, the noble and the rich, in the English Constitution, an evil worth any struggle to get rid of.

Autobiography (1873)

No great improvements in the lot of mankind are possible, until
a great change takes place in the fundamental constitution of
their modes of thought.

Autobiography (1873)

The art of sacrificing the non-essential to preserve the essential.

On compromise, *Autobiography* (1873)

An aristocratic party in opposition, coquetting with popular
principles for the sake of popular support.

On the Whigs, *Autobiography* (1873)

I had what might truly be called an object in life; to be a
reformer of the world.

Autobiography (1873)

The legislature instead of being weeded of individual
peculiarities and entirely made up of men who simply represent
the creed of great political or religious parties, will comprise a
large proportion of the most eminent individual minds in the
country placed there without reference to party by voters who
appreciate their individual eminence.

On the potential benefits of proportional representation, *Autobiography*
(1873)

It is, no doubt, a very laudable effort, in modern teaching,
to render as much as possible of what the young are required to
learn, easy and interesting to them. But when this principle is
pushed to the length of not requiring them to learn anything
but what has been made easy and interesting, one of the chief
objects of education is sacrificed.

Autobiography (1873)

In the case of most men, the only inducement which has been
found sufficiently constant and unflagging to overcome the ever-
present influence of indolence and love of ease, and induce men
to apply themselves unrelaxingly to work for the most part in

itself dull and unexciting, is the prospect of bettering their own economic condition and that of their family.

Fortnightly Review, April 1879

[Toryism] is *tout bonnement* a reverence for government in the abstract. It means ... it is good for man to be ruled; to submit both his body and mind to the guidance of a high intelligence and virtue. It is, therefore, the direct antithesis of Liberalism, which is for making every man his own guide and sovereign master, and letting him think for himself, and do exactly as he judges best for himself, giving other men leave to persuade him if they can by evidence, forbidding him to give way to authority; and still less allowing them to constrain him more than the existence and tolerable necessity of every man's person and property renders indispensably necessary.

Cited in R. H. Murray, *Studies in English Social and Political Thinkers of the Nineteenth Century* (1929)

The government of a people by itself has a meaning and a reality, but such a thing as government of one people by another does not and cannot exist.

R. Wollheim (ed.), *Three Essays* (1975)

One person with a belief is a social power equal to ninety-nine who have only interest.

R. Wollheim (ed.), *Three Essays* (1975)

The despotism of custom is everywhere the standing hindrance to human advancement, being in unceasing antagonism to that disposition to aim at something better than customary, which is called, according to circumstances, the spirit of liberty, or that of progress or improvement ... The only unfailing and permanent source of improvement is liberty, since by it there are as many possible independent centres of improvement as there are individuals.

R. Wollheim (ed.), *Three Essays* (1975)

The contented man, or the contented family, who have no ambition to make anyone else happier, to promote the good of their country or their neighbourhood, or to improve themselves in moral excellence, excite in us neither admiration or approval.

R. Wollheim (ed.), *Three Essays* (1975)

John Milton

1608–74; poet

The land had once enfranchised herself from this impertinent yoke of prelaty, under whose inquisitorious and tyrannical duncery no free and splendid wit can flourish.

The Reason of Church Government, book 2 (1642)

Since knowledge and survey of vice in this world is so necessary to the consistency of human virtue, and the scanning of errors to the confirmation of truth, how can we move safely and with less danger, out of the regions of sign and falsity, than by reading all kinds of tractates and hearing all manner of reasons?

Areopagitica (1644)

For this is not the liberty which we can hope, that no grievance ever should arise in the Commonwealth, that let no man in this world expect; but when complaints are freely heard, deeply considered, and speedily reformed, then is the utmost bound of civil liberty attained that wise men look for.

Areopagitica (1644)

Give me the liberty to know, to utter, and to argue freely according to conscience, above all liberties.

Areopagitica (1644)

Where there is much desire to learn, there of necessity will be much arguing, much writing, many opinions; for opinion in good men is but knowledge in the making.

Areopagitica (1644)

No man who knows aught, can be so stupid to deny that all men naturally were born free.

The Tenure of Kings and Magistrates (1649)

None can love freedom heartily, but good men; the rest love not freedom, but licence.

The Tenure of Kings and Magistrates (1649)

Baron de Montesquieu

1689–1755; French philosopher

Political liberty in a citizen is that tranquillity of spirit which comes from the opinion each one has of his security, and in order for him to have this liberty the government must be such that one citizen cannot fear another citizen.

The Spirit of the Law (1748)

[Commerce] cures destructive prejudices, and it is an almost general rule that wherever manners are gentle there is commerce and that wherever there is commerce manners are gentle.

The Spirit of the Law (1748)

Charles Moore

b. 1956; editor of the *Daily Telegraph* 1995–2003

The actual programme for tenderness is a bit thin. Every time David Owen enthuses about bombs and the free market he carries conviction. Every time he talks of welfarism and public services he sounds bored.

Comment on Owen's 'tough and tender' slogan, *The Spectator*, 17 September 1983

John Morley

1838–1923; MP (Liberal) Newcastle-upon-Tyne 1883–95, Montrose
1896–1908; created Viscount Morley of Blackburn 1908; Secretary of
State for India 1905–10, Lord President of the Council 1910–14

You have not converted a man because you have silenced him.

On Compromise (1874)

Our main text has been that men should refuse to sacrifice their
opinions and ways of living out of regard for the status quo, or
the prejudices of others.

On Compromise (1874)

The great body of English voters, so far as they have political
ideas or interests at all, are left centre. They have a general
feeling that the world ought to be made a little better, while
they listen sometimes with profound apathy, sometimes with
faint intellectual interest, usually with the bitterest suspicion
and the most resentful distrust to every proposal for making it
better.

Fortnightly Review, February 1875

I am bound to say that it is when I come northward that I am in
the presence of that kind of Liberalism which I, for one, most
sympathise with, most rejoice in, and to which I look forward
most confidently for the safe progress of the fortunes of our
country.

At Newcastle, reported in *The Times*, 5 April 1888

Although in Cabinet all its members stand on an equal footing,
speak with equal voices and, on the rare occasions when a
division is taken, are counted on the fraternal principle of one
man, one vote, yet the head of the Cabinet is *primus inter pares*,
and occupies a position which, so long as it lasts, is one of
exceptional and peculiar authority.

Walpole (1889)

Talk of the Liberal Party? Why, it consists of Mr G. After him it will disappear and all will be chaos.

1891, cited in D. A. Hamer, *Liberal Politics in the age of Gladstone and Rosebery* (1972)

Simplicity of character is no hindrance to subtlety of intellect.

Life of Gladstone (1903)

Foreign ideas reached us of that generation in glorious mould. England was the refuge of two famous exiles between 1849 and 1871, a great Italian and a great Frenchman, voices of the most energetic and imaginative genius since Byron and Shelley. Mazzini and Victor Hugo imparted activity, elevation and generous breadth of cosmopolitan outlook to the most ardent spirits of the new time in our own island ... If we seek a word for the significance of it all, it is not hard to find. Alike with those who adore and those who detest it, the dominating force in the living mind of Europe for a long generation after the overthrow of the French monarchy in 1830 has been that marked way of looking at things, feeling them, handling them, judging main actors in them, for which, with a hundred kaleidoscopic turns, the accepted name is Liberalism.

Recollections (1917)

The proper memory for a politician is one that knows what to remember and what to forget.

Recollections (1917)

Respect for the dignity and worth of the individual is [Liberalism's] root. It stands for pursuit of social good against class interest or dynastic interest. It stands for the subjection to human judgement of all claims of external authority, whether in an organised Church, or in more loosely gathered societies of believers, or in books held sacred.

Recollections (1917)

Do you know, I am sometimes amazed, and a trifle horrified,
when I contrast the loose free-and-easy way in which politicians
form their judgements with the strict standards of proof,
evidence, fact observed by every conscientious critic or
historian. So little evidence goes such a long way when once
your mind is made up, and circumstances are calling for decision
and act.

　Recollections (1917)

But have you ever heard of this account of a political speech and
its contents? Success depends on three things: who says it, what
he says, how he says it; and of these three things what he says is
the least important.

　Recollections (1917)

One great spring of mischief in these high politics is to suppose
that the situation of to-day will be the situation tomorrow. If
I were writing a manual for a statesman, I should say to him.
'Remember that in the great latitudes of policy, all is fluid
elastic, mutable; the friend to-day, the foe to-morrow; the ally
and confederate against your enemy, suddenly *his* confederate
against you.'

　Recollections (1917)

I have faith in mankind, placed under free institutions.

　Cited in D. A. Hamer, *John Morley: Liberal Intellectual in Politics* (1968)

While cultivating a balanced habit of mind – a disposition to
hearken to both sets of arguments – don't forget that you have
to decide – and that the decision is at last the most important
part of the matter.

　Cited in D. A. Hamer, *John Morley: Liberal Intellectual in Politics* (1968)

The state represents physical force together with moral
authority. The state is most civilised where moral authority is
most potent, and physical force least required.

　Cited in D. A. Hamer, *John Morley: Liberal Intellectual in Politics* (1968)

It is important that a young man should start life with a general
faith in the principle of social improvement; he may decline
in the energy of his faith, as the years wear out the edge of
his mind. But if a man starts with a predisposition to regard
improvement as moonshine, there is no limit to the hold which
stupidity and obstruction may get upon him.

Cited in D. A. Hamer, *John Morley: Liberal Intellectual in Politics* (1968)

Samuel Morley

1809–86; MP (Liberal) Nottingham 1865–66, Bristol 1868–85

A party of progress, a party whose desire it is to keep pace with
the times and with the requirements of the nation – not seeking
change for the sake of change, but for improvement.

On the Liberal Party, cited in I. Bradley *The Optimists* (1980)

Rhys Hopkin Morris

1888–1956; MP (Liberal) Cardiganshire 1923–32, Carmarthenshire
1945–56

There is no man alive who is sufficiently good to rule the life of
the man next door to him.

Cited in R. Douglas, *The History of the Liberal Party 1895–1970* (1971)

William Morris

1834–96; writer, artist and designer

The Liberal Party, a nondescript and flaccid creation of
bourgeois supremacy, a party without principles or definition,
but a thoroughly adequate expression of English middle-class
hypocrisy, cowardice, and short-sightedness, engrossed the
whole of the politically progressive movement in England, and

dragged the working classes along with it, blind as they were to their own interests and the solidarity of labour.

> On politics after the collapse of Chartism, 1885 lecture 'The Signs of Change', cited in M. Morris (ed.), *The Collected Works of William Morris*, Vol. 23 (1915)

Wayne Lyman Morse
1900–74; American writer

The liberal, emphasising the civil and property rights of the individual, insists that the individual must remain so supreme as to make the state his servant.

> *New Republic*, 22 July 1946

Ramsay Muir
1872–1941; Liberal thinker; MP (Liberal) Rochdale 1923–24; President, National Liberal Federation 1933–36

I believe we have thought too much about leaders and organisation and enquired too little: this has been the malady of the Liberal Party for a long time. I put it down to the tremendous personal ascendancy of Gladstone, which was mischievous in the long run.

> To H. A. L. Fisher, February 1923, cited in J. Campbell, 'Liberalism without Liberals', in *The Politics of Reappraisal 1918–39* (1975)

What we [Liberals] ought to aim at is not public ownership but popular ownership.

> 'Government under the Three Party System', Liberal Summer School 1929

The price of liberty is eternal watchfulness, because when men get power into their hands they nearly always abuse it.

> *The Faith of a Liberal* (1933)

Liberalism means generosity of mind, a readiness to recognise and to uphold the just claims of other nations, other classes, and other interests than our own. It stands for persuasion rather than dictation, for discussion rather than force; and it is only on this basis that fear can be banished, and effective cooperation brought about, between the nations of an interdependent world, or the diverse classes and interests of an interdependent society. For, now that we are all 'members one of another' we can only be safe or prosperous if we realise that the well-being of each depends on the well-being of all.

Introduction to *The Liberal Way* (1934)

The electoral system must be reformed. But we must avoid the Continental form of Proportional Representation, which intensifies instead of qualifying the undue power of political parties.

The Liberal Way (1934)

The Liberal social ideal ... is governed by two principles. The first is a belief in the sacredness of individual human personality, a belief that every unnecessary restriction of the expression of personality, and of individual energy, is an evil which will sooner or later bring punishment upon the society which encourages or permits it. The second is a belief that the State, as the mouthpiece of the Community, can alone create the conditions which will make a reasonable life possible, but that these conditions must be such as to permit of and encourage the maximum development of individual powers. The State exists for the sake of the individual, not the individual for the sake of the State.

The Future for Democracy (1939)

By liberty, I mean the secure enjoyment by individuals, and by natural or spontaneous groups of individuals (such as nations, churches, trades unions) of the power to think their own thoughts, and to express and act upon them, using their own gifts in their own way, under the shelter of the law, provided they do not impair the rights of others.

Civilisations and Liberty (1940)

Sheelagh Murnaghan

1924–93; barrister and civil rights activist; MP, Northern Ireland Parliament (Liberal) Queen's University Belfast 1961–69

In Northern Ireland politics, I don't know which is the greatest obstacle: to be a woman, a Catholic or a Liberal. I am all three.

Comment to Jeremy Thorpe, c. 1961, cited in *Mothers of Liberty: Women Who Built British Liberalism* (2012)

Gilbert Murray

1866–1957; Regius Professor of Greek, Oxford University, 1908–36; first chairman of the executive committee of the League of Nations; President of Liberal International 1947–49

No one can be really at peace in his own mind now until he has in some way offered his life to his country.

Letter to J. L. Hammond, 17 November 1915, cited in M. Pugh, *The Making of Modern British Politics 1867–1939* (1982)

To be merely free is not much. To be able to do whatever you want to do does not in itself produce a good life or a fine character. All you can say is that without freedom the real problem of a good life cannot even begin.

World Review, February 1950

A very large part of Liberalism consists in extending goodwill to your opponents, trusting their sincerity, leaving them free, understanding their point of view and eradicating one's own prejudices.

The Meaning of Freedom (1956)

N

Harry Nathan

1889–1963; solicitor; MP (Liberal, Labour), Bethnal Green North East
1929–35, (Labour) Wandsworth Central 1937–40; created Baron Nathan
of Churt, 1940

It has not been that Liberalism has abdicated its task. In election
after election Liberals have preached the cause of the forlorn
and the miserable. Their common aim has been to defend the
oppressed and raise up the beggar, to cleanse our towns from
the hideous leprosy of poverty, to make the state of our villages
a less cruel mockery on the green loveliness with which God has
surrounded them, to make industrial toil more of a service and
less of a servitude.

Liberalism and Some Problems of Today (1929)

New Orbits Group

Liberals are too independent-minded to tolerate caucus rule.

Statement of the Joint Political Committee of the National League of
Young Liberals and the Union of University Liberal Students forming
the New Orbits group, March 1959

There is a tendency for Liberals to glory in their amateurism.

High Time for Radicals (1960)

New Statesman

Leading the Liberal Party must rank as the most thankless job
in British politics. The man who shoulders it gets no money for
his pains. His role at Westminster is little more than a prominent

backbencher. At the same time, in the country at large, he must figure as the Messiah.

20 January 1967

Thomas Pelham-Holles, Duke of Newcastle

1693–1768; became Baron Pelham of Laughton 1712, created Duke of Newcastle-upon-Tyne 1715; Prime Minister 1754–56, 1757–62

I shall not, therefore, think the demands of the people a rule of conduct, nor shall ever fear to incur their resentment in the prosecution of their interest. I shall never flatter their passions to obtain their favour, or gratify their revenge for fear of their contempt.

Cited in D. Englefield, J. Seaton & I. White, *Facts About The British Prime Ministers* (1996)

John Henry Newman

1801–1890; theologian; Cardinal 1879–90

By Liberalism, I mean false liberty of thought, or the exercise of thought upon matters, in which, from the constitution of the human mind, thought cannot be brought to any successful issue and therefore is out of place ... Liberalism is the mistake of supposing that there is a right to private judgement, that is, that there is no existing authority on earth competent to interfere with the liberty of individuals in reasoning and judging for themselves.

Apologia Pro Vita Sua, cited in I. Bradley, *The Optimists* (1980)

Emma Nicholson

b. 1941; MP (Conservative, Liberal Democrat) Devon West & Torridge
1987–97; created Baroness Nicholson of Winterbourne 1997; MEP
(South East) 1999–2009

The Conservative Party has changed so much, while my
principles have not changed at all. I would argue that it is not so
much a case of my leaving the party, but the party leaving me.

On television, discussing her defection from the Conservative Party to
the Liberal Democrats, 29 December 1995

Privacy is a right mistrusted by those in authority in the modern
age.

John Stuart Mill Lecture, 16 November 1998

It's hard to distinguish the difference between the Conservative
Party and the BNP.

The Independent, 10 June 1999

Harold Nicolson

1886–1968; MP (National Labour) Leicester West 1935–45; author,
diarist and politician

Kingsley [Martin] and Aneurin [Bevan] start a hare by saying that
Ll. G. was a finer man than Churchill. Churchill is 'adolescent',
which is suitable in times of emotional strain. Ll. G. is the wise
statesman. I say that Ll. G., if he had not been so gaga, would
have been our Pétain. They agree to this, but still say he is a
great man.

Diary, 29 January 1943

I met Beveridge in the lobby, looking like the witch of Endor.
I said, 'Well, are you enjoying this?' He said, 'I am having
the fun of my life'. 'Upsetting Governments and wrecking
constitutions?' He said, 'My two previous reports led to the fall

of two Ministers. This one may bring down a Government'. He is a vain man.

During the debate on the Beveridge Report, Diary, 18 February 1943

We had a coal debate at which Gwilym Lloyd George made a heavy impressive speech. His old father sat opposite, smiling in affectionate pride. In the lobby afterwards I bumped into the old man. 'Well,' I said, 'what did you think of Gwilym?' 'He lacks my fire', the old man answered. 'You see, Nicolson, he is not a Welshman. He is a Scandinavian. You only have to look at him to see that he is pure Scandinavian. His mother is directly descended from the Vikings.' It amused him saying that, and for an instant the old charm and vigour reappeared, but then once again there fell on his face that mask of extreme and inarticulate old age. He is now a yellow old man with a mane of dead-white hair, and uncertain movements of his feet and hands.

Diary, 23 June 1943

[Violet Bonham Carter] abuses the Government for abandoning all moral principle. Until now she had believed that the Liberal Party were closer to the Socialists than to any other party. Now she doubts it. The Government now only lack ability and courage but also integrity ... She feels closer to the left-wing Tories today. All of which suggests that the Liberal Party are about to create a common anti-communist front.

Diary, 29 October 1947

Simon was a man who wished to be agreeable, but could never inspire confidence in his sincerity.

On the death of Viscount Simon, Diary, 11 January 1954

Friedrich Nietzsche
1844–1900; German philosopher

Freedom is the will to be responsible to ourselves.

Twilight of the Idols (1888)

Liberal institutions straightaway cease from being liberal the
moment they are soundly established.

Twilight of the Idols (1888)

People demand freedom only when they have no power.

The Will to Power (1888)

The surest way to corrupt a youth is to instruct him to hold
in higher esteem those who think alike than those who think
differently.

Attributed

Philip Noel-Baker

1889–1982; MP (Labour) Coventry 1929–31, Derby, later Derby South
1936–70; Secretary of State for Commonwealth Relations 1947–50 and
for Fuel and Power 1950–51

Inherently, he's quite useless.

On Clement Davies, letter to Megan Lloyd George, 20 March 1951

Liberalism is a spent force as a party ... you must work with us.

Letter to Megan Lloyd George, advocating that she join the Labour
Party, 28 October 1951

For Violet, it is the final and devastating end; for Clem D, the
last step but one down the Gadarene slope.

On the result of the 1951 general election, letter to Megan Lloyd
George, 29 October 1951

The Nonconformist

The Liberal Party has striven to follow the fiery pillar of
conscience into this promised land. It has striven to be the party
of moral principle as against that of selfish and corrupt interests,
the party of peace as against that of violence, the party of

popular improvement and reform as against that of resistance to progress, the party of justice as against that of despotic force or social disorder. The backbone of this party has been the religious Protestantism and Puritanism of England for a very good reason, because a party whose object it is to rule men's action by a moral principle in legislation and government derives its force from conscience.

1 January 1880

Kathleen Nott

1905–99; writer and broadcaster

Disapproval of war, disapproval of capitalism, disapproval of Labour: disapproval of God (and since he happened to be a first-class choir bass, mild contempt of vicars); and a Utopian chiliasm based on a belief in Original Virtue, that looked forward to lotus eating rather than general prosperity.

Description of her father's Victorian-style Liberal beliefs on the eve of the First World War, *The Good Want Power: Essays in the Psychological Possibilities of Liberalism* (1977)

Tommy Nudds

Long-time Secretary of the Liberal Central Association

An aristocrat to his fingertips, but a radical of the first water.

On Harcourt Johnstone, cited in R. Douglas, *The History of the Liberal Party 1895–1970* (1971)

O

Barack Obama
b. 1961; American President 2009–

In the end, that's what this election is about. Do we participate in a politics of cynicism or a politics of hope? I'm not talking about blind optimism here … No, I'm talking about something more substantial. It's the hope of slaves sitting around a fire singing freedom songs; the hope of immigrants setting out for distant shores; the hope of a young naval lieutenant bravely patrolling the Mekong Delta; the hope of a millworker's son who dares to defy the odds; the hope of a skinny kid with a funny name who believes that America has a place for him, too. The audacity of hope!

    Keynote address, Democratic National Convention, 27 July 2004

Hope is the bedrock of this nation. The belief that our destiny will not be written for us, but by us, by all those men and women who are not content to settle for the world as it is, who have the courage to remake the world as it should be.

    Victory speech, Iowa caucus, 3 January 2008

This is our moment. This is our time, to put our people back to work and open doors of opportunity for our kids; to restore prosperity and promote the cause of peace; to reclaim the American dream and reaffirm that fundamental truth, that, out of many, we are one; that while we breathe, we hope. And where we are met with cynicism and doubts and those who tell us that we can't, we will respond with that timeless creed that sums up the spirit of a people: yes, we can.

    Victory speech upon election as 44th US President, Grant Park, Chicago, 4 November 2008

Each nation gives life to democracy in its own way and in line with its own traditions. But history offers a clear verdict: governments that respect the will of their own people, that govern by consent, and not coercion, are more prosperous, they are more stable, and more successful than governments that do not.

Address to Ghanaian Parliament, Accra, 11 July 2009

Nor is the question before us whether the market is a force for good or ill. Its power to generate wealth and expand freedom is unmatched, but this crisis has reminded us that without a watchful eye, the market can spin out of control – and that a nation cannot prosper long when it favors only the prosperous. The success of our economy has always depended not just on the size of our gross domestic product, but on the reach of our prosperity; on our ability to extend opportunity to every willing heart – not out of charity, but because it is the surest route to our common good.

First inaugural address, Washington DC, 20 January 2009

We, the people, declare today that the most evident of truths – that all of us are created equal – is the star that guides us still; just as it guided our forebears through Seneca Falls and Selma and Stonewall; just as it guided all those men and women, sung and unsung, who left footprints along this great Mall, to hear a preacher say that we cannot walk alone; to hear a King proclaim that our individual freedom is inextricably bound to the freedom of every soul on Earth.

Second inaugural address, Washington DC, 21 January 2013

The Observer

They would become a political society, devoted to finding, working out and promoting certain ideas, and seeking to get these adopted, either in full by one of the other parties, or in part by both.

> Suggesting a role for the Liberal Party following the 1951 general election, cited in M. Baines, 'Survival of the British Liberal Party 1932–59', D.Phil, Oxford University, 1989

José Ortega y Gasset
1883–1955; Spanish philosopher

Liberalism is the supreme form of generosity; it is the right which the majority conceded to minorities and hence it is the noblest cry that has ever resounded on this planet.

> Attributed

David Owen
b. 1938; MP (Labour) Plymouth Sutton 1966–74, (Labour, SDP) Plymouth Devonport 1974–92; Foreign Secretary 1977–79; leader of the SDP 1983–87; created Baron Owen of Plymouth 1992

We will not be tempted by the siren voices from outside, from those who have given up the fight from within.

> On the possibility of leaving the Labour Party to form or join a centre party, 1980, cited in D. Healey, *The Time of My Life* (1989)

We are fed up with fudging and mudging, with mush and slush.

> At the Labour Party conference, Blackpool, 2 October 1980

We are going to have a Socialist Party, a genuine SDP seen to be on the left, with strong links with the trade unions.

> At the Campaign for Labour Victory conference, 25 October 1980

If you want a manifesto, go and join one of the other parties.

> When asked what the SDP's manifesto contained on the day of the party's launch, 26 March 1981

To those in the Social Democratic Party: we have retained our individual identity; we have established a Social Democratic tradition; we have laid down roots for the future and this tree will blossom and grow until eventually we become with or without Liberal partners the Government of this country.

In Plymouth on election night, 9 June 1983, cited in *The Social Democrat*, 24 June 1983

To create and defend an open, classless and more equal society.

Pledge to the party on succeeding Roy Jenkins as leader of the SDP, *The Social Democrat*, 24 June 1983

From the beginning, I knew it would have been better without involving Roy, but Bill and Shirley were vacillating ... in the beginning, it was truly a Gang of Three, and we should have kept it that way.

1984, cited in P. Lee Sykes, *Losing from the Inside: The Cost of Conflict in the British SDP* (1990)

I do not believe the Dimbleby Lecture has any major significance in the creation of the SDP ... I found the Dimbleby Lecture an impediment for concentrating people's minds on the need to try and fight genuinely from within.

1984, cited in P. Lee Sykes, *Losing from the Inside: The Cost of Conflict in the British SDP* (1990)

I was against going to bed with the Liberals from the beginning. We should have run against them in the early by-elections and beat them into the ground. Then we would have had more clout in the negotiations.

1984, cited in P. Lee Sykes, *Losing from the Inside: The Cost of Conflict in the British SDP* (1990)

Conviction politics must not become a monopoly of Mrs Thatcher. The SDP was founded on convictions, better than the convictions of Mrs Thatcher – and we should not be ashamed of them or run away from them.

At the Council for Social Democracy, concerning defence policy and the nuclear deterrent, 17 May 1986

A far more potent libel for me than being accused of having it off with someone.

On being accused by Mrs Thatcher of being vague on nuclear weapons, 21 May 1987

Whether the Alliance is in government on its own or with others, we will ensure a national coalition which will unite this nation.

Launching the Alliance campaign for the 1987 general election with David Steel, *The Social Democrat*, 15 June 1987

Jumping out of the frying pan into the cotton wool.

Assessing the possibility of joining the Liberal Party in 1981 rather than forming the SDP, *Time to Declare* (1991)

with Bill Rodgers and Shirley Williams

We will not support a Centre Party for it would lack roots and a coherent philosophy. But if the Labour Party abandons its democratic and internationalist principles, the argument may grow for a new democratic socialist party to establish itself as a party of conscience and reform.

Open letter to Labour Party members, *The Guardian*, 1 August 1980

with David Steel

The Alliance represents the coming together of the two major reforming traditions in British politics. Our Alliance is a synthesis of our beliefs in individual freedom, pluralism and diversity with the values of social reform and justice.

The Time Has Come (1987)

Frank Owen

1905–79; MP (Liberal) Hereford 1929–31; journalist

Guilty Men

    Title of influential pamphlet condemning appeasement and its
proponents, co-authored by Owen, M. Foot and P. Howard, 1940

In 1929 the wise, far-seeing electors of my native Hereford
sent me to Westminster and, two years later, in 1931, the lousy
bastards kicked me out.

    Cited in D. Brack et al. (eds), *Dictionary of Liberal Biography* (1998)

Oxford Guardian

Greta Garbo is about to join the Liberal Party. Doubtless to
satisfy the desire to be alone.

    October 1937

P

Thomas Paine
1737–1809; radical writer

Government, even in its best state, is but a necessary evil; in its
worst state, an intolerable one. Government, like dress, is the
badge of lost innocence; the palaces of kings are built upon
the ruins of the bowers of paradise.

    Common Sense (1776)

A long habit of not thinking a thing wrong gives it a superficial
appearance of being right, and raises at first a formidable outcry
in defence of custom.

    Common Sense (1776)

One of the strongest natural proofs of the folly of hereditary
right in kinds, is that nature disapproves it, otherwise she would
not so frequently turn it into ridicule, by giving mankind an ass
for a lion.

    Common Sense (1776)

Freedom hath been hunted round the globe. Asia and Africa
have long expelled her. Europe regards her like a stranger,
and England hath given her warning to depart. O! receive the
fugitive, and prepare in time an asylum for mankind.

    On America, *Common Sense* (1776)

We have it in our power to begin the world over again.

    Common Sense (1776)

As to religion, I hold it to be the indispensable duty of
government to protect all conscientious professors thereof,

and I know of no other business which government hath to do therewith.

Common Sense (1776)

Those who expect to reap the blessings of freedom must, like men, undergo the fatigue of supporting it.

The American Crisis (1776–83)

I am a farmer of thoughts, and all the crops I raise I give away.

Letter to Henry Laurens, 1778

A total reformation is wanted in England. She wants an expanded mind – a heart which embraces the universe. Instead of shutting herself up in an island, and quarrelling with the world, she would derive more lasting happiness, and acquire more real riches, by generously mixing with it, and bravely saying, I am the enemy of none.

Letter to the Abbé Raynal (1782)

The idea of hereditary legislators is as inconsistent as that of hereditary judges, as hereditary juries; and as absurd as an hereditary mathematician or an hereditary wise man; as absurd as an hereditary Poet Laureate.

Cited in *Modernising Parliament, Reforming the House of Lords*, Cm 4183 (1999), from *The Rights Of Man* (1791)

[In France] all that class of equivocal generation, which in some countries is called aristocracy, and in others nobility, is done away, and the peer is exalted as MAN.

The Rights of Man (1791)

Persecution is not an original feature of any religion; but it is always the strongly marked feature of all law-religions, or religions established by law.

The Rights of Man (1791)

What were formerly called revolutions were little more than a change of persons ... what we now see in the world, from the revolutions of America and France, is a renovation of the natural order of things.

The Rights of Man (1791)

All hereditary government is in its nature tyranny ... to inherit a government, is to inherit the people, as if they were flocks and herds.

The Rights of Man, Part 2 (1792)

I compare it to something kept behind a curtain, about which there is a great deal of bustle and fuss, and a wonderful air of seeming solemnity; but when, by any accident, the curtain happens to be open, and the company see what it is, they burst into laughter.

On monarchy, *The Rights of Man*, Part 2 (1792)

When in countries that are called civilised, we see age going to the workhouse and youth to the gallows, something must be wrong in the system of government.

The Rights of Man, Part 2 (1792)

I do not believe that any two men, on what are called doctrinal points, think alike who think at all. It is only those who have not thought that appear to agree.

The Rights of Man, Part 2 (1792)

My country is the world, and my religion is to do good.

The Rights of Man, Part 2 (1792)

As he rose like a rocket, he fell like a stick.

On Edmund Burke losing a parliamentary debate on the French Revolution to Charles James Fox, *Letter to the Addressers on the Late Proclamation* (1795)

He that would make his own liberty secure must guard against even his enemy from oppression; for if he violates this duty he establishes a precedent that will reach himself.

Dissertation on First Principles of Government (1795)

To elect, and to reject, is the prerogative of the free people.

National Intelligencer, 29 November 1802

When moral principles, rather than persons, are candidates for power, to vote is to perform a moral duty, and not to vote is to neglect a duty.

Trenton True-American, April 1803

A share in two revolutions is living to some purpose.

Cited in E. Foner, *Tom Paine and Revolutionary America* (1976)

Where Liberty is not, there is my country.

Cited in J. Keane, *Tom Paine* (1995)

Henry John Temple, Viscount Palmerston

1784–1865; MP (Tory) Newport, Isle of Wight 1807–11, (Tory, Whig) Cambridge University 1811–31, (Whig) Bletchingley 1831–32, Hampshire South 1832–35, (Whig, Liberal) Tiverton 1835–65; Foreign Secretary 1830–34, 1835–41, 1846–51, Home Secretary 1852–55, Prime Minister 1855–58, 1859–65

The interests of civilisation, the interests of commerce, and the interests of political independence are all the interests of England, and all have been signally promoted by the emancipation of Greece.

In the House of Commons, 8 August 1832

Ineffective protest is better than tacit acquiescence in wrong.

Referring to the occupation of Frankfurt, May 1834, cited in D. Southgate, *The Most English Minister* (1966)

A wise government in its home policy considers the reasonable wants of the people; in its foreign policy it is prepared to resist the unjust demands and the unreasonable views of foreign powers. The present government inverts this method; it is all resistance at home, all concession abroad.

In the House of Commons, 28 July 1843

For my part, I believe that if any nation should be found not to be fit for constitutional government, the best way to fit such a nation for it would be to give it to them.

On the revolution in Greece, in the House of Commons, 14 March 1844, but also quoted in correspondence from around the same time in variations

We have no eternal allies and we have no perpetual enemies. Our interests are eternal and perpetual and those interests it is our duty to follow.

In the House of Commons, 1 March 1848

Large republics seem to be essentially and inherently aggressive.

Letter to Lord Normanby, 5 March 1848

Sir, my answer is, opinions are stronger than armies. Opinions, if they are founded in truth and justice, will in the end prevail against the bayonets of infantry, the fire of artillery, and the charges of cavalry.

On the attempt by Hungary to secure independence from Austria, in the House of Commons, 21 July 1849

I therefore fearlessly challenge the verdict which this House, as representing a political, a commercial, a constitutional country, is to give on the question now brought before it; whether the principles on which the foreign policy of Her Majesty's Government has been conducted, and the sense of duty which has led us to think ourselves bound to afford protection to our fellow subjects abroad, are proper and fitting guides for those who are charged with the Government of England; and whether, as the Roman, in days of old, held himself free from indignity, when he could say *Civis Romanus sum*; so also a British subject, in whatever land he may be, shall feel confident that the watchful eye and the strong arm of England, will protect him against injustice and wrong.

In the House of Commons, after he ordered Greek ports blockaded when the Greek government refused compensation to the Portuguese Jewish trader David (Don) Pacifico (1784–1854), who had been born a British subject at Gibraltar – the justification for gunboat diplomacy, 25 June 1850

It has always been the fate of advocates of temperate reform and of constitutional improvement to be run at as the fomenters of revolution. It is the easiest mode of putting them down; it is the received formula ... Now there are revolutionists of two kinds in the world. In the first place there are those violent, hot-headed and unthinking men who fly to arms, who overthrow established Government, and who recklessly, without regard to consequences, and without measuring difficulties or comparing strength, deluge their country with blood and draw down the greatest calamities on their fellow-countrymen ... But there are revolutionists of another kind; blind-minded men, who, animated by antiquated prejudices, and daunted by ignorant apprehensions, dam up the current of human improvement until the irresistible pressure of accumulated discontent breaks down the opposing barriers, and overthrows and levels to the earth those very institutions which a timely application of renovating means would have rendered strong and lasting. Such revolutionists as these are the men who call us revolutionists.

In the House of Commons, 25 June 1850

I believe weakness and irresolution are, on the whole, the worst faults that statesmen can have. A man of energy may make a wrong decision, but, like a strong horse that carries you rashly into a quagmire, he brings you by his sturdiness out on the other side.

December 1850, cited in D. Englefield, J. Seaton & I. White, *Facts About the British Prime Ministers* (1996)

Taking a leap in the dark.

On Lord John Russell's proposals for parliamentary reform, 1854

England is one of the greatest powers in the world, no event
or series of events bearing on the balance of power, or on
probabilities of peace or war can be matters of indifference to
her, and her right to have and to express opinions on matters
thus bearing on her interests is unquestionable.

Letter to Queen Victoria, 23 August 1859

Let us try to improve all these countries by the general
influence of our commerce, but let us all abstain from a crusade
of conquest which would call upon us the condemnation of all
the other civilised nations ... We do not want Egypt any more
than any rational man with an estate in the north of England and
a residence in the south, would have wished to possess the inns
on the north road. All he could want would have been that the
inns should be well kept, always accessible, and furnishing him,
when he came, with mutton chops and post horses.

Letter to Earl Cowley, 25 November 1859, cited in E. Ashley, *The Life
of Henry John Temple, Viscount Palmerston, 1846–65* (1876)

What is merit? The opinion one man entertains of another.

Cited in T. Carlyle, *Shooting Niagara: and After?* (1867)

Yes we have. Humbug.

On being told that English has no word equivalent to *sensibilité*, cited
in E. Latham, *Famous Sayings and their Authors* (1904)

The function of a government is to calm, rather than to excite
agitation.

Cited in P. Guedalla, *Gladstone and Palmerston* (1928)

Lord Palmerston, with characteristic levity had once said that
only three men in Europe had ever understood [the Schleswig-
Holstein question], and of these the Prince Consort was dead, a

Danish statesman (unnamed) was in an asylum, and he himself
had forgotten it.

Cited in R. W. Seton-Watson, *Britain in Europe 1789–1914* (1937)

Die, my dear doctor? That's the last thing I shall do.

Last words, apparently attributed in error, see D. Englefield, J. Seaton
& I. White, *Facts about the British Prime Ministers* (1996)

John Pardoe

b. 1934; MP (Liberal) North Cornwall 1966–79

Everything was arranged down to the size of our wellingtons.
Only no one had given any thought as to what we were
supposed to be saying.

On the Liberals' October 1974 general election campaign, cited in
D. Steel, *Against Goliath* (1989)

[The Social Democrats] appear to have been taught about
Liberalism by the same people who teach my son A Level
politics and who manage to convey a view of Liberalism as if
Keynes and Beveridge had never existed.

The Guardian, 2 February 1981

In 1983 the two-leader thing was a problem ... So, you see, we
had to have the Ettrick Bridge meeting ... At the same time,
we thought the problem was simply Jenkins ... We thought we
dealt with the central problem when we got rid of Roy. Didn't
work. The problem was not Roy. It was dual leadership itself.

1987, cited in P. Lee Sykes, *Losing from the Inside: The Cost of Conflict in
the British SDP* (1990)

By the end I was forced to admit to myself that I did not much want to be governed by either [David Steel or David Owen] and the thought of being governed by both was too appalling for words.

On his experience as Chair of the Alliance Planning Group in the 1987 general election, cited in R. Douglas, *Liberals: The History of the Liberal and Liberal Democrat Parties* (2005)

Dorothy Parker

1893–1967; American poet and writer

The affair between Margot Asquith and Margot Asquith will live as one of the prettiest love stories in all literature.

Cited in R. E. Drennan, *Wit's End* (1968)

Matthew Parris

b. 1949; MP (Conservative) Derbyshire West 1979–86; journalist and author

To witness the destruction of a human being at a by-election is the closest modern Britons come to the joys of a public execution ... watching fox cubs having their tails pulled off is tame by comparison. But with Liberal Democrats, as with foxes, you must remember that they'd do the same to you.

After the Ribble Valley by-election, *The Times*, March 1991

C. Hubert Parry

1848–1918; composer

The violence with which the family ... talk about Gladstone is perfectly astounding. As Eddie said, it is quite indecent. According to their views, everything he does is for the sake of popularity ... Their way of talking is so extraordinary that I can only listen with gaping mouth and answer not a word, for I simply don't know what to say to such a torrent of invective. If one attempts to say a word in his defence one is gaped at as if one were a lunatic.

Diary, 18 April 1878, cited in J. Dibble, *C. Hubert H. Parry: His Life and Music* (1992)

Alan Paton

1903–88; South African writer

To give up the task of reforming society is to give up one's responsibility as a free man.

Saturday Review, 9 September 1967

Chris Patten

b. 1944; MP (Conservative) Bath 1979–92; Secretary of State for the Environment 1989–90, Chancellor of the Duchy of Lancaster 1990–92; Governor of Hong Kong 1992–97; European Commissioner 1999–2004; created Baron Patten of Barnes, 2005

Attacking the Liberals is a difficult business, involving all the hazards of wrestling with a greasy pig at a fair and then insulting the vicar.

Cited in Bruce Anderson, *The Independent*, 19 April 2010

Alfred Pease

1857–1939; MP (Liberal) York 1885–92, Cleveland 1892–1902

The idea that the State can take from one class and give to other classes and take the place of individual enterprise is a very corrupting one.

Letter to Herbert Samuel, 19 August 1908, cited in M. Pugh, *The Making of Modern British Politics 1867–1939* (1982)

Henry Pelham

1694–1754; MP (Whig) Seaford 1717–22, Sussex 1722–54; Prime
Minister 1743–54

A great unwieldy body which requires great art and some
cordials to keep it together.

On the House of Commons, cited in R. Ellis & G. Treasure, *Britain's
Prime Ministers* (2005)

David Penhaligon

1944–86; MP (Liberal) Truro 1974–86

Turkeys don't vote for Christmas.

To the Liberal Party's special assembly, urging Liberal Party members
not to vote against the Lib–Lab Pact, January 1978

If you have something to say, stick it on a piece of paper, and
stuff it through a letter box.

On how to communicate a message to the electorate, at the Liberal
assembly, 1979

I have always said that I only got elected because I was too naïve
to realise it was impossible.

On BBC Radio, *Desert Island Discs*, broadcast January 1987

There is only one hope for regions such as mine – namely, quick
and powerful decentralisation of government.

Cited in A. Penhaligon, *Penhaligon* (1989)

Hubert Phillips

1891–1964; author, journalist and broadcaster; Liberal candidate

Which is the Liberal army? Is it those who are at any one
moment marching under the Liberal banner, divergent, perhaps,
as may be the objectives that they have in view? Is it those who

seek that ultimate goal to which the traditions or the philosophy of Liberalism inevitably point? Or is it those who, whether under the Liberal banner or some other, or under no banner at all, are marching in step with Liberal ideals and to the rhythm of Liberal drums? Liberalism has always been something bigger than the Liberal Party. It has not always been under Liberal leadership that the citadels of reaction and privilege have been overthrown, but it is Liberals who have planned the advance and who have heartened to the attack the conscript armies of a rival faith.

The Liberal Outlook (1929)

Wendell Phillips
1811–84; American orator and abolitionist

Whether in chains or in laurels, liberty knows nothing but victories.

1 November 1859

William Pitt, the elder, Earl of Chatham
1708–78; MP (Whig) Old Sarum 1735–47, Seaford 1747–54, Aldborough 1754–56, Okehampton 1756–57, Bath 1757–66; created Viscount Pitt of Burton Pynsent and Earl of Chatham 1766; Prime Minister 1766–68

The poorest man may in his cottage bid defiance to all the forces of the Crown. It may be frail – its roof may shake – the wind may blow through it – the storm may enter – the rain may enter – but the king of England cannot enter!

Speech, 1763

Unlimited power is apt to corrupt the minds of those who possess it.

In the House of Lords, 9 January 1770

There is something behind the throne greater than the King himself.

In the House of Lords, 2 March 1770

If I were an American, as I am an Englishman, while a foreign troop was landed in my country, I never would lay down my arms – never – never – never – never!

In the House of Lords, 18 November 1777, cited in D. Englefield,
J. Seaton & I. White, *Facts About The British Prime Ministers* (1996)

Our watchword is security.

Attributed

Francis Place

1771–1854; radical reformer

To stop the Duke, go for gold.

Advocating a run on the banks in order to prevent the possibility of the Duke of Wellington becoming Prime Minister again, May 1832

Poor Man's Guardian

The Whigs have too much to lose to desire real reform. The only difference between them and the Tories is this – the Whigs would give the shadow to preserve the substance; the Tories would not give the shadow, because, stupid as they are, they know, that the principle of Reform once admitted, the millions will not stop at shadows, but proceed onwards to substance ... [The Whigs] know the old system could not last, and desiring to establish another as like it as possible, and also to keep their places, they framed the BILL, in the hope of drawing to the feudal aristocrats and yeomanry or counties a large reinforcement of the middle class.

On the Reform Bill, 27 October 1832

Karl Popper
1902–94; philosopher

What we need and what we want is to moralise politics and not to politicise morals.

The Open Society and its Enemies (1945)

I believe that the injustice and inhumanity of the unrestrained 'capitalist system' described by Marx cannot be questioned ... We must construct social institutions, enforced by the power of the state, for the protection of the economically weak from the economically strong.

The Open Society and its Enemies (1945)

Only freedom can make security secure.

The Open Society and its Enemies (1945)

Enoch Powell
1912–98; MP (Conservative) Wolverhampton South West 1950–74, (Ulster Unionist) Down South 1974–87; Minister for Health 1960–63

All political lives, unless they are cut off in midstream at a happy juncture, end in failure, because that is the nature of politics and of human affairs. The career of Joseph Chamberlain was not an exception.

Joseph Chamberlain (1977)

John O'Connor Power
1846–1919; Irish lawyer and politician

The mules of politics: without pride of ancestry, or hope of posterity.

On the Liberal Unionists, cited in H. H. Asquith, *Memories and Reflections* (1928)

Pravda

Would I be right if I told my readers that this marks the start of American-style politics in Britain?

Question asked by *Pravda* journalist at the press conference launching the SDP, 26 March 1981

John Prescott

b. 1938; MP (Labour) Hull East 1970–2010; deputy Prime Minister and Secretary of State for the Environment, Transport and the Regions 1997–2001, First Secretary of State 2001–07; created Baron Prescott of Kingston upon Hull 2010

I am not a fan of Lib–Lab deals … It is fundamentally clear that Labour's manifesto is the one that was endorsed by the electorate and those with minority votes should take that into account.

Following the results of the elections for the Scottish Parliament and Welsh Assembly, *The Independent*, 8 May 1999

Richard Price

1723–91; Nonconformist minister

Now, methinks, I see the ardour of liberty catching and spreading; a general amendment beginning in human affairs; the dominion of kings changed for the dominion of laws and the dominion of priests giving way to the dominion of reason and conscience.

A Discourse on the Love of our Country (1790)

Private Eye

What does the SDP stand for? Liberal seats.

Cartoon caption, 1982

Punch

You speak, Mr Asquith, the suffragist said,
Of the will of the People wholesale;
But has the idea ever entered your head
That the People are not wholly male?

1910 cartoon, cited in M. G. Fawcett, *The Women's Victory and After*
(1920)

Francis Pym

1922–2008; MP (Conservative) Cambridgeshire, later Cambridgeshire
South East 1961–87; Foreign Secretary 1982–83; created Baron Pym of
Sandy 1987

Stale claret in new bottles – it is a confidence trick not to be
mistaken for the elixir of life.

On the SDP, cited in G. Knight, *Honourable Insults* (1990)

John Pym

1584–1643; MP Calne 1614–22, 1624–25, Brymore 1622–24, Tavistock
1629 and 1640–43; one of the five MPs whom Charles I tried to arrest in
the House of Commons, 1641

To have granted liberties, and not to have liberties in truth and
realities, is but to mock the kingdom.

After the battle of Edgehill, at the Guildhall, drawing attention to the
illusory nature of Charles I's promises, in Pym's entry to the *Dictionary
of National Biography*

R

Radical Reform Group

We need greater responsibility – and humility – towards
the material resources of the world. A characteristic of the
mentality of a free economy is profligacy with resources …
Planning of the use of the resources of the world, for the benefit
of all men, ignoring the motive of personal profit, is necessary if
future generations are not to pay the cost.

*Radical Aims – Social Reform without Socialism, A Statement of Policy by the
Radical Reform Group* (1953)

Let Labour abandon nationalism and class consciousness, and
what is left to distinguish it from the cautiously reformist wing
of the Conservative Party?

Radical Challenge (1960)

A movement of revolt and protest against the establishment.

A definition of radicalism, *Radical Challenge* (1960)

Thomas Rainsborough
c. 1610–48; Civil War soldier and MP Droitwich 1646–48

For really I think that the poorest he that is in England hath a life
to live, as the greatest he; and therefore truly, I think it is clear
that every man that is to live under a government ought first by
his own consent to put himself under that government.

Army Debates at Putney, 29 October 1647

William Rathbone

1819–1902; MP (Liberal) Liverpool 1868–80, Caernarvonshire 1880–85, Caernarvonshire North 1885–95

There was a large amount of treating going on, a great number of small bribes in the form of payments of 5/- as a day's wage to everyone who chose to claim it by voting Conservative; the Liberal side were absolutely pure, not a penny or a glass of beer being given.

> Recollection of his first election campaign, cited in E. F. Rathbone,
> *William Rathbone: A Memoir* (1905)

Andrew Rawnsley

b. 1962; journalist

He has been wounded by polls suggesting that voters still preferred Kennedy drunk to Campbell sober.

> On Menzies Campbell's leadership, *The Observer*, 17 September 2006

John Mead Ray

Minister to the congregation of Protestant Dissenters, Sudbury, Suffolk 1773–1837

In the following address, I design:
I To maintain, and defend the right of private judgement, and of a free enquiry after truth.
II Shew that it is the duty of every one to follow his convictions, and steadily adhere to those principles which appear to him to be just, and scriptural.
- And consequently
III That no one ought to suffer any disgrace or punishment for the exercise of that liberty, which the gospel not only allows, but requires us to maintain.

> Sermon on the Repeal of the Corporation and Test Acts, at
> Stowmarket, 1 December 1789

Russell Rea

1846–1916; MP (Liberal) Gloucester 1900–10, South Shields 1910–16

The questions the Social Reformer would ask are not one, but two. Has it tended to equality? Then it is *so far* good. And, more important still, has this surrender of liberty secured a larger liberty for the individual? Has it given him a better and a freer life? *This is the test*.

On the New Liberalism, *Social Reform versus Socialism* (1912)

David Rendel

b. 1949; MP (Liberal Democrat) Newbury 1993–2005

I was not especially good at anything, and politics seems to be just about the only career in which it is important to be some good at everything but not particularly good at anything.

Cited in D. Brack et al. (eds), *Dictionary of Liberal Biography* (1998)

David Ricardo

1771–1823; economist

All taxes are bad and, except to avoid a deficit, I will vote for none, considering that a surplus would be an insuperable temptation to increase expenditure.

1822, cited in D. Brack et al. (eds), *Dictionary of Liberal Biography* (1998)

Ivor Richard

b. 1932; MP (Labour) Barons Court 1964–74; European Commissioner 1981–84; created Baron Richard of Ammanford 1990; leader of the House of Lords and Lord Privy Seal 1997–98

He was the man who gave politics a good name.

About Jo Grimond, on his death, 1993

Jeff Roberts
Liberal Councillor in Hackney

A trick to get elected without doing any work.
> On the proposed Liberal–SDP Alliance, at the Liberal assembly,
> Llandudno, 1981

Roger Roberts
b. 1935; President, Welsh Liberal Party 1980–83, Welsh Liberal
Democrats 1990–93; created Baron Roberts of Llandudno 2004

It is far better to change your name and keep your principles
than to keep your name and abandon your principles.
> Attacking the Labour Party, at the Liberal Democrat conference,
> September 1990

Tommy Rhys Roberts
1910–75; popular entertainer

Lloyd George knew my father,
My father knew Lloyd George.
> Comic song, to tune of *Onward Christian Soldiers*

J. M. Robertson
1856–1933; writer; MP (Liberal) Tyneside 1906–18

'Wherever feasible', remember – the whole secret of practical
Liberalism is in that modifying clause. The broad, practical
differentiation between Liberalism in this sense and Socialism in
anything like a precise sense lies in that principle of feasibility.
> *The Mission of Liberalism* (1908)

The permanent vindication of Liberalism as against
Conservatism must lie in the profession of general standards and

ideals which are founded on an inclusive
as against an exclusive bias, or rooted in
a general sympathy and not in antipathy, in aspiration and not in
ill-will. Liberal movement or impulse starts in a simple desire
for 'better life' for those who lack it.

The Meaning of Liberalism (1912)

Laissez-faire is not done with as a principle of rational limitation
of state interference, but it is quite done with as a pretext for
leaving uncured deadly social evils which admit of curative
treatment by state action.

The Meaning of Liberalism (1912)

Lawrence Robson

1904–82; accountant and politician; President, Liberal Party, 1953–54

We Liberals accept the fact that men are both social and
individualistic beings, whose spiritual health is more important
than their material well-being. We perceive that without a
spiritual or moral approach to the problems of the day we
cannot hope to relieve the tensions which divide the world.
Re-armament can only be a sterile and highly dangerous
undertaking unless the time which it buys is used by statesmen
to create the institutions without which we shall continue to live
in the shadow of a third world war.

'Fear or Faith – the choice which confronts the world', as President of
the Liberal Party, 1953

Duc de la Rochefoucauld

1613–80; French soldier, courtier and man of letters

For society to run smoothly it is necessary for every man to
preserve his liberty.

Maximes (1665)

Charles Watson-Wentworth, Marquess of Rockingham

1730–1782; became 2nd Marquess Rockingham 1750; Prime Minister
1765–66, 1782

The King can have no interests, no dignity, no views whatever,
distinct from those of his people.

In the House of Lords, 9 March 1778

Bill Rodgers

b. 1928; MP (Labour, SDP) Stockton-on-Tees 1962–83; created Lord
Rodgers of Quarry Bank 1992; leader of the Liberal Democrat peers
1997–2001

I am full of admiration for the way Liberals got onto the
doorsteps to wake up councils dominated and depressed by
long-term single party rule. They challenged the conventional
civic wisdom and put service before the size of the mayoral car.

The Social Democrat, No. 1, May 1982

Like others, I was much influenced by R. H. Tawney's classic
Religion and the Rise of Capitalism and I am amused by the
controversy that surrounds the adoption of his name for the
SDP's answer to the Fabian Society. I remember an earlier
controversy, over twenty years ago, when Tawney's endorsement
of the campaign in support of Hugh Gaitskell brought forth a
disbelieving and choleric snort from the Labour left.

The Social Democrat, No. 1, May 1982

Politicians have failed largely because they have been prisoners –
sometimes willing prisoners – of a political divide which is itself
based on outworn assumptions.

The Politics of Change (1982)

Fourth Among Equals

Title of autobiography (2000)

Marie-Jeanne Roland

1754–93; French revolutionary

Oh liberty, what crimes are committed in your name!

Before her execution, 8 November 1793

Eleanor Roosevelt

1884–1962; American human rights campaigner; wife of Franklin
Roosevelt

Where, after all, do universal human rights begin? In small
places, close to home – so close and so small that they cannot
be seen on any maps of the world. Yet they *are* the world of
individual persons; the neighbourhood he lives in; the school
or college he attends; the factory, farm or office where he
works. Such are the places where every man, woman or child
seeks equal justice; equal opportunity, equal dignity without
discrimination. Unless those rights have meaning there, they
have little meaning anywhere. Without concerned citizen action
to uphold them close to home, we shall look in vain for progress
in the larger world.

At the United Nations, New York, 27 March 1958, cited in

E. C. Phillips, *You in Human Rights* (1967)

Franklin Roosevelt

1882–1945; American President 1933–45

These unhappy times call for the building of plans that ... build
from the bottom up and not from the top down, that put
their faith in the forgotten man at the bottom of the economic
pyramid.

Radio address, 7 April 1932

The country needs and, unless I mistake its temper, the country
demands bold, persistent experimentation. It is common sense

to take a method and try it. If it fails, admit it frankly and try another. But above all, try something.

At Oglethorpe University, Atlanta, 22 May 1932

I pledge you, I pledge myself, to a new deal for the American people.

Convention speech, Chicago, 2 July 1932

Let me assert my firm belief that the only thing we have to fear is fear itself.

Inaugural address to Congress, 4 March 1933

In the field of world policy I would dedicate this Nation to the policy of the good neighbour.

Inaugural address to Congress, 4 March 1933

In the truest sense, freedom cannot be bestowed, it must be achieved.

Greeting to the 74th anniversary of the Emancipation Proclamation, 16 September 1936

The only sure bulwark of continuing liberty is a government strong enough to protect the interests of the people, and a people strong enough and well enough informed to maintain its sovereign control over its government.

Radio address, 14 April 1938

No democracy can long survive which does not accept as fundamental to its very existence the recognition of the rights of minorities.

Letter to the National Association for the Advancement of Colored People, 25 June 1938

A radical is a man with both feet planted firmly in the air. A reactionary is a somnambulist walking backwards. A conservative is a man with two perfectly good legs who, however, has never learned how to walk forward. A liberal is a man who uses his legs and his hands at the behest – at the command – of his head.

Radio address, 26 October 1939

We look forward to a world founded upon four essential human freedoms. The first is freedom of speech and expression – everywhere in the world. The second is freedom of every person to worship God in his own way – everywhere in the world. The third is the freedom from want … everywhere in the world. The fourth is freedom from fear … everywhere in the world.

Message to Congress, 6 January 1941

We, too, born to freedom, and believing in freedom, are willing to fight to maintain freedom. We, and all others who believe as deeply as we do, would rather die on our feet than live on our knees.

On being awarded the degree of Doctor of Civil Law from Oxford, 19 June 1941

Books cannot be killed by fire. People die, but books never die. No man and no force can abolish memory … in this war, we know, books are weapons. And it is part of your dedication always to make them weapons for man's freedom.

Message to the Booksellers of America, 6 May 1942

True individual freedom cannot exist without economic security and independence. People who are hungry and out of a job are the stuff of which dictatorships are made.

Message to Congress, 11 January 1944

You sometimes find something good in the lunatic fringe. In fact, we have got as part of our social and economic government today a whole lot of things which in my boyhood were considered lunatic fringe, and yet they are now part of everyday life.

Press conference, 30 May 1944

Archibald Philip Primrose, Earl of Rosebery

1847–1929; Foreign Secretary 1886, 1892–94, leader of the Liberal Party
1894–96, Prime Minister 1894–95

There is no need for any nation, however great, leaving the
Empire, because the Empire is a Commonwealth of Nations.

At Adelaide, Australia, 18 January 1884

Before Irish Home Rule is conceded by the Imperial Parliament,
England as the predominant member of the three kingdoms will
have to be convinced of its justice and equity.

In the House of Lords, 11 March 1894

I have never known the sweets of place with power; but of place
without power, of place with the minimum of power – that is a
purgatory, and if not a purgatory it is a hell.

Shortly after the defeat of his government, *The Spectator*, 6 July 1895

The people will come back to us. Liberalism has always been
founded among the masses not on aspiration but on discontent.
The masses are, comparatively speaking, contented just now.
May they remain so, even if Liberalism should suffer thereby.

Letter to Canon Scott Holland, 21 August 1895, following the Liberal
Party's defeat in the general election

I count too as clear gain the defeat of Socialism of the rabid kind
and the separation of Socialism from Liberalism. But it is always
possible that that may happen which has happened in Belgium
– the elimination of Liberalism, leaving the two forces of
Socialism and Reaction face to face. Whether that shall happen
here depends on the Liberal Party.

Letter to Canon Scott Holland, following the Liberal Party's defeat in
the general election, 21 August 1895

Imperialism, sane Imperialism, as distinguished from what I may call wild-cat Imperialism, is nothing but this – a larger patriotism.

   At the City of London Liberal Club, 5 May 1899

There are two supreme pleasures in life. One is ideal, the other real. The ideal is when a man receives the seals of office from his Sovereign. The real pleasure comes when he hands them back.

   Sir Robert Peel (1899)

A First Minister has only the influence with the Cabinet which is given him by his personal argument, his personal qualities, and his personal weight. All his colleagues he must convince, some he may have to humour, some even to cajole; a harassing, laborious, and ungracious work.

   Sir Robert Peel (1899)

For the present, at any rate, I must proceed alone. I must plough my furrow alone, but before I get to the end of that furrow it is possible that I may not find myself alone.

   On remaining outside the Liberal Party leadership, at the City Liberal
   Club, 19 July 1901

There are men who sit still with the fly-blown phylacteries, obsolete policies bound round their foreheads, who do not remember that while they have been mumbling their incantations to themselves, the world has been marching and revolving, and that if they have any hope of leading it or guiding it they must march and move with it too.

   On certain members of the Liberal Party which he considered bound
   to the outmoded policies of the Newcastle Programme and to Home
   Rule, at Chesterfield, 16 December 1901

What is the advice I have to offer you? The first is this – that you have to clean your slate. It is six years since you were in office ... the primary duty of the Liberal Party is to wipe its slate clean.

   At Chesterfield, 16 December 1901

The end of all, the negation of faith and family, of property, of Monarchy, of Empire.

> On the 1909 'People's' Budget, cited in M. Foot, *Loyalists and Loners* (1986)

A gentleman will blithely do in politics what he would kick a man downstairs for doing in ordinary life.

> 1914, cited in J. Green, *Dictionary of Insulting Quotations* (1996)

There was no retirement, no concealment. He died by inches in public, sole mourner at his own protracted funeral.

> Attributed, about Lord Randolph Churchill

C. S. Roundell
1827–1906; MP (Liberal) Grantham 1880–85, Skipton 1892–95

Legislation which encourages the people rather to rest upon State help than to rely upon themselves, however well-intentioned, will prove incalculably mischievous in the end, and to every measure which is brought forward with the object of improving the condition of the people, this simple test should be applied – will it tend to encourage them to rely upon self-help?

> Cited in M. Richter, *The Politics of Conscience: T. H. Green and his Age* (1964)

Jean-Jacques Rousseau
1712–78; French philosopher

To renounce liberty is to renounce being a man, to surrender the rights of humanity and even its duties.

> *Contrat Social* (1762)

The English people believes itself to be free; it is gravely mistaken; it is free only during the election of members of parliament; as soon as the members are elected, the people is enslaved; it is nothing. In the brief moment of its freedom, the English people makes such a use of that freedom that it deserves to lose it.

Attributed

John Ruskin

1819–1900; art and social critic

Consider, for instance, the ridiculousness of the division of parties into 'Liberal' and 'Conservative'. There is no opposition whatever between these kinds of men. There is opposition between Liberals and Illiberals; that is to say, between people who desire liberty, and who dislike it. I am a violent Illiberal; but it does not follow that I must be a Conservative. A Conservative is a person who wishes to keep things as they are; and he is opposed to a Destructive, who wishes to destroy them, or to an Innovator, who wishes to alter them. Now, though I am an Illiberal, there are many things I should like to destroy.

Fors Clavigera (1871)

Bertrand Russell

1872–1970; philosopher and mathematician

Too little liberty brings stagnation, and too much brings chaos.

Authority and the Individual (1949)

The essence of the Liberal outlook lies not in *what* opinions are held, but in *how* they are held: instead of being held dogmatically, they are held tentatively, and with a consciousness that new evidence may at any moment lead to their abandonment.

Unpopular Essays (1950)

Conrad Russell

1937–2004; historian and Liberal Democrat peer; became 5th Earl
Russell 1987

Utopianism is at all times a threat to freedom, and a party
concerned with liberty must be concerned not to impose a
single ideal but to hold the ring between different ideals.

> Lecture to the John Stuart Mill Institute, 29 October 1992, published
> as *John Stuart Mill: The Free Market and the State* (1993)

The loudest cheer I have ever had from a party audience was
for saying: 'if we were in power, we would be just as bad as the
others; we'd need control just as much'. I am proud of my party
for that cheer.

> Cited in D. Brack (ed.), *Why I am a Liberal Democrat* (1996)

A defence of nonconforming aldermen under Queen Anne may
not sound like an attack on black unemployment in 1997, yet
the principle of non-discrimination is the same under the wig.
The ideological continuity is clearer than the change in its dress
will show.

> Founder's Day Lecture, Hawarden 1997; published as 'Liberalism
> and Liberty from Gladstone to Ashdown', *Journal of Liberal Democrat
> History*, Issue 20, autumn 1998

Liberalism has always been about power – how it is to be
controlled and dispersed and used to help the powerless and the
underprivileged help themselves. It is a philosophy which does
not easily fit into a Left-Right spectrum based on social class.

> *The Times*, 11 June 1999

Libertarians believe that 'anything goes': Liberals believe that
we should enjoy liberty while doing no harm to others. This is
a bigger limitation than is often realised ... Libertarians are for
minimum government; Liberals are for minimum oppression.
We want to see all power subject to control; not just the power

of the state but also that of Monsanto, a bent copper, or a violent husband.

The Times, 11 June 1999

G. W. E. Russell

1853–1919; MP (Liberal) Aylesbury 1880–85, Bedfordshire North 1892–95; writer

My hearers are very keen about the blasphemy laws and the grant to Princess Beatrice, but for the physical and moral welfare of themselves and their neighbours they did not seem to care a straw.

On the lack of appeal of New Liberal policies of social reform, even to working men, in the 1885 election, *Nineteenth Century* XXVI (1889)

Child: Mama, are Tories born wicked, or do they grow wicked afterwards?
Mother: They are born wicked, and grow worse.

Collections and Recollections (1898)

From the day when Bradlaugh's case was first mooted, it became apparent that the Liberal Party contained a good many men who had only the frailest hold on the primary principles of Liberalism, and who, under the pressure of social and theological prejudice, were quite ready to join the Tories in a tyrannical negation of Religious Liberty. Gladstone, though deserted and defeated by his own followers, maintained the righteous cause with a signal consistency and courage. There was no one in the world to whom Bradlaugh's special opinions could have been more abhorrent but he felt – and we who followed him felt the same – that the cause of God and morality can never be served by the insolent refusal of a civil right.

Fifteen Chapters of Autobiography (1914)

Lord John Russell

1766–1839; MP (Whig) Tavistock 1788–1802 and 1830–31; became 6th
Duke of Bedford 1802

There are circumstances in which you give great offence to
your followers ... in the House of Commons by not being
courteous to them, by treating them superciliously, and de haut
en bas, by not listening to them with sufficient patience to their
solicitations or remonstrances.

Letter to his son, Lord John Russell, 1838

Lord John Russell

1792–1878; MP (Liberal) Tavistock 1813–20, Huntingdon 1820–26,
Bandon 1826–30, Devonshire 1831–32, Devon South 1832–35, Stroud
1835–41, City of London 1841–61; created 1st Earl Russell 1861;
Home Secretary 1835–39, Prime Minister 1846–52, 1865–66, Foreign
Secretary 1852–53, 1859–65

Wherever the aristocracy resides, receiving large incomes,
performing important duties, relieving the poor by charity,
and evincing private worth and public virtue, it is not in human
nature that they should not possess a great influence upon public
opinion, and have an equal weight in selecting persons to serve
their country in Parliament.

In the House of Commons, 1 March 1831, during the debate on the
Reform Bill

When I am told that the government of a country does not
affect the condition of its people, I say, look to Ireland.

In the House of Commons, 24 June 1831

It is impossible that the whisper of a faction should prevail
against the voice of a nation.

Letter to Thomas Attwood after the rejection of the Reform Bill by the
House of Lords, October 1831

Neither a Government nor a legislature can ever regulate the corn market with the beneficial effects which the entire freedom of sale and purchase are sure of themselves to produce.

Public letter from Edinburgh which precipitated a crisis in Peel's government and made inevitable the repeal of the Corn Laws, 22 November 1845

I cannot look with indifference to the statement that the great proportion of the people of this country have only to work, to sleep, to eat and to die. In my opinion, it is a duty of the state to endeavour that you should have a population, in the first place, aware of the doctrines of religion; that, in the next place, they should be able to cultivate domestic habits and domestic affections; and that, in the third place, they should be likely to look up to the laws and government of the country as their protectors from undue inflictions upon the young of this country.

On factory legislation, in the House of Commons, 17 March 1847

If peace cannot be maintained with honour, it is no longer peace.

At Greenock, in the run-up to the Crimean War, 19 September 1853

Among the defects of the Bill, which were numerous, one provision was conspicuous by its presence and another by its absence.

To the electors of the City of London during the general election of April 1859, about the unsuccessful Reform Bill whose failure brought down Derby's government and paved the way for the foundation of the modern Liberal Party

I have made mistakes, but in all I did my object was the public good.

To his wife, 1878

'Is it true, Lord John,' the Queen is reported to have asked, 'that you hold a subject is justified in certain circumstances in disobeying his sovereign?' To which Lord John replied, 'Well, speaking to a sovereign of the House of Hanover I can only say that I suppose he is.'

Cited in A. Wyatt Tilby, *Lord John Russell* (1930)

A proverb is one man's wit and all men's wisdom.

Cited in D. Englefield, J. Seaton & I. White, *Facts About the British Prime Ministers* (1996)

S

Sa'di
c. 1200–1292; Persian poet

The hand of liberality is stronger than the arm of power.
>*Gulistan* (1258)

Robert Arthur Talbot Gascoyne-Cecil, 3rd Marquess of Salisbury
1830–1903; MP (Conservative) Stamford 1853–68; became 3rd
Marquess of Salisbury 1868; Foreign Secretary 1878–80, 1885–86,
1887–92, 1895–1900, Prime Minister 1885–86, 1886–92, 1895–1902

The duty of making political speeches is an aggravation of the
labours of your Majesty's servants which we owe entirely to Mr
Gladstone.
>1887, cited in M. Pugh, *The Making of Modern British Politics 1867–1939*
>(1982)

Hartington is at Newmarket and all political arrangements have
to be hung up till some quadruped has run faster than some
other quadruped.
>Letter to A. J. Balfour, 15 October 1891, cited in R. H. Williams (ed.),
>*The Salisbury-Balfour Correspondence 1869–1892* (1988)

Sobriety is a very good thing and philanthropy is a very good
thing, but freedom is better than either.
>Cited in P. T. Marsh, *The Discipline of Popular Government: Lord Salisbury's
>Domestic Statecraft 1881–1902* (1978)

Anthony Sampson

1926–2004; writer and journalist

The Liberals remained an odd mixture. There were rich country Whigs who looked back to Asquith and saw freedom in terms of escape from bureaucracy and high taxation. There were individualists and windbags who could not submit to the discipline of the big parties. There were leaders in the traditional liberal regions of the 'Celtic fringe' – Scotland, Wales and the West Country – who resented the London hegemony. And there were radical young Liberals who regarded Labour as too hidebound for their crusades against apartheid and pollution. In some ways the Liberals were actually more class-based than the other two: they had proportionately more public-school candidates and a fruitier style. Some of them, standing repeatedly for hopeless seats, seemed actually to *prefer* losing. But the Liberals also included many original and dedicated politicians who were determined to maintain their concern for individual liberties and human rights against the encroachments of bureaucracy and corporate politics.

On the Liberal Party in the early 1980s, *The Changing Anatomy of Britain* (1982)

Herbert Samuel

1870–1963; MP (Liberal) Cleveland 1902–18, Darwen 1929–35; Home Secretary 1916 and 1931–32; created Viscount Samuel of Mount Carmel and Toxteth 1937, leader of the Liberal peers 1944–55

The trunk of the tree of Liberalism is rooted in the soil of ethics.

Liberalism: an attempt to state the principles and proposals of contemporary Liberalism in England (1902)

The general feeling on our side seems to be one of frightened satisfaction, the kind of feeling one has on being launched down an exhilarating steep and unknown toboggan run.

On the People's Budget, remark to Herbert Gladstone, 29 April 1909

[To disarm] would merely be to hand over to the militarists the control of the world's affairs.

   Speech, 5 March 1935, cited in G. Mander, *We were not all wrong* (1941)

Confine the expression of popular feeling within rigid limits, surround it with iron bands, and a spark may cause a terrific explosion. Leave it free and, like gunpowder scattered in the open air, even if set alight it will do no more damage.

   Viscount Samuel's Book of Quotations (1947)

No nation resents firmness in its Government, provided it is combined with understanding and sympathy.

   Viscount Samuel's Book of Quotations (1947)

The true nature of Freedom is often not understood. It is usually regarded as a single and simple idea: let men be free to lead their lives as they will – provided always that they do not interfere with the equal liberties of others. And one conflict only confronts it – with its opposite, Tyranny. But if that had really been the situation, Liberty would easily have been triumphant, everywhere and long ago. Past history and present experience, however, show clearly enough that that has not been the situation. There has been no such happy simplicity. Liberty is not a single idea; it includes many ideas, which sometimes conflict with one another. Indeed it frequently happens that one kind of liberty may have to be sacrificed, in greater or lesser degree, in order to make others secure. Then the friends of Liberty themselves may be divided as to the right course to take: their dissensions may even reduce them to impotence in face of the common enemy.

   Introduction to *The Meaning of Freedom* (1956)

[The Civil Service had] a difficulty for every solution.

   Cited in G. Knight, *Honourable Insults* (1990)

Michael Sandel

b. 1953; American political philosopher

The virtues in democratic life – community solidarity, trust, civic friendship – these virtues are not like commodities that are depleted with use. They are, rather, the muscles that develop and grow stronger with use.

BBC Reith Lecture 2009

Democracy does not require perfect equality, but it does require that citizens share in a common life. What matters is that people of different backgrounds and social positions encounter one another, and bump up against one another, in the course of everyday life. For this is how we learn to negotiate and abide our differences, and how we come to care for the common good. And so, in the end, the question of markets is really a question about how we want to live together. Do we want a society where everything is up for sale? Or are there certain moral and civic goods that markets do not honour and money cannot buy?

What Money Can't Buy: The Moral Limits of Markets (2012)

Friedrich Schiller

1759–1805; German dramatist, writer and historian

When the artisan lays hands upon the formless mass in order to shape it to his ends, he has no scruple in doing it violence. The natural material he is working merits no respect for itself, his concern is not with the whole for the sake of the parts but with the parts for the sake of the whole. The political or educational artist, however, must learn to approach his medium with genuine respect for its individuality and potential for dignity ... and beware of damaging its natural variety.

1794, cited in F. Gladstone, *Voluntary Action in a Changing World* (1979)

C. P. Scott

1846–1932; editor of the *Manchester Guardian* 1872–1929; MP (Liberal)
Leigh 1895–1906

No man who is responsible for [embarking upon war] can lead
us again.

> Letter to David Lloyd George, 3 August 1914, cited in M. Pugh, *The
> Making of Modern British Politics 1867–1939* (1982)

Asquith will never fight for a principle.

> On Asquith's unwillingness to oppose Lloyd George's plan to
> introduce conscription in Ireland and thereby risk a general election,
> letter to L. T. Hobhouse, 12 April 1918

If there is a future for the Liberal Party it surely rests on the
rock of Free Trade.

> Letter to J. L. Hammond, 12 December 1931

Nancy Seear

1913–97; politician and academic; President, Liberal Party 1965–66;
created Baroness Seear of Paddington 1971; leader of the Liberal peers,
1984–88

For forty years we Liberals have prophesied that the country
would come to recognise the need for a non-Socialist
progressive party. We have not spent these years isolated but
undefiled in the wilderness to choose this moment, of all
moments, to go, in a biblical phrase, 'a-whoring after foreign
women'.

> At the Liberal assembly, 22 September 1965, following talk of a Lib–
> Lab coalition

I never want to meet another bloody pensioner again!

> During the 1987 general election campaign (when Seear was 74), cited
> in D. Brack et al. (eds), *Dictionary of Liberal Biography* (1998)

I'm very cross that I am typecast with 'Women'.
> Quoted in her obituary in *The Independent*, April 1997

J. E. B. Seely

1868–1947; MP (Conservative) Isle of Wight 1900–04 (Liberal)
1904–06, 1923–24, Liverpool Abercromby 1906–10, Ilkeston 1910–22;
created Baron Mottistone 1933

The committee have seen a good deal this evening of the
opposition of the overfed Members to the underfed child.
> On Tory opposition to the provision of free school meals, cited in
> G. Knight, *Honourable Insults* (1990)

W. C. Sellar and R. J. Yeatman

Sellar 1898–1951;Yeatman 1898–1968; writers

Meanwhile, at home, fresh attempts to galvanise the Queen
resulted in the promotion of Lord Palmerston ('Pal') to the
Premiership – a rather matey minister who always wore green
gloves and sucked a straw and altered the despatches after the
Queen signed them, so that they became surprises for her. It
was not, however, until he conceived and carried through his
heartless Conspiracy to Murder Bill that the Good (but now
Horrified) Queen dismissed him. After which 'Pal' spent his
time taking special trains in all directions and galloping to
Harrow on a cream-coloured pony, thus endearing himself to
the People and becoming an object of terror and admiration to
all foreign governments.
> *1066 and All That* (1930)

Gladstone, on the other hand, endeavoured (quite
unsuccessfully) to please Her Majesty by chewing a milk
pudding seventy-nine times every day, and by his memorable
inventions; amongst the latter were an exceptionally
uncomfortable collar which he inhabited for sixty-two years

on the floor of the House of Commons, and an extremely simple kind of bag which he designed to enable the Turks to be driven out of Europe Bag and Baggage. Gladstone also invented the Education rate by which it was possible to calculate how soon anybody could be educated, and spent his declining years trying to guess the answer to the Irish Question; unfortunately, whenever he was getting warm, the Irish secretly changed the Question, so that as he grew older and older Gladstone became angrier and angrier, grander and grander, and was ultimately awarded the title 'G. P. O.' Gladstone was thus clearly a Good man but a Bad thing (or, alternatively, a Bad man but a Good thing).

1066 and All That (1930)

Seneca
c. 4 BC–AD 65; Roman philosopher, statesman and dramatist

Freedom can't be bought for nothing. If you hold her precious, you must hold all else of little worth.

Letters to Lucilius (1st century AD)

Anthony Ashley Cooper, Lord Shaftesbury
1621–83; MP Tewkesbury 1640, Wiltshire 1653–59, 1660–61; Chancellor of the Exchequer 1661–72, Lord Chancellor 1672–73; created Earl of Shaftesbury 1672

There is no place or condition will invite me to court during this parliament, nor until I see the king thinks frequent parliaments as much his interest as they are the people's rights.

Letter to the Earl of Carlisle, 3 February 1675

A land may groan under a multitude of laws ... and when laws grow so multiplied, they prove oftener snares than directions and security to the people.

In the House of Lords, 20 October 1675

My principle is 'that the king is king by law, and by the same law that the poor man enjoys his cottage'; and so it becomes the concern of every man in England that has but his liberty, to maintain and defend, to his utmost, the king in all his rights and prerogatives.

In the House of Lords, 20 October 1675

George Bernard Shaw
1856–1950; Irish playwright

Liberty means responsibility. That is why most men dread it.

Man and Superman (1903)

We must be thoroughly democratic and patronise everybody without distinction of class.

John Bull's Other Island (1907)

Charles Shaw-Lefevre
1794–1888; MP (Liberal) Downton 1830, Hampshire North 1831–57; Speaker 1839–57

What is that fat gentleman in such a passion about?

As a boy, on hearing Charles James Fox speak in the House of Commons, cited in G. W. E. Russell, *Collections and Recollections* (1898)

William Petty, Earl of Shelburne
1737–1805; MP (Whig) Chipping Wycombe 1760–61; became 2nd Earl of Shelburne 1761; Prime Minister 1782–83

The country will neither be united at home nor respected abroad, 'til the reins of government are lodged with men who have some little pretensions to common sense and common honesty.

In the House of Lords, 22 November 1770

I avow that monopoly is always unwise, but if there is any nation under heaven who ought to be the first to reject monopoly, it is the English.

Defending the provisional treaties he had negotiated with the American States, 1783

Percy Bysshe Shelley
1792–1822; romantic poet

Government is an evil; it is only the thoughtlessness and vices of men that make it a necessary evil. When all men are good and wise, government will of itself decay; so long as men continue foolish and vicious, so long will government, even such a government as that of England, continue necessary in order to prevent the crimes of bad men.

An Address to the Irish People (1812)

The man
Of virtuous soul commands not, nor obeys.
Power, like a desolating pestilence
Pollutes whate'er it touches; and obedience,
Bane of all genius, virtue, freedom, truth,
Makes slaves of men, and of the human frame
A mechanised automaton.

Queen Mab, Vol. 3 (1813)

Richard Sheridan
1751–1816; dramatist; MP (Whig) Stafford 1780–1806, Westminster 1806–07, Ilchester 1807–12

The throne we honour is the people's choice.

Pizarro (1799)

The Right Honourable gentleman is indebted to his memory for his jests, and to his imagination for his facts.

In the House of Commons, in reply to Dundas, cited in T. Moore, *Life of Sheridan*, Vol. 2 (1825)

Elizabeth Shields

b. 1928; MP (Liberal) Ryedale 1986–87

The Mother of Parliaments had seen many fine sons, not least those who sat on the Liberal benches, but the number of daughters was far too few for the health of the nation.

Maiden speech in the House of Commons, May 1986

Algernon Sidney

1622–83; Republican; MP Cardiff 1646 Parliament; executed for his part in the Rye House plot 1683

There can be no peace without justice. Nor any justice if the government instituted for the good of a nation be turned to its ruin.

1680

Ernest Simon

1879–1960; industrialist; MP (Liberal) Manchester Withington 1923–24, 1929–31; created Baron Simon of Wythenshawe 1947

What a party! No leaders. No organisation. No policy. Only a Summer School!

On the foundation of the Liberal Summer School, 1921; cited in D. Brack & E. Randall (eds), *Dictionary of Liberal Thought* (2007)

We cannot, even in the best democracy, expect *everybody* to take an active interest in public affairs. But unless the great majority do so, and unless the tasks of citizenship are generally held to be among the highest duties of man, we can never hope to succeed in the most difficult task before mankind: the building of a just and efficient social order.

Constructive Democracy (1938)

John Simon

1873–1954; MP (Liberal) Walthamstow 1906–18 (Liberal, Liberal National) Spen Valley 1922–40; Home Secretary 1915–16, 1935–37, Foreign Secretary 1931–35, Chancellor of the Exchequer 1937–40, Lord Chancellor 1940–45; created Viscount Simon of Stackpole Elidor 1940

We have been snowed under, but snow melts.

Responding to the party's defeat in the 1918 general election

But while snow melts, it may in the meantime crush the life out of that which it has buried.

Commenting on the above thirty years later, cited in D. Dutton, *A History of the Liberal Party* (2004)

I am myself enough of a pacifist to take this view that, however we handle this matter, I do not intend my own country to get into trouble about it.

Reacting to the Japanese invasion of Manchuria, which the League of Nations did not intervene to prevent or reverse, and which was widely seen as the beginning of the policy of appeasement, in the House of Commons, 27 February 1933

There are two reasons why Ministers are given new offices:
1. Because they filled the old one so well.
2. Because they filled the old one so badly.

Cited in J. Wheeler-Bennett, *Sir John Anderson* (1962)

Democracy encourages the minority to decide things about which the majority is ignorant.

Attributed

Archibald Sinclair

1890–1970; MP (Liberal) Caithness & Sutherland 1922–45, Liberal Chief
Whip 1930–31, Secretary of State for Scotland 1931–32, for Air 1940–
45; leader of the Liberal Party 1935–45; created Viscount Thurso 1952

The outbreak of war between any two great Powers would
undoubtedly, inevitably lead to a world-wide conflagration
from which no country, least of all a country like Britain with
possessions in every part of the globe and trade relations
with every country of the world, could be immune.

   In the House of Commons, 28 November 1934

We shall once more draw into our counsels and into our
political activities all men and women who hate tyranny,
whether of the Right or of the Left, whether of privilege and
monopoly or of officialdom and Governments, and all those
who love freedom, justice and peace, and mean to create a new
and better order in which men and women shall live in
peace and freedom, a fuller and richer life.

   'The Modern Mission of the Liberal Party', Liberal Convention,
   18 June 1936

Aggression is an appetite that grows by what it feeds on. The
Government's policy puts a premium on successful aggression,
and makes the world safe for dictatorship.

   In the House of Commons, 23 June 1936

I am sure that peace cannot be bought by sacrifices to aggressive
military Powers at the expense of small and weak nations. Peace
must be based upon justice and it must be defended against
aggression. Peace must be built upon justice buttressed by force,
but force must the servant, not the master, of justice.

   At the Liberal Party Council, 21 September 1938

The Liberal National has neither eyes to see, nor ears to hear,
nor tongue to speak, save as his local Conservative Association
directs him ... But you mustn't call them Tories. I have never

called them Tories. A Liberal National is no more a Tory than a ventriloquist's dummy is a ventriloquist.

At the National Liberal Club, 26 January 1938

We shall have to make a great effort to preserve the essential foundations of freedom and order in the world, to preserve democracy, that form of government which is inspired by consciousness of the dignity of man and the use of power only for good and lawful ends. To our generation it falls to guard that flame. Let His Majesty's Government call upon the men and women of this country to rally to the defence of freedom and justice, and we may yet save ourselves by our exertions, and democracy by our example.

In the Munich debate in the House of Commons, 3 October 1938

It is the people whom the Liberal Party exists to serve – not a section or a class, nor an abstraction like a State or an Empire – but the individual men and women and their families in which they live. To serve them – to create for them an environment of peace and justice, of beauty and happiness, and of health and freedom – freedom to express themselves in worship, in art, in literature, in craftmanship, in commercial enterprise, or on farming the land from which they sprang, and freedom to enjoy the works of others – that is our aim and purpose.

At Caxton Hall, London, 5 September 1942

The only means of preserving the life, and securing the independence, of the Liberal Party.

On electoral reform, letter to Clement Davies, 1950, cited in
J. G. Jones, *National Liberal of Wales Journal*, 23, No. 4

The National Liberals are like a mule, in that they have no pride of ancestry and no hope of posterity.

Attributed, cited in J. Thorpe, *In My Own Time* (1999)

I never care for conferences.

Attributed, while he was Liberal leader

Adrian Slade

b. 1936; President, Liberal Party 1987–88

[Don't] be persuaded to join some sort of lemming tendency
hurtling in a manner reminiscent of a doctor in another place
towards a Liberal cliff of electoral oblivion.

> Urging support for merger of the Liberal Party and SDP, at the Liberal
> special assembly, Blackpool, 16 January 1988

O true believers, take your necessary precautions against your
enemies and either go forth in separate parties or go forth all
together in a body.

> Quoting the Koran in order to advocate the merger of the Liberal
> Party and SDP, *The Guardian*, 25 January 1988

Samuel Smiles

1812–1904; writer and social reformer

We often discover what will do by finding out what will not
do; and probably he who never made a mistake never made a
discovery.

> *Self-Help, with Illustrations of Conduct and Perseverance* (1859)

The spirit of self-help is the root of all genuine growth in the
individual; and, exhibited in the lives of the many, it constitutes
the true source of national vigour and strength.

> *Self-Help, with Illustrations of Conduct and Perseverance* (1859)

If the nation is only an aggregate of individual conditions ...
then it follows that the highest patriotism and philanthropy
consist, not so much in altering laws and modifying institutions,
as in helping and stimulating men to elevate and improve
themselves by their own free and individual action.

> *Self-Help, with Illustrations of Conduct and Perseverance* (1859)

Adam Smith

1723–90; philosopher and economist

Little else is requisite to carry a state to the highest degree of opulence from the lowest barbarism, but peace, easy taxes, and a tolerable administration of justice; all the rest being brought about by the natural course of things.

1755, cited in *Essays on Philosophical Subjects* (1795)

[The man of systems] seems to imagine that he can arrange the different members of a great society with as much ease as the hand arranges the different pieces upon a chessboard; he does not consider that the pieces upon the chessboard have no other principle of motion besides that which the hand impresses upon them; but that, in the great chessboard of human society, every single piece has a principle of motion of its own, altogether different from that which the legislator might choose to impress upon it.

Theory of Moral Sentiments (1759)

There is no art which one government sooner learns of another than that of draining money from the pockets of the people.

Wealth of Nations (1776)

Every individual necessarily labours to render the annual revenue of the society as great as he can. He generally, indeed, neither intends to promote the public interest, nor knows how much he is promoting it. By preferring the support of domestic to that of foreign industry, he intends only his own security; and by directing that industry in such a manner as its produce may be of the greatest value, he intends only his own gain, and he is, in this, as in many other cases, led by an invisible hand to promote an end which was no part of his intention.

The concept of the 'invisible hand' of the market has become a central economic tenet, *Wealth of Nations* (1776)

It is the highest impertinence and presumption, therefore, in kings and ministers, to pretend to watch over the economy of private people, and to restrain their expense ... They are themselves always, and without any exception, the greatest spendthrifts in society. Let them look well after their own expense, and they may safely trust private people with theirs. If their own extravagance does not ruin the state, that of their subjects never will.

Wealth of Nations (1776)

What is prudence in the conduct of every private family, can scarce be folly in that of a great kingdom. If a foreign country can supply us with a commodity cheaper than we ourselves can make it, better buy it of them with some part of the produce of our own industry, employed in a way in which we have some advantage.

Wealth of Nations (1776)

The natural effort of every individual to better his own condition ... is so powerful, that it is alone, and without any assistance, not only capable of carrying on the society to wealth and prosperity, but of surmounting a hundred impertinent obstructions with which the folly of human laws too often encumbers its operations.

Wealth of Nations (1776)

Commerce and manufactures gradually introduced order and good government, and with them, the liberty and security of individuals.

Cited in J. M. Beattie, *Crime and the Courts in England, 1660–1800* (1986)

Chris Smith

b. 1951; MP (Labour) Islington South & Finsbury 1983–2005; created Baron Smith of Finsbury 2005

Liberal democracy is the only way of organising society that allows it to experiment fully, proceeding through trial and error, allowing government to change along with circumstances and without violence.

Suicide of the West (2006)

Many Western liberals are perversely unwilling to recognise the unprecedented virtues of Western liberal society – something that other societies could not have produced, something that is worth defending and, by mutual consent, extending. Perversely, the most dangerous enemy of liberalism is liberalism.

Suicide of the West (2006)

Cyril Smith

1928–2010; MP (Liberal) Rochdale 1972–92, Liberal Chief Whip 1976–77

It's a two-horse race and the carthorse will win.

Predicting the outcome of the Rochdale by-election, 1972

The euphoria wagon was not only dragged out of its stable, but was pushed off on a tearing, whooping, cheering downhill charge.

On the Liberal Party's February 1974 general election campaign, cited in *Big Cyril: The Autobiography of Cyril Smith* (1977)

He could not make a bang with a firework in both hands.

On David Steel, 1976, cited in Lord Norton of Louth, *The House*, 19 July 1999

Shot any dogs lately?

To Jeremy Thorpe, 1976

A veritable kingfisher, nattily dressed, his gold watch-chain swinging from his double-breasted waistcoat, his trilby at a jaunty angle.

On Jeremy Thorpe, cited in *Big Cyril: The Autobiography of Cyril Smith* (1977)

The longest running farce in the West End.

> On the House of Commons, cited in *Big Cyril: The Autobiography of Cyril Smith* (1977)

There is only room for one centre party, not two. That is why I urge Liberals to strangle at birth any fourth party.

> At Newbury, 4 March 1981

If the fence is strong enough, I'll sit on it.

> Attributed

F. E. Smith

1872–1930; MP (Conservative) Liverpool Walton 1906–18, Liverpool West Derby 1918–19; created Baron Birkenhead 1919, Viscount Birkenhead 1921, Earl Birkenhead 1922; Lord Chancellor 1919–22, Secretary of State for India 1924–28

These Liberals came floating into Parliament like corks on the top of a dirty wave.

> On the outcome of the 1906 general election, cited in G. Knight, *Honourable Insults* (1990)

The Government has turned its back on the country and now has the impertinence to claim the country is behind it.

> On the 1910 government, cited in G. Knight, *Honourable Insults* (1990)

Only the certitude that he would never be called upon to prove his claim, can have permitted him, at the last general election, to declare that he could cure unemployment in a year without the expenditure of public money.

> On Lloyd George and the 1929 general election, cited in G. Knight, *Honourable Insults* (1990)

The Liberals do not want to abolish the House of Lords when it opposes the people – but wish to abolish the people when they oppose the Liberal Party.

Cited in G. Knight, *Honourable Insults* (1990)

Sydney Smith
1771–1845; clergyman and Whig essayist

The prize of supreme power is too tempting to admit of fair play in the game of ambition; and it is wise to lessen its value by dividing it.

Edinburgh Review, 1803

The moment the very name of Ireland is mentioned, the English seem to bid adieu to common feeling, common prudence, and common sense, and to act with the barbarity of tyrants, and the fatuity of idiots.

Letters of Peter Plymley 1807–08

Toleration never had a present tense, nor taxation a future one.

Edinburgh Review, 1808

It is the easiest of all things, too, in this country, to make Englishmen believe that those who oppose the Government wish to ruin the country.

Edinburgh Review, 1809

Brougham's review is not in good taste; he should have put on an air of serious concern, not raillery and ridicule; things are too serious for that. But it is very able. It is long yet vigorous, like the penis of a jackass.

Brougham was the lawyer to Queen Caroline and contributor to the *Edinburgh Review*, letter, 1809

Nothing dies so hard and rallies so often as intolerance.

Edinburgh Review, 1811

All establishments die of dignity. They are too proud to think themselves ill, and to take a little physic.

Edinburgh Review, 1811

All great alterations in human affairs are produced by compromise.

Edinburgh Review, 1827

I love liberty, but I hope that it can be so managed that I shall have soft beds, good dinners, fine linen, etc., for the rest of my life.

Letter, 1830

We are told, by Mr Dundas, that there is no eagerness for Reform. Five minutes before Moses struck the rock, this gentleman would have said that there was no eagerness for water.

Speech, 1831

Tory & Whig in turns shall be my host,
I taste no politics in boiled and roast.

Letter to John Murray, 1834, cited in *Letters of Sydney Smith* (1953)

You say that you are not convinced by my pamphlet. I am afraid that I am a very arrogant person. But, I do assure you that, in the fondest moments of self-conceit, the idea of convincing a Russell that he was wrong never crossed my mind.

Letter to Lord John Russell 1837

There is not a better man in England than Lord John Russell; but his worst failure is that he is utterly ignorant of all moral fear; there is nothing he would not undertake. I believe he would perform the operation for the stone – build St. Peter's – or assume (with or without ten minutes' notice) the command of the Channel Fleet; and no one would discover by his manner that the patient had died – the Church tumbled down – and the Channel Fleet had been knocked to atoms.

Letters to Archdeacon Singleton 1837–40

Before this Reform agitation commenced Lord John was over six feet high. But, engaged in looking after your interests, fighting the peers, the landlords, and the rest of your natural enemies, he has been so constantly kept in hot water that he is boiled down to the proportions in which you now behold him.

Referring to Lord John Russell, cited in D. Englefield, J. Seaton & I. White, *Facts About the British Prime Ministers* (1996)

The Social Democrat

Social Democrat activists are mainly brainy, middle-class professionals who see themselves as moderately left of centre, and are passionately committed to helping the poor and supporting the welfare state.

Summary of a survey undertaken at the Scottish Social Democrats' assembly by David Denver of the University of Lancaster, 8 April 1983

John Sparrow

1906–92; Warden of All Souls College, Oxford

This stone, with not unpardonable pride
Proves by its record what the world denied:
Simon could do a natural thing – he died.

A suggested epitaph for Viscount Simon, cited in H. Nicolson, *Diary*, 11 January 1954

The Spectator

The Liberals' strongest card is precisely that they have no vested interests to protect and can therefore claim to be the only party which is free to come to current problems with an open mind. It is a card which neither Labour nor Tories can easily wrest from them.

September 1963, cited in H. Cowie, *Why Liberal?* (1964)

J. A. Spender

1862–1942; editor of the *Westminster Gazette* 1896–1921

CB never disguised his opinion that London society was bad for Radical politics.

On Sir Henry Campbell-Bannerman, cited in D. Brack et al. (eds),
Dictionary of Liberal Biography (1998)

Lancelot Spicer

Chairman of Radical Action, a campaigning group within the Liberal Party during the Second World War

Without radicals, Liberals would become dilettantes.

'Some Critical Thoughts on the White Paper on Employment',
June 1944

Baruch Spinoza

1632–77; Dutch philosopher

Human freedom consists solely in the fact that men are conscious of their own desire, but are ignorant of the causes whereby that desire has been determined.

Letter to Schuller, October 1674

The virtue of a free man appears equally great in refusing to face difficulties as in overcoming them.

Ethics (1677)

Madame de Staël

1766–1817; French writer

A nation has character only when it is free.

De la littérature (1800)

James Stansfeld

1820–98; MP (Liberal) Halifax 1859–95; President of the Board of Local Government 1871–74, 1886

[Liberalism is] robust and hopeful. It represents the natural mental attitude and condition of manly educated intelligence in youth and manhood.

Cited in A. Reid (ed.), *Why I am a Liberal* (1885)

Liberalism believes in individuality, in the capacity for liberty and progress of the individual man. There is no Liberalism without this as the basis of its faith.

Cited in A. Reid (ed.), *Why I am a Liberal* (1885)

W. T. Stead

1849–1912; Liberal editor of the *Pall Mall Gazette*; drowned with the *Titanic*

I was a thorough-going Gladstonian of a very stalwart fighting kind, with a wholesome conviction that Tories were children of the Devil, and that the supreme duty of a Liberal journalist was to win as many seats as possible for the Liberal Party.

When editor of the *Northern Echo*, cited in E. Stead, *My Father* (1913)

The germ of a federated continent exists in the Concert of Europe. To foster that germ until it attains its full development in the establishment of the Federated United States of Europe is the special role of English statesmanship.

Cited in F. Whyte, *The Life of W.T. Stead* (1925)

To vivify the stagnant squalor of the life of great masses of the population by associated effort, voluntary, municipal and imperial.

Aims of the New Liberalism, cited in F. Whyte, *The Life of W.T. Stead* (1925)

David Steel

b. 1938; MP (Liberal, Liberal Democrat) Roxburgh, Selkirk & Peebles, later Tweeddale, Ettrick & Lauderdale 1965–97; Liberal Chief Whip 1970–76, leader of the Liberal Party 1976–88; created Baron Steel of Aikwood 1997; MSP Lothian 1999–2003; presiding officer of the Scottish Parliament 1999–2003

We are in being as a political party to form a government so as to introduce the policies for which we stand. I do not expect to lead a nice debating society ... we shall probably have – at least temporarily – to share power with somebody else to bring about the changes we seek.

At the Liberal assembly, Llandudno, September 1976

The road I intend to travel may be a bumpy one, and I recognise the risk that in the course of it we may lose some of the passengers, but I don't mind so long as we arrive at the end of it reasonably intact and ready to achieve our goals.

At the Liberal assembly, Llandudno, September 1976

I said last year that the road I intended to travel would be a bumpy one and that we might therefore lose some of the passengers. Some of them must have had a pretty tenuous hold on the vehicle, for they fell off at the first pot-hole.

On the impact of the Lib–Lab Pact on the Liberal Party, at the Liberal assembly, Brighton, 26 September 1977

Great Liberals have always recognised that Liberty does not exist in a vacuum. Each man's liberty depends on respect for every man's rights and obligations. People talk of 'rights' easily; they talk of 'freedom' almost glibly. Yet how often do you hear of 'responsibility?' I fear for a liberal society when it is not also a responsible society.

At the Liberal assembly, Brighton, September 1977

The social democratic tradition has run into the sands.

At the Liberal assembly, Brighton, September 1977

[This] has been an appallingly difficult time for Liberals. We face an electorate brainwashed into seeing politics as a contest between a pair of mighty adversaries.

On the difficulties of the Lib–Lab Pact, at the Scottish Liberal Party conference, June 1978

Liberalism is not just the creed of a political party. It is the expression of a profoundly moral view of human nature and its possibilities. For too long the Liberal values of tolerance, mutual respect and cooperation have been on the defensive against the zealots of right and left. Liberals themselves have sometimes been defensive, with the attitudes and concerns of a persecuted minority. There has even been a tendency to say: keep Liberalism out of politics. But that time is over. The relevance of Liberalism, which has sometimes been drowned out by the clamour of the extremists, is sharp and clear today.

At the Liberal assembly, Llandudno, 18 September 1981

I have the good fortune to be the first Liberal Leader for over half a century who is able to say to you at the end of our annual Assembly: go back to your constituencies and prepare for government!

At the Liberal assembly, Llandudno, 18 September 1981

Go back to your constituencies and bloody well stay there!

To Liberal activists; attributed (humorously) to David Steel by the Liberal Revue team, at the Liberal assembly, Dundee, 1985

I am not attracted by power without principle but, equally, I am only faintly attracted to principles without power.

At the Liberal assembly, Eastbourne, 1986

Neither David Owen nor I are prepared to arrive at any election policy as a result of some botched up bargaining process. We wouldn't convince the country. We wouldn't convince you. We wouldn't convince ourselves.

At the Liberal assembly, Eastbourne, 1986

I have spoken this morning as a Liberal about liberalism. That is as it should be. Opponents of merger sometimes talk as if the Liberal Party is going to be abolished, that the new Party will not be Liberal. If that were so, I would be voting against merger ... But it is precisely because we shall carry our Liberalism proud and intact into the new party, because our chance to achieve Liberal aims will be increased and because the SDP are our natural partners that I do support merger now.

At the Liberal special assembly, Blackpool, 23 January 1988

Scotland has no need of a spurious 'independence' – as though such a concept had much reality in the Europe of today. Our literature, our education, and our political talents are already appreciated around the globe. The task of the Scottish Parliament will be to provide the focus and voice for that identity.

Cited in *Liberal Democrat News*, 23 April 1999

This is the start of a new sang.

May 1999, on the election of the new Scottish Parliament ('Now there's ane end of ane auld sang' was Lord Seafield's comment when the Act of Union was introduced in the Scottish Parliament in 1706)

I ... believe that we need as a country to recapture a sense of common purpose and mutual interdependence and to rediscover what Adam Smith unashamedly called our benevolent instincts.

Kirkgate Lecture, Linlithgow, 25 September 2012

For the future I favour what has been described as a 'New Union' within the UK – a Holyrood with appropriate powers to raise the majority of its revenue, a permanence of our institutions so that they exist in a union created in a written constitution, not in a tenancy agreement with the Westminster landlord.

The Scotsman, 3 April 2013

Politicians at their peril dictate identity and culture. People can quite comfortably consider themselves both Scots and British and European, a combination of all. Indeed for the citizen is it empowering to have ownership of their own identity.

The Scotsman, 3 April 2013

James Fitzjames Stephen
1829–94; barrister

So we may put him [John Dalton] down as a Liberal-Conservative, which perhaps may be defined as a man who thinks things ought to progress, but would rather they remained as they were.

Liberty, Equality, Fraternity, second edition (1874)

Adlai Stevenson
1900–65; American politician; Democrat candidate in 1952 and 1956 US Presidential contests

Why is it that when political ammunition runs low, inevitably the rusty artillery of abuse is always wheeled into action?

At New York, 22 September 1952

We have confused the free with the free and easy.

Putting First Things First (1960)

He's the kind of politician who could cut down a tree and then mount the stump and make a speech for conservation.

On Richard Nixon, cited in G. Knight, *Honourable Insults* (1990)

Self-criticism is the secret weapon of democracy and candour and confession are good for the political soul.

Attributed

Frances Stevenson

1888–1972; mistress and second wife of David Lloyd George

The PM is absolutely devoid of all principles except one – that of retaining his position as Prime Minister. He will sacrifice everything except No. 10 Downing Street. D says he is for all the world like a sultan with his harem of twenty-three, using all his skills and wiles from preventing one of them from eloping.

Referring to H. H. Asquith (D was David Lloyd George), *Diary*, 30 November 1916

'The reason that I like Lloyd George,' said Carson, 'is that he always put his cards on the table. Then you know exactly what he is playing.' 'That is all very well,' was my remark when D told me this: 'You may put your cards on the table, but you take good care to keep one or two up your sleeve in case of emergency.' D laughed. 'You give me credit for a great deal more craft than I am capable of!' 'I think you are a past master in craft,' I replied, laughing. And D knows he is, too.

Cited in M. Foot, *Loyalists and Loners* (1986)

No one was ever able to persuade him to do something he did not want to do, or conversely, not to do anything he wanted to do. He had a will of granite.

On David Lloyd George, cited in M. Foot, *Loyalists and Loners* (1986)

Never once did I imagine that he would be in the wilderness for thirteen years at least. When D said 'Ten' in 1922 I laughed, and did not believe it or think that he meant it.

Cited in M. Foot, *Loyalists and Loners* (1986)

D has gone to Downing Street in a very truculent mood. If this state of things goes on much longer, he will burst – or someone else will.

Before 1935 election, cited in M. Foot, *Loyalists and Loners* (1986)

John Stevenson

b. 1946; academic and author

A great future behind it and no obvious hope of better things to come.

Assessing the Liberal Party in 1945, *Contemporary Record*, Vol. 2, No. 3 (1988)

Harold Storey

Liberal Party official, thinker and writer, 1920s; editor of *The Liberal Magazine*

Liberals are not opposed to the national ownership of this or that industry, where special conditions call for it; we can contemplate the disappearance of rich men without a tremor; we do not greatly care whether the nation is wealthy enough to be a terror to its neighbours. But we care for liberty. Our idea of progress is a movement towards social conditions in which liberty is a secure and universal possession. Socialism, on the other hand, is a desperate surrender of liberty.

The Liberal Handbook (1923)

Lytton Strachey

1880–1932; writer

In Asquith's case the inveterate lack of ideals and imagination seems really unredeemed; when one peels off the brown-paper wrapping of phrases and compromises – just nothing at all.

Cited in J. Green, *Dictionary of Insulting Quotations* (1996)

Arthur Street

1892–1966; writer

If I vote Liberal they've got no darned policy at all. Voting
Liberal is about as satisfying as kissing your sister.

> On BBC Radio, *Any Questions*, 1959, cited in J. Rattue, *Kissing Your Sister*
> (1993)

G. H. Stuart

Independent candidate for Dundee, 1908

He is a slippery gentleman – a fraudulent and dishonest
politician and no friend to the workers.

> On Winston Churchill, cited in G. Knight, *Honourable Insults* (1990)

The Sun

The most dangerous party in Britain.

> On the Liberal Democrats, 17 July 2004

Sunday Times

Today his supporters revere him as a political Moses leading
them to the promised land, while his opponents deride him
as a peddler of dreams, a national figure by accident because
a frustrated Poujadism has been making its hive in a Liberal
revival.

> On Jo Grimond, 15 June 1958

The Liberal resurgence had as much impact on solidly working-
class seats as a soggy pancake.

> 8 April 1962

By far the most sexually enlightened and the most sexually active.

Comparing SDP female political activists with those of other parties, 6 March 1984

Jonathan Swift

1667–1745; poet and satirist

Of what use is freedom of thought if it will not produce freedom of action?

Cited in H. Bool & S. Carlyle, *For Liberty* (1914)

A. J. Sylvester

1889–1989; Lloyd George's private secretary

But for you, there would have been no parliamentary Liberal Party.

Letter to Clement Davies, 1950, cited in J. G. Jones, *National Library of Wales Journal*, 23, No. 4

T

Peter Tatchell

b. 1952; left-wing and gay rights' activist, Labour candidate in the
Bermondsey by-election, 1983

Liberal community politics is the politics of drains and dustbins. It is
not really politics at all. Instead of focusing on the issues, the Liberals
indulge in a glorified form of social work which deals more or less
exclusively with people's individual problems. With an insatiable
appetite for 'parish pump' and negative 'knocking' propaganda,
usually against Labour councils, the Liberals take up a few individual
cases of broken windows and cracked paving-stones and then make
a huge blaze of publicity about them through their *Focus* newsletter.
By this means, they project the appearance of being much more
concerned and successful than they really are, while dodging the far
trickier questions about what they actually stand for.

The Battle for Bermondsey (1983)

Simon Hughes is an average Liberal candidate with all the
political deficiencies this implies.

The Battle for Bermondsey (1983)

Mark Tavener

1963–2007; writer

Climb every staircase
Try every door
Canvass every voter
'Til you find one more

Chorus from 'Climb Every Staircase' (sung to the tune 'Climb Every
Mountain'), written in 1984 and now sung regularly at Liberal
Democrat conferences

A. J. P. Taylor
1906–90; historian

He aroused every feeling except trust.

On David Lloyd George, *English History 1914–45* (1965)

Norman Tebbit
b. 1931; MP (Conservative) Epping 1970–74, Chingford 1974–92;
Secretary of State for Employment 1981–83, Trade and Industry 1983–
85; created Baron Tebbit of Chingford 1992

Yes. We did make one tactical error. We under-estimated the
capacity of the Alliance to make a mess of its own campaign.

At press conference after the 1987 election, cited in P. Lee Sykes,
Losing from the Inside: the cost of conflict in the British SDP (1990)

Liberals are Enid Blyton Socialists – a dustbin for undecided
votes.

Cited in G. Knight, *Honourable Insults* (1990)

Vera Terrington
1889–1973; MP (Liberal) Wycombe 1923–24

If I am elected to Westminster I intend to wear my best clothes.
I shall put on my ospreys and my fur coat and my pearls.
Everyone here knows I live in a large house and keep men
servants, and can afford a motor-car and a fur coat. Every
woman would do the same if she could. It is sheer hypocrisy to
pretend in public life that you have no nice things and not to
display them in your home.

Daily Express, 3 December 1923; Terrington sued the *Express* for libel
for printing this comment (particularly the headline, 'Aim if elected –
furs and pearls'), part of a campaign to trivialise her contest against an
anti-feminist Tory, but lost; however, she won the election

Margaret Thatcher
1925–2013; MP (Conservative) Finchley 1959–92; Prime Minister
1979–90; created Baroness Thatcher of Kesteven 1992

The one thing you never get from parties which deliberately
seek the middle way between left and right is new ideas and
radical initiatives. We were the mould-breakers, they the mould.

The Downing Street Years (1993)

The SDP were retread socialists who had gone along with
nationalisation and increased trade union power when in office,
and had only developed second thoughts about socialism when
their ministerial salaries stopped in 1979. The Liberals have
always, for their part, been the least scrupulous force in British
politics, specialising in dubious tactics – fake opinion polls
released on the eve of by-elections to suggest a non-existent
Liberal surge were a well-loved classic. Another tactic, which
the SDP quickly borrowed, was to support one policy when
talking to one group and a quite different one when talking to
another.

The Downing Street Years (1993)

They were excellent campaigners, particularly effective in local
government elections.

On Finchley Liberals, led by John Pardoe, *The Path to Power* (1995)

Although the Lib–Lab pact did the Liberals a good deal of harm,
while doing Jim Callaghan no end of good, it did allow Liberal
Party spokesmen the thrilling illusion that they were important.

The Path to Power (1995)

Bishop Thomas of Strängnäs
1380–1443; Swedish scholar and theologian

Freedom is the fairest thing
To which a man may have a liking

355

In the wide world's dominions.
Who loveth freedom more than wealth
He tendereth his honour's health;
For they be good companions.

> Extract from poem praising Karl Knutson, 1439, translation from
> M. Roberts, *On Aristocratic Constitutionalism in Swedish History* (1966)

Mike Thomas

b. 1944; MP (Labour, SDP) Newcastle-upon-Tyne East 1974–83

Social democracy is a distinct approach to politics, not the same as liberalism, well developed on the Western European mainland, but lost in Britain through the progressively syndicalist/state socialist tendencies of the Labour Party ... These honest differences – differences which many of us care very deeply about – were after all why we formed the new party in the first place; why we refused to settle for a 'plague on both your houses' rootless, policy-less, centre-party approach to British politics.

> *The Social Democrat*, 22 July 1983

Merger mania is a shallow based recipe for deep and bitter internal conflict in both parties. We should stop it now.

> Speech to the Luxembourg area party, reported in *The Social Democrat*,
> 22 July 1983

Dorothy Thompson

1893–1961; American journalist

It is not the fact of liberty by the way in which liberty is exercised that ultimately determines whether liberty itself survives ... When liberty is taken away by force it can be restored by force. When it is relinquished voluntarily by default it can never be recovered.

> Attributed

Henry David Thoreau

1817–62; American writer

That Government is best which governs least.
Civil Disobedience (1849)

Disobedience is the true foundation of liberty. The obedient must be slaves.
Civil Disobedience (1849)

The man for whom law exists – the man of forms, the Conservative – is a tame man.
Civil Disobedience (1849)

Under a government which imprisons any unjustly, the true place for a just man is also a prison.
Civil Disobedience (1849)

The law will never make men free; it is men who have got to make the law free.
Civil Disobedience (1849)

We can never have enough of Nature.
Walden (1854)

Jeremy Thorpe

b. 1929; MP (Liberal) North Devon 1959–79, leader of the Liberal Party 1967–76

The Butcher of Bouverie Street.
In the House of Commons, October 1960, describing Lawrence Cadbury, last proprietor of the *News Chronicle*, in *In My Own Time* (1999)

Bunnies can (and will) go to France.
Letter to Norman Scott, 13 February 1962

Greater love hath no man than this, that he lay down his friends for his political life.

> In the House of Commons after Harold Macmillan sacked most of his cabinet, 14 July 1962

The main supply of oil now travels on the rail line which crosses the border at Malvernia. If that supply were to continue it might be necessary to consider whether with the backing of a United Nations resolution it might be feasible for that line of communication to be nipped on Rhodesian soil by the use of high flying planes, under United Nations command.

> At the Liberal assembly, 23 September 1966, on the Rhodesian situation; the speech earned Thorpe the nickname 'Bomber' Thorpe

We'll shake this old party up. I'll lead it as ruthlessly as Lloyd George. Harold and Ted won't know what hit them. No more farting about. Now it's a crusade.

> To Peter Bessell when Thorpe became Liberal leader, cited in
> P. Bessell, *Cover Up: The Jeremy Thorpe Affair* (1980)

There are some people who say that the Liberal MPs should spend all their time demonstrating outside the House. I say bluntly to them when they have won a seat and held it against all the odds in two successive general elections, I will believe them.

> At the Royal Albert Hall, 26 March 1968

We are not helped by the antics of that small minority in our midst who believes that the British electorate want Marxism in a new dress – what they call 'non-state socialism'. In so far as they are noticed they play into the Tories' hands by making the progressive side of politics seem absurd.

> On the 'Red Guard', 27 May 1968, cited in S. Freeman & B. Penrose,
> *Rinkagate: The Rise and Fall of Jeremy Thorpe* (1996)

The Liberal Party pioneered the movement towards European unity in this country, and it is a sign of the cynicism to which

politics has now sunk that we should have been expected to
throttle it tonight.

> Statement following the second reading of the European Communities
> Bill, when Liberal votes saved the government from defeat,
> 17 February 1972

Looking around the House, one realises that we are all
minorities now – indeed, some more than others.

> In the House of Commons, following the inconclusive result of the
> 1974 general election, 6 March 1974

John the Baptist, the prophet and forerunner of great events.

> Describing Christopher Mayhew, on his defection to the Liberal Party,
> cited in C. Mayhew, *Time to Explain* (1987)

His offer was a complete coalition with the Liberal Party and
a seat in the Cabinet. I can state with utter conviction that no
specific ministry was mentioned or suggested … I later learnt
from a reliable source that what he had in mind was a Foreign
Office job with specific responsibility for Europe.

> *In My Own Time* (1999). Edward Heath, in his memoirs, claimed
> Thorpe had requested the Home Office during coalition talks after the
> February 1974 election

You should dress to the right and look to the left.

> Attributed

Ursula Thorpe

1903–92; mother of Jeremy Thorpe

He carried all before him, except his degree.

> On Jeremy Thorpe's university career (he got a third), 1952, cited in
> S. Freeman & B. Penrose, *Rinkagate: The Rise and Fall of Jeremy Thorpe*
> (1996)

The Times

Free trade is henceforth, like parliamentary representation or ministerial responsibility, not so much a prevalent opinion as an article of national faith.

Editorial, 1859

Lord Palmerston, in truth, represents the precise state of the national mind in opposing unnecessary changes without setting up resistance as a principle, and in countenancing all foreign approximations to the political theories and systems of England.

1861, cited in N. Gash, *Aristocracy and People 1815–65* (1979)

We have an instinctive dislike of 'caucuses'. We do not want any party to get the management of the constituencies or of public affairs into its own hands, and this, probably, even more than hostility to particular measures, has been the secret of a good deal of Conservative reaction of late years.

Referring to the development of the Liberal organisation in Birmingham under Joseph Chamberlain, cited in A. Dasent, *T. Delane*, Vol. 2 (1908)

That ten days' waterspout dealing with all human affairs.

On Gladstone's first Midlothian campaign, 1879

It is significant that ... the reformed constituency of Westminster should have preferred the unknown Conservative who sold books [W. H. Smith] to the famous Liberal – John Stuart Mill – who wrote them.

On Mill's defeat by Smith in the 1868 general election, 7 October 1891, cited in M. Pugh, *The Making of Modern British Politics 1867–1939* (1982)

Louth Reduces Sex Prejudice.

Headline, after Mrs Margaret Wintringham became the first Liberal woman MP by winning a by-election at Louth, 23 September 1921

The two-headed party is a stranger in the British political bestiary, and the animal appears the odder when the heads are snapping at each other.

On the Liberal–SDP Alliance, editorial, 1986

The Liberal Parliamentary Party was lined up behind the two leaders like warders surrounding a pair of newly-recaptured prisoners. Bob Maclennan was asked whether any of them would comment on the founding policy document. 'They will not be allowed to open their mouths', he replied.

On the press conference to announce the withdrawal of the original merger policy document, January 1988

It is given to few actors at Westminster to choose their time to leave the stage. But yesterday, by announcing his resignation as Liberal Democrat leader, Paddy Ashdown chose to shape a day's events rather than submit to them. In that respect, his going matches his tenure as leader. More than any other Liberal leader in living memory, Mr Ashdown shaped the party of his time.

Leader, 21 January 1999

Alexis de Tocqueville
1805–59; French historian and politician

The strength of free peoples lies in the municipality. Municipal institutions are to liberty what primary schools are to learning; they put it within reach of the people.

Democracy in America (1835)

Not what is done by a democratic government but what is done under a democratic government by private agency is really great. Democracy does not confer the most skilful kind of government upon the people but it produces that which the most skilful governments are frequently unable to awaken, namely an all-pervading and restless activity – a superabundant force – an energy which is never seen elsewhere and which may, under favourable circumstances, beget the most amazing benefits. These are the true advantages of democracy.

Democracy in America (1835)

When I refuse to obey an unjust law, I do not contest the right of the majority to command, but I simply appeal from the sovereignty of the people to the sovereignty of mankind.

Democracy in America (1835)

Arnold Toynbee

1889–1975; historian

We have not abandoned our old belief in liberty, justice and self-help, but we say that under certain conditions the people cannot help themselves, and that then they should be helped by the state representing directly the whole people. In giving this State help, we make three conditions: first, the matter must be one of primary social importance; next, it must be proved to be practicable; thirdly, the State interference must not diminish self-reliance. Even if the chance should arise of removing a great social evil, nothing must be done to weaken those habits of individual self-reliance and voluntary association which have built up the greatness of the English people.

'Are Radicals Socialists?', lecture to working men in 1882, *Lectures on the Industrial Revolution in England* (1884)

Polly Toynbee

b. 1946; journalist

Walking a perilous path above the rocks of mockery, he reaches for the highest redoubt on the moral high ground in search of justification for his party's existence.

On Paddy Ashdown's leadership of the Liberal Democrats, *The Independent*, 8 April 1997

C. P. Trevelyan

1870–1958; MP (Liberal) Elland 1899–1918, (Labour) Newcastle-upon-Tyne Central 1922–31; President of the Board of Education 1924 and 1929–31

The Liberal Party is not a free trade party. It is only satisfied with Free Trade as an economic base to work from ... The whole *raison d'être* of present day Liberalism is constructive reform ... What I want to know is how much common ground can you find with reforming Liberals on economic and social questions? ... The reform forces in the party are vastly stronger than ten years ago and I am certain will never check themselves for the sake of a few Tory votes.

Note to Winston Churchill, 1903, cited in M. Pugh, *The Making of Modern British Politics 1867–1939* (1982)

Anthony Trollope

1815–82; writer

It is the highest and most legitimate pride of an Englishman to have the letters MP written after his name. No selection from the alphabet, no doctorship, no fellowship, be it ever so learned or royal a society, no knightship, not though it be of the Garter, confers so fair an honour.

Can You Forgive Her (1864)

It has been the great fault of our politicians that they have all wanted to do something.

Phineas Finn (1869)

You are a Liberal because you know that it is not as it ought to be, and because you would still march on to some nearer approach to equality.

Duke of Omnium to Phineas Finn, *The Prime Minister* (1876)

Equality would be a heaven, if we could attain it.

The Prime Minister (1876)

From morning to evening every day I was taken round the lanes and byways of that uninteresting town, canvassing every voter exposed to the rain, up to my knees in slush, and utterly unable to assume that air of triumphant joy with which a jolly, successful candidate should be invested. At night, every night, I had to speak somewhere, – which was bad; and to listen to the speaking of others, – which was much worse ... it was the most wretched fortnight of my manhood.

On contesting Beverley, Yorkshire, as a Liberal, in the 1868 general
election – he was not elected, *An Autobiography* (1883)

But there is a fine career open to you. You will spend £1,000, and lose the election. Then you will petition, and spend another £1,000. You will throw out the elected members. There will be a commission, and the borough will be disenfranchised. For a beginner such as you are, that will be a great success.

In the event Trollope only spent £400 but, as forecast, the elected MPs
were unseated and the borough disenfranchised, *An Autobiography* (1883)

But perhaps my strongest sense of discomfort arose from the conviction that my political ideas were all leather and prunella to the men whose votes I was soliciting. They cared nothing for my doctrines, and could not even be made to understand that I should have any.

An Autobiography (1883)

I have always thought that to sit in the British Parliament should be the highest object of ambition to every educated Englishman.

An Autobiography (1883)

I consider myself to be an advanced, but still a conservative Liberal, which I regard not only as a possible but as a rational and consistent phase of political existence.

An Autobiography (1883)

Make all men equal to-day and God has so created them that they shall be all unequal to-morrow.

An Autobiography (1883)

[The Liberal] is ever willing to help the many ascend the ladder a little, though he knows, as they come up towards him, he must go down to meet them.

An Autobiography (1883)

Pierre Trudeau

1919–2000; leader of the Canadian Liberal Party, 1968–84; Prime Minister of Canada 1968–79, 1980–84

Liberal philosophy places the highest value on freedom of the individual. And that in practice, the first consequence of freedom is change. Hence a liberal is a man of the left. He can seldom be a partisan of the status quo. A liberal tends to be a reformer – attempting to move society, to modify its institutions, to liberate its citizens. At the same time, the liberal is not an anarchist because he does not believe that a free man can live as a total individual outside society. Nor is the liberal a revolutionary who believes that society must perpetually be scrubbed clean of the tracings of the past, must always begin again from an antiseptic tabula rasa. I like to repeat that a liberal is on the left, but no farther.

At the Liberal International colloquium, Ottawa, 29 April 1974

The Liberal is an optimist at heart, who trusts people. He does not see man as an essentially perverse creature, incapable of moral progress and happiness. Nor does he see him as totally or automatically good. The liberal prizes man's inclinations to good but knows such inclinations must be cultivated and supported. While understanding as well as any other man the limits of government and the law, the liberal knows that both are powerful forces for good and does not hesitate to use them.

At the Liberal International colloquium, Ottawa, 29 April 1974

Mark Twain

1835–1910; American writer

It is by the goodness of God that in our country we have those three unspeakably precious things: freedom of speech, freedom of conscience, and the prudence never to practice either of them.

Following the Equator (1897)

It is a worthy thing to fight for one's freedom; it is another sight finer to fight for another man's.

Letter to the Reverend Joseph Twichell, 1898

The radical invents the views. When he has worn them out, the conservative adopts them.

Attributed

Whenever you find that you are on the side of the majority, it is time to reform.

Attributed

Paul Tyler

b. 1941; MP (Liberal) Bodmin 1974, (Liberal Democrat) Cornwall North 1992–2005; Liberal Democrat Chief Whip 1997–2001; created Baron Tyler of Linkinhorne 2005

It is too early to say which instinct of this schizophrenic party is going to win. If Mr Blair is a pluralist, his henchmen would seem to be control freaks.

On the Labour Party, to the Lloyd George Society, February 1998

U

Universal Declaration of Human Rights
All human beings are born free and equal in dignity and rights.
Article 1

V

Paul Valéry

1871–1945; French poet and man of letters

It must be admitted that liberty is the hardest test that one can inflict on a people. To know how to be free is not given equally to all men and all nations.

Reflections on the World Today (1931)

Luc de Vauvenargues

1715–47; French soldier and man of letters

Reason and freedom are incompatible with weakness.

Maximes (1746)

Guy Verhofstadt

b. 1953; Prime Minister of Belgium 1999–2008; MEP 2009–, leader of the Alliance of Liberals and Democrats for Europe, European Parliament 2009–

What is sovereignty? In the old days, sovereignty meant the ability to impose one's will over a defined territory. Today, sadly, it is too often mixed up with concepts such as 'nation', 'nation-states' and 'nationalism'. The so-called nation's ability to fulfil its obligation, to exercise power ... But what about the irrevocable loss of power? Do you not think that in today's world we are in danger of losing power, losing power to globalisation, to the markets, in short, to the modern world? On this huge loss of power, nobody has been consulted. Nobody has agreed. Indeed, the people haven't been asked. People too often are not even aware of it ... And this is precisely the 'raison d'être', the reason of the European project. Integrating Europe is a vast project in regaining sovereignty. It is a project to give citizens ... back control over the world we are living in.

> At Hannover, 18 September 2012

Queen Victoria
1819–1901; Queen 1837–1901

Those two dreadful old men.

> On Palmerston and Russell, 1864, cited in N. Gash, *Aristocracy and People 1815–65* (1979)

I will sooner abdicate than send for or have anything to do with that half-mad firebrand who would soon ruin everything and be a dictator.

> Referring to W. E. Gladstone, letter to Sir Henry Ponsonby, 1880

The danger to the country, to Europe, to her vast Empire, which is involved in having all these great interests entrusted to the shaking hand of an old, wild, and incomprehensible man of 82, is very great!

> Letter to Lord Lansdowne, 12 August 1892

He speaks to me as if I were a public meeting.

> Referring to W. E. Gladstone, cited in G. W. E. Russell, *Collections and Recollections* (1898)

Kaspar Villiger
b. 1941; Swiss businessman and politician; Liberal President of the Swiss Confederation

Liberalism is not an easy formula. It is an attitude of mind whose characteristic feature is an incessant search for new ways of teaching the aim of a liberal constitutional, economic and social order. Liberalism is a permanent intellectual discussion.

There is no final definition, no ultimate truth. Liberalism is a political vision.

At the Liberal International Executive Committee, 19 May 1995

Voltaire

1694–1778; French writer and philosopher

The true charter of liberty is independence, maintained by force.

Philosophical Dictionary (1764)

Every abuse ought to be reformed, unless the reform is more dangerous than the abuse itself.

Philosophical Dictionary (1764)

I disapprove of what you say, but I will defend to the death your right to say it.

Attributed by S. G. Tallenture, *The Friends of Voltaire* (1907); they are a summary of Voltaire's views towards Helvétius following the burning of the latter's *De l'Esprit* (1759)

Man is free at the moment he wishes to be.

Attributed

W

Donald Wade

1904–88; MP (Liberal) Huddersfield West 1950–64; Liberal Chief Whip 1956–62; created Baron Wade of Huddersfield 1964; President, Liberal Party 1967–68

Liberalism is often described as an attitude of mind or a faith. As such it is to be found in every age and generation and in all classes of society. There are times when it flourishes and times when it is despised and persecuted; but it never perishes; it never has and never will become extinct. There always will be some who prefer liberty to authority – who prefer persuasion to dictatorship and brute force, and who believe that the well-being of the part depends upon the well-being of the whole, as opposed to those whose primary concern is to maintain the interests of a section or class.

Liberalism: Its Task in the Twentieth Century (1944)

The curious fact about political groupings is that the further one gets to the extreme Right and to the extreme Left the more the two opposing sides have in common. There are many similarities between Communist and Right Wing dictators. The extreme Left and the extreme Right are both totalitarian and both despise liberal democracy.

Our Aim and Purpose (1961)

The aim of Liberalism is always liberty – and liberty for more people. This constant liberal aim ... springs naturally from something fundamental in liberal philosophy, that is, the belief in the value of individual personality.

Our Aim and Purpose (1961)

Richard Wainwright

1918–2003; MP (Liberal) Colne Valley 1966–70, 1974–87

We are being made into a nation of teachers' pets in which
the keynote is obedience and conformity, instead of gumption
and initiative. Millions of us carry out imposed routines which
we cannot justify to our own intelligence or conscience. In
business, words such as 'ethical' are stood on their heads to
denote restrictive practices, for which the real word should be
'corrupt.'

Oldham Evening Chronicle, 14 March 1966

We have the almost nightly experience as to whose company
we should keep in the lobby and from time to time it causes us
revulsion.

On the problems of being a Liberal MP, *Colne Valley Hansard*, 17
December 1969

Why has not Mr Thorpe sued for libel, which is the proper
way in England for clearing one's name? Why does he not sue
for libel Mr Scott and others who have made these allegations
outside the court, in public? I must emphasise that this is not
tittle-tattle. It is a serious matter, and the truth – I do not know
what the truth is – but the truth has to be brought out.

On BBC Radio Leeds, in a broadcast which was significant in forcing
Jeremy Thorpe to resign as leader of the Liberal Party over the
Norman Scott allegations, 8 May 1976

Frances, Lady Waldegrave

1821–79; Whig political hostess

No one is fit to govern who does not know how to serve. This is
true for the individual, who cannot serve himself, if he cannot
govern himself.

Letter to Sir William Harcourt, 11 December 1873, cited in A. G.
Gardiner, *The Life of Sir William Harcourt* (1923)

Jim Wallace

b. 1954; MP (Liberal, Liberal Democrat) Orkney & Shetland 1983–2001; MSP (Liberal Democrat) Orkney 1999–2007; Liberal Democrat Chief Whip 1987–92, leader, Scottish Liberal Democrats 1992–2005; Deputy First Minister of Scotland 1999–2005; created Baron Wallace of Tankerness 2007; Advocate General for Scotland 2010–

We are not going to put ourselves in a position where we support the Government's programme from the Opposition benches and get the blame when things go wrong and none of the credit when things go right.

The Independent, 5 May 1999

That is why, as Scottish Liberal Democrats, we are prepared to go into government, and put these principles into practice. And that is why I want this day to be remembered not as the end of fifty years out of government, but the start for the Liberal Democrats of fifty years and more at the very heart of government.

At the Liberal Democrat conference, Harrogate, 20 September 1999

I've had a pretty exciting time. But I always think it's probably better that you go when people are saying 'why are you going?' than 'when is he going?'

On his decision to stand down as Scottish Liberal Democrat leader, 9 May 2005

Labour deserves great credit for delivering a Scottish Parliament, in spite of nationalist taunts that they couldn't deliver a pizza. But it's a rich paradox that Labour could devolve power within a nation, while remaining incapable of devolving power within itself.

The Observer, 17 August 2008

Robert Walpole
1676–1745; MP (Whig) Castle Rising 1701–02, Kings Lynn 1702–42;
created Earl of Orford 1742; Prime Minister 1721–42

The balance of power.
> In the House of Commons, 13 February 1741

All these men have their price.
> Usually quoted as 'Every man has his price', cited in W. Coxe, *Memoirs of Sir Robert Walpole* (1798)

George Washington
1732–99; American President 1789–97

Free men have virtue to withstand the highest bidder.
> Letter, 17 August 1779

Liberty, when it begins to take root, is a plant of rapid growth.
> Attributed

Alan Watkins
1933–2010; journalist and author

An extraordinary rag-bag of assorted discontents.
> On the Liberal Party, *Sunday Express* 29 April 1962

Many of the arguments of J. S. Mill ... are plausible only on the
assumption that society consists solely of middle-aged bachelors,
in good health and the possession of adequate incomes.
> *Independent on Sunday*, 30 May 1999

Graham Watson
b. 1956; MEP (Liberal, Liberal Democrat) Somerset & North Devon,
later South West England 1994–; leader of the Alliance of Liberals and

Democrats for Europe, European Parliament 2004–09; President, European Liberal Democrat and Reform Party 2011–

Ensuring the future well-being of our people, as well as the capacity of our planet to sustain life, requires a level of global cooperation never before seen … [I]nsistence on national sovereignty simply fans the flames of global anarchy. Issues of this kind can only be addressed by bodies which represent the interests of the world's citizens in a democratic, fair, and proportional manner … For far too long decisions affecting billions of people – particularly the world's poor – have been made by bodies which are spuriously representative at best, and fragrantly unrepresentative at worst … In a world where global governance lacks even the thinnest veneer of democratic legitimacy the need for the UN as a powerful player is greater than ever before.

'Advocating a United Nations Parliamentary Assembly', *The Case for Global Democracy* (September 2007)

Beatrice Webb

1858–1943; Fabian and socialist pioneer, wife of Sidney Webb

This ministry of all the talents wandered in and out of the trenches of the old individualists and the scouting parties of the new Socialists.

On Gladstone's second administration 1880–85, *My Apprenticeship* (1926)

Sidney Webb

1859–1947; Fabian and socialist pioneer, husband of Beatrice Webb

A Liberal reform is never simply a social means to a social end, but a struggle of good against evil.

Nineteenth Century, September 1901

Steve Webb

b. 1965; academic; MP (Liberal Democrat) Northavon, then Thornbury &
Yate 1997–; Minister of State, Department of Work and Pensions 2010

Intervention, where it can be shown to be effective, is justified
by an enabling state that seeks to empower its citizens and
not simply to stand by as a passive spectator and occasional
policemen. And once you view full-blooded liberalism as
implying positive action to ensure equality of opportunity and
the maximising of individual potential, you will find as your
fellow travellers those whose starting point was a passion for
social justice.

'Free to be fair or fair to be free?', in J. Margo (ed.), *Beyond Liberty*
(2007)

Wei Jingsheng

b. 1950; Chinese dissident We want no more gods or emperors,
no more saviours of any kind. Democracy, freedom and
happiness are the only goals of modernisation.

Attributed

Rebecca West

1892–1983; feminist and writer

To be wiped out by the Liberal Party is a more inglorious end
than to be run over by a hearse.

The Clarion, 25 October 1912

Shirley Williams has such an advantage over her [Margaret
Thatcher] because she's a member of the upper-middle class and
can achieve the kitchen-sink revolutionary look that one cannot
get unless one has been to a really good school.

To Jilly Cooper, *Class* (1979)

Edward Wheeler

Liberal Chief Agent, 1960s

A sedan chair – no wheels at all!
> On the Liberal Party Organisation, following Harold Wilson's
> comparison of the Labour Party with a penny farthing bicycle, in *The*
> *Guardian*, 9 April 1965

E. B. White

1899–1985; American writer and humourist

Liberty is never out of bounds or off limits; it spreads wherever
it can capture the imagination of men.
> *The Points of my Compass* (1960)

Henry Graham White

1880–1965; MP (Liberal) Birkenhead East 1922–24, 1929–45; President,
Liberal Party 1954–55

The preservation of peace is the first and most urgent task
which lies before us but after that the most important and social
problem ahead of a democratic people is the question whether
'full employment' can be maintained in a free society.
> 'The Economic Situation is Grim', in *The Middle Road*, January 1951

Michael White

b. 1945; journalist

Colleagues would grumble about Kennedy's lack of strategic
vision and organisational drive. To which I would mutter that
voters seemed to like the 'sort of bloke you could imagine
meeting in a pub and having a drink, possibly two'.
> Reviewing Greg Hurst, *Charles Kennedy: A Tragic Flaw* (2006), *The*
> *Guardian*, 23 September 2006

Paul Whiteley, Patrick Seyd and Antony Billinghurst

Whiteley: Professor of Government, University of Essex; Seyd: Professor of Government, University of Sheffield; Billinghurst: civil servant

We see that the image of the Liberal Democrats that was often conveyed by the media in times past as predominantly sandal-wearing, bearded male eccentrics concerned about marginal issues is far from the truth. While we did not ask our respondents about their footwear or shaving habits, we did ask them enough about their background and attitudes to know that such an image is a caricature. Liberal Democrat members are relatively mature, highly educated professionals whose attitudes reflect the core beliefs of modern Liberal Democracy.

Paul Whiteley, Patrick Seyd & Antony Billinghurst, *Third Force Politics: Liberal Democrats at the Grassroots* (2006)

Walt Whitman

1819–92; American poet

The shallow consider liberty a release from all law, from every constraint. The wise see in it, on the contrary, the potent Law of Laws.

Notes Left Over (1881)

Samuel Wilberforce

1805–73; Bishop of Oxford and Winchester

That wretched Pam seems to me to get worse and worse. There is not a particle of veracity or noble feeling that I have ever been able to trace in him. He manages the House of Commons by debauching it, making all parties laugh at one another ... by substituting for principle an openly-avowed vainglorious imbecile vanity as a panoply to guard himself from the attacks of all thoughtful men. I think, if his life last long, it must cost us the slight remains of Constitutional Government which exist among us.

> On Lord Palmerston, cited in G. W. E. Russell, *Sixty Years of Empire* (1897)

Oscar Wilde
1854–1900; Irish playwright and poet

As for Mill as a thinker – a man who knew nothing of Plato and Darwin gives me very little. His reputation is curious to me. I gain nothing, I have gained nothing from him – an arid, dry man with moods of sentiment – a type that is poor, and, I fancy, common. But Darwinism has of course shattered many reputations besides his, and I hope that individual liberty has had its day, for a time. His later religious views show an outstanding silliness and sentimentality.

> Letter to W. L. Courtney, 1889

Lady Bracknell: 'What are your politics?'
Jack: 'Well, I am afraid I really have none. I am a Liberal Unionist.'
Lady Bracknell: 'Oh, they count as Tories. They dine with us. Or come in the evening at any rate.'

> *The Importance of Being Earnest* (1895)

John Wilkes
1725–97; radical orator; MP Aylesbury 1757–64, Middlesex 1768–69, 1774–90

That depends, my Lord, whether I first embrace your Lordship's principles, or your Lordship's mistresses.

> After being told by the Earl of Sandwich, 'I don't know whether you'll die upon the gallows or of the pox', cited in C. Petrie, *The Four Georges* (1935)

Kenneth Williams

1926–88; actor

I see now that the obvious answer is to vote Liberal. The other two are obviously the 'choix d'embarras' & there is something innocent and honest about the Libs.

> Days before voting Conservative in the 1964 general election, *Diary*, 12 October 1964

Kirsty Williams

b. 1971; AM (Liberal Democrat) Brecon & Radnorshire 1999–; leader of the Welsh Liberal Democrats 2008–

My test for a Liberal administration is not how far we shrink the state. How far do we roll back the state is not the right question for Liberals. It is how far we are able to make the state the agent of change, the instrument of political reform, the vehicle of economic renewal and the guarantor of social justice. After all, size doesn't matter, it's what you do with it that counts.

> At the Liberal Democrat conference, Liverpool, September 2010

The smaller party in government has to be able to show it has made a difference. Not just on issues of concern to their core supporters but across government, and in particular on those issues that matter most to voters. Our core voters may be satisfied by delivery on fringe issues. But fringe supporters will only take notice when we deliver on the core issues.

> At the Liberal Democrat conference, Birmingham, September 2011

And this is the thing that irks me most about Labour. Labour uses the language of equality. But the poor services they provide do poor people down. If you fail to crack down on poor standards in schools, it isn't the well-off that suffer. They play the system, they move house, they go private – whatever they need to get their kids the best education. And the poorest in our society, the people Labour profess to care about, put up with substandard services.

At the Liberal Democrat conference, Birmingham, September 2011

Shirley Williams
b. 1930; MP (Labour) Hitchin 1964–74, Stevenage 1974–79, (SDP) Crosby 1981–83; Secretary of State for Consumer Protection 1974–76 and for Education and Science 1976–79; created Baroness Williams of Crosby, 1993; leader of the Liberal Democrat peers 2001–04

There are hazards in anything one does, but there are greater hazards in doing nothing.

1974

No roots, no principles, no philosophy and no values. I am not interested in a third party. I do not believe it has a future.

On the possibility of a new party being formed, 1979

The party I loved and worked for over so many years no longer exists.

Letter of resignation from the Labour Party to Ron Hayward, General Secretary of the Party, 10 February 1981, quoted in *The Social Democrat*, 10 September 1982

Nothing less than a new beginning for Britain and for our battered and unhappy world.

Describing the proposed SDP–Liberal Alliance, at a fringe meeting at the Liberal Assembly in Llandudno, 1981, the night before the vote which endorsed the Alliance, cited in *SDP Newsletter*, No. 3, 1981

The nation state, which dominated the history of the nineteenth and twentieth centuries, is being pulled apart by centrifugal pressures, pressures for power to be devolved downwards to regional and local government, pressures for power to be transferred upwards to international and supranational bodies. The nation state can yield a good deal of power without threatening its own survival and their functions in the modern post-industrial world.

Politics is for People (1981)

The commitment to persuasion is of the essence of social democracy.

Politics is for People (1981)

Politics isn't all made up of Mrs Thatchers and Richard Nixons. I don't believe in macho struttings and high noons.

1981, cited in A. Sampson, *The Changing Anatomy of Britain* (1982)

A valiant political campaigner, despite his inability to dissemble or gladhand the electors; an eloquent orator, a sensitive and gracious writer; an honest politician who remains his own man; the foremost champion of Britain's role in Europe; the first leader of the SDP, who will have a lasting place in history, more significant than that of most Prime Ministers; these are the characteristics of Roy Jenkins, and we thank him for all he has done for this party and for this nation.

On Jenkins's resignation as SDP leader, *The Social Democrat*, 24 June 1983

One of the reasons I was in the Labour Party for so many years was its commitment to social justice, I'm not saying it's not there any more but they are not prepared to spell out the consequences of it. They are not prepared to say to comfortable middle Britain that it has to make sacrifices. Without rubbishing Labour, we owe more to the people who are losing in our society than just words.

Cited in *The Independent*, 13 April 1997

Women bring fresh values to politics. Where they play a large part in shaping the culture of public life, as in Scandinavia, politics begin to change ... Our voices should be heard. In a

world wracked by violence and by poverty, we cannot abandon
the struggle.

The Independent, 5 April 1999

My preferred choice – which may have been very irresponsible
of me – was for a minority Conservative government … It
was a slightly selfish position. We wouldn't have been forced to
support things we didn't agree with. It was about protecting
the legacy of the Lib Dems. I didn't want to see the Lib Dems,
who I've always regarded as a left-of-centre party, suddenly
becoming a right-of-centre party.

Interview, *The Guardian*, on the formation of the Conservative–Liberal
Democrat coalition government, 14 August 2010

I always felt that because, for all that I'm a Liberal Democrat,
I suppose I'm fundamentally and always will be a Social
Democrat.

Ad Lib, November 2012

Des Wilson

b. 1941; campaigner; President, Liberal Party 1986–87

I cannot believe there is anybody who was centrally involved in
the Alliance campaign who would wish to repeat the experience
of having two leaders in two buses in two different parts of
the country with two different views on strategy, effectively
conducting two different campaigns.

On the Liberal–SDP Alliance 1987 election campaign, cited in I.
Crewe & M. Harrop (eds), *Political Communications: The General Election
of 1987* (1989)

As dead as John Cleese's parrot.

Referring to the policy declaration made and then withdrawn by David
Steel and Robert Maclennan before the merger of the Liberal Party
and the SDP, January 1988; the policy document was later referred to
as the 'dead parrot'

383

Harold Wilson

1916–95; MP (Labour) Ormskirk 1945–50, Huyton 1950–83; President
of the Board of Trade 1947–51, Prime Minister 1964–70, 1974–76;
created Baron Wilson of Rievaulx 1983

A man who could inspire all who came under his dominating
sway with a love of work for its own sake, of the discovery of
truth for its own sake and the application of that truth for the
betterment of his fellow citizens.

On William Beveridge, cited in K. Harris, *Conversations* (1967)

We are not even the natural party of opposition.

1982, following the SDP victory at Crosby, cited in A. Sampson, *The
Changing Anatomy of Britain* (1982)

[I hoped] to convert them to my ideas of radical socialism.

Explaining why he had joined the Liberal Club at Oxford University,
cited in *Memoirs: Making of a Prime Minister 1916–64* (1986)

He was a devil to work for. He was absolutely certain that he
was right about everything but he was a political innocent.
As a practical administrator he was a disaster because of his
arrogance and rudeness and his total inability to delegate.

On William Beveridge, cited in *Memoirs: Making of a Prime Minister
1916–64* (1986)

Robert Anton Wilson

1932–2007; American writer

It only takes twenty years for a liberal to become a conservative
without changing a single idea.

Attributed

Woodrow Wilson

1856–1924; American President 1913–21

The history of liberty is a history of limitation of government power, not the increase of it.
At New York, 9 September 1912

Liberty is its own reward.
12 September 1912

You cannot tear up ancient rootages and safely plant the tree of liberty in soil that is not native to it.
25 September 1912

Liberty does not consist in mere general declarations of the rights of men. It consists in the translation of those declarations into definite action.
At Philadelphia, 4 July 1914

A Conservative is a man who just sits and thinks – mostly just sits.
Cited in G. Knight, *Honourable Insults* (1990)

The highest and best form of efficiency is the spontaneous cooperation of a free people.
Attributed

Patrick Wintour

b. 1954; journalist

Few organisations can debate for three days whether to stage a debate, hold a debate, have a vote and then proceed to have a debate about what they have debated. But that is why the Liberal Democrats hold a special place in the British constitution.
On the debate on NHS reform at the Liberal Democrat conference, Gateshead, *The Guardian*, 11 March 2012

Margaret Wintringham

1879–1955; MP (Liberal) Louth 1921–24

The barbarians did give me welcome.

On the reception given to her by male Members of Parliament
following her victory in the Louth by-election, *Daily Telegraph*, 18 May
1922

Mary Wollstonecraft

1759–97; writer and women's rights activist

The divine right of husbands, like the divine right of kings, may,
it is hoped, in this enlightened age, be contested without danger.

A Vindication of the Rights of Women (1792)

Charles Wood

1800–1885; MP (Liberal) Grimsby 1826–31, Wareham 1831–32, Halifax
1832–65, Ripon 1865–66; Chancellor of the Exchequer 1846–52;
created Viscount Halifax of Mount Bretton 1866

Our quiet days are over, no more peace for us.

At the death of Palmerston, referring to the likelihood of Lord
John Russell becoming Prime Minister and parliamentary reform
again becoming a dominant political issue, October 1865, cited in
A. Dasent, *T. Delane*, Vol. 2 (1908)

I am convinced that many of us old public men must make up
our minds to see public questions dealt with in a very different
fashion from the days of our youth. The people generally were
ignorant in those days and the old Whigs were far in advance of
the people ... Now the people are more educated – all public
questions are freely and universally discussed in the press as
soon as they can be considered and before they can be taken
up by the heads of parties. It may not be wise to say it, but in
practice it cannot be helped. Public opinion will direct the

course of public men – it may be to a great extent formed by them – but able writers in the public press will do much more than any man can do in Parliament.

Letter to Lord Fortescue, 25 December 1877, cited in T. A. Jenkins, *Parliament, Party and Politics in Victorian Britain* (1996)

Maurice Woods

1882–1929; private secretary to Lord Beaverbrook

Mr Chamberlain liked good work better than abstract theories, and this alone proves that he was never at heart a Liberal.

In an obituary of Joseph Chamberlain, reflecting a popular view of Liberalism at the time, cited in M. Woods, 'Mr Chamberlain', *Fortnightly Review*, Vol. 46 (1914)

Tom Woolley

Architect and community activist

Many political changes and reforms can be brought about for people, or on their behalf, by elites, minority pressure groups and 'parties' but without the physical and thinking involvement of the mass of people, then those changes and reforms are merely improvements in the management of a passive population, not their liberation.

'The Politics of Intervention', *New Outlook*, November 1972

Robert Worcester

b. 1933; founder of MORI polling organisation

There is no such thing as a natural Lib Dem voter. It is not a calling or a commitment but an opt-out, or else a tactical vote. People float in and out of this station. If you are angry with your natural party, you turn to the Lib Dems. It is the dustbin vote.

The Independent, 8 April 1997

William Wordsworth

1770–1850; poet

Our duty is – our aim ought to be – to employ the true means of liberty and virtue for the ends of liberty and virtue.

    Attributed

George Worman

Liberal councillor in St Mary Cray, Orpington, 1960

Faith, hope and canvassing – and the greatest of these is canvassing.

    Explaining his surprise victory in the 1960 local elections, cited in
    D. Newby, *The Orpington Story* (1963)

Peregrine Worsthorne

b. 1923; journalist

In a sense the very quality of simple, boyish straightforwardness with which Mr Grimond answers questions is the most sinister thing about him. For, although he is actually in the business of seduction, he preserves the manner of the innocent flirt.

    On Jo Grimond, *Sunday Telegraph* 20 May 1962

Y

Hugo Young
1938–2003; journalist and author

It revealed a failure of leadership on such a scale to put to question whether Mr David Steel or Mr Robert Maclennan is the more incompetent politician. Neither of them, on this showing, is fit to run a whelk stall.

> On the policy declaration, abortively launched in advance of the merger of the Liberal Party and SDP, *The Guardian*, 14 January 1988

Index

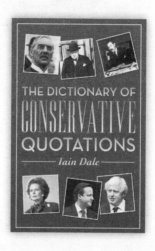

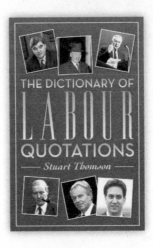